H. P. BLAVATSKY:
THE MYSTERY

H. P. BLAVATSKY: THE MYSTERY

By

Gottfried de Purucker

in collaboration with Katherine Tingley

POINT LOMA PUBLICATIONS, INC.
P.O. Box 6507
San Diego, California 92166

Copyright ©1974 by Point Loma Publications, Inc.

ISBN: 0-913004-14

Printed in the United States of America by—
STOCKTON TRADE PRESS, INC.
Santa Fe Springs, California

EDITORIAL FOREWORD

The world is more ready to understand Helena Petrovna Blavatsky now than it was forty years ago when the chapters of this book first appeared serially in *The Theosophical Path*. Deeper study of the subtle reaches of psychology and hitherto little-probed areas of consciousness has prepared the Western mind for what before has been carefully guarded and considered largely esoteric. Because of this perhaps the long delay in this publication may be held opportune since the minds of today are more in harmony with the tempo of an awakening cycle.

Readers will recognize, especially with regard to science, that the commentary here is based on the science of the 1920's and the more philosophical scientific attitudes of those days. Science fluctuates in its trend and emphasis, and today's science is more strictly materialistic than that of half a century ago when pronouncements of leading scientists seemed almost intuitionally to echo pages of the esoteric Wisdom-Religion. But Science, like everything else, moves in cycles. The time will inevitably come again when it reflects more faithfully the wholeness of the evolutionary process which would embrace also concepts which are philosophical and religious.

Because the theme is unusual, not easily yet acceptable to the pragmatic Western mind, the reader will recognize that ideas set forth in this volume are not simply bluntly stated and then hurriedly dropped, but like phrases of a musical theme they appear and reappear with fascinating variation and elaboration. Again and again you hear the challenging signature and recognize the central theme. Again and again you hear overtones and undertones and, we may say, innertones. And with each hearing the theme becomes clearer in meaning, richer in significance. We are listening to a symphony of thought revealing key-sounds, key-chords, and we hear their harmonious progression reaching ever towards what may seem to us some far off but essentially basic resolution. In the end the reader, the listener, receives an over-all understanding and feeling of composition not obtainable by ordinary methods of exposition or orchestration.

This point and counterpoint should be borne in mind as one moves first from a study of the being, H. P. Blavatsky, to that of the great ideas of esoteric teaching she enunciated. We step beyond the psychological into the realm of pneumatology. The curtain of 'mystery' is drawn aside to reveal that H. P. Blavatsky, Founder of the Theosophical Movement, was, because of the work she performed, *a type* of avatâra. She brought key-thoughts, ideas that are universal, not hers, she declared, but those of the timeless Archaic Wisdom-Religion-Philosophy for which she was only a channel. She moved the intransigent, the heavy materialistic, and — daring thought perhaps for Western minds — she became through her composite self that Force needed to initiate for mankind a new Cycle. Misunderstood, unappreciated except by the few, reviled and persecuted, she wrought her great work. And its momentum rolls on.

The basic tenets she boldly enunciated constitute the very essence of all occult doctrine. To begin to understand them is to begin to know her; and to know the doctrine she taught is to begin to know Truth.

Helen Todd
W. Emmett Small

Contents

Editorial Foreword v

Preface xiii

The Theosophical Religion-Philosophy-Science explains the nature of things as they are; only with the knowledge it gives can H. P. Blavatsky be understood. True biographical story of H.P.B., as the inaugurator of a new civilization founded on spiritual ideals and cosmic verities.

PART I: MYSTICAL AND PSYCHOLOGICAL

CHAPTER I

A Spiritual-Psychological Mystery 1

The biography of a soul rather than a mere human personality. H.P.B. a great psychological mystery. Attracted into membership in the Theosophical Society a large number of spiritually-minded people. Her inner Self one of the Great Ones of the ages. The nature of man's inner constitution. Maeterlinck quoted, *"Ernst ist das Leben"*. The rationale and meaning of a Bodhisattva, a Buddha, a Christ.

CHAPTER II

The Threshold of the Mystery 10

The constitution of man and universe can be divided into three parts. Some great Teachers enumerated. Great Ones work in silence and retirement. H. P. Blavatsky a Messenger of the Association of Great Ones.

CHAPTER III

Pausing on the Threshold of the Mystery 19

Three elements of man's constitution separable each from the other two without causing death. Temporary disjunction of psychological portion of human constitution from the vital-astral-physical, enabling the monadic element to dominate and inspire the individual, the case of H. P. Blavatsky. H.P.B. a vehicle of a lofty Master-Intelligence, her own Inner Divinity or Spiritual Self. Hpho-wa explained. H.P.B. the chosen Messenger and Mouthpiece of the Association of Great Sages and Seers.

CHAPTER IV

OVER THE THRESHOLD 29

Cycles of spiritual barrenness and spiritual fertility. H. P. Blavatsky's spiritual and intellectual inspiration came from her own Inner Spiritual Inspirer made possible by a complete stilling of the brain-mind. The subordination of personality to quasi-divinity. The essence of H.P.B.'s message. Secrets of nature and philosophical deductions made by modern science. Einstein instanced; also Eddington and Sir James Jeans. Latter on 'singular points' or 'laya centers'.

CHAPTER V

APPROACHING THE LIGHT 41

H. P. Blavatsky one of a long line of World-Teachers, not a will-less instrument but agent of free will. Human beings may be divided into three Classes: Ordinary men, Messengers and disciples of Sages, Avatâras. The word 'avatâra' explained. Śankarâchârya and Jesus examples of avatâras.

CHAPTER VI

CLOTHED WITH THE LIGHT: THE INNER GOD 51

Teaching of man's essential divinity back of all systems of mystic training in various lands and ages by individuals and schools. Destiny of the human race to transfer the seat of consciousness upwards from the brain-mind to the noëtic or spiritual-intellectual part. Living reality of the inner god. The pathway is within yourself.

PART II: PHILOSOPHIC AND SCIENTIFIC

CHAPTER VII

THE GREAT SAGES AND SEERS 61

Graduated scale of beings in Universe divided into seven stages of evolution from First Elemental Kingdom to Gods. In seven-principled Man the psychological and spiritual unite. The Mahâtmas are perfected men. The evolutionary *idea* caught from the invisible thought-reservoir of the planet by Lamarck, Darwin, and others. H. P. Blavatsky, quoting from vast area of world's literatures in support of Theosophy, aroused animosity of critics.

CONTENTS

CHAPTER VIII

THE GREAT SAGES AND SEERS (continued) 75

The Fine Flower of the Human Race called the 'Guardian Wall' of protection around humanity; their task. The value of myth and legend. The Theosophist the most truly religious, scientific, philosophic, and also freest-thinking type of mind.

CHAPTER IX

THE GREAT SAGES AND SEERS (concluded) 87

Why the Great Teachers do not appear openly before the world. Gautama Buddha and Jesus cited as Great Teachers. All Teachers face ridicule and even hatred. H.P.B. did not 'invent' existence of the Masters.

CHAPTER X

THE HIERARCHICAL CONSTITUTION OF NATURE 95

"The Universe is worked and *guided* from *within outwards*" (quotation from *The Secret Doctrine*). Examination of the teachings H. P. Blavatsky brought giving proof of her mission. Scientists today on illusory nature of the physical universe. Teaching of Chain of Causation. Matter and Energy two forms of an underlying Reality. Practically no real knowledge of Nature during last fifteen hundred years. Theories of Einstein, Millikan, Eddington. The hierarchies of Nature are the cosmos itself.

CHAPTER XI

THE HIERARCHICAL CONSTITUTION OF NATURE (continued) 107

In the Theosophical teachings can be found the explanation of who and what H. P. Blavatsky was. This world the general reflection of what the invisible worlds or planes contain. Quotations from Professor A. Wolf of London University on the nature of 'things'; defines a quantum. The Pythagorean cosmic Monad. H.P.B. quoted in *The Secret Doctrine* on invisible worlds *within* our own world as objective and material to their respective inhabitants as ours is to us. Circulations of the Kosmos take place through 'critical points' or laya-centers. Evolution a Habit of Nature. Theosophy an objective-idealism. Constitution of the Universe a self-expression of the worlds of evolving Monads.

CHAPTER XII

WORLDS INVISIBLE AND VISIBLE:
THE HEAVEN-WORLDS AND THE HELL-WORLDS 118

The so-called Heavens and so-called Hells not eternal but temporary. Free Will inherent in degree in all beings. Ancient literatures quoted. St. Paul echoes Wisdom of the archaic Ages. Lokas and Talas in Brahmanical literature. 'Heavens' represent ascending stages in pathways of the Circulation of the Cosmos.

CHAPTER XIII

THE VISIBLE WORLDS 130

Hierarchical structure of universe. Brahmanical table of Lokas. Universal life-consciousness-substance pervades everything. H. P. Blavatsky quoted showing identity of physical and chemical constituents in the forms of all kingdoms. Origen's opinions condemned by Ecumenical Council in 553 A.D. Nebula, sun, star, a focus or psycho-electric lens. Laya centers, Sir James Jeans' 'singular points'. All worlds are living beings. Morals based on fact of hierarchical structure of universe.

CHAPTER XIV

EVOLUTION 143

Evolution means unfolding, unwrapping of what is within. Postulates of the Ancient Wisdom on Evolution enumerated. Evolution on three planes: monadic, psycho-intellectual, and astral-physical. The drive to better is universal. Distinction between Darwinism and the Theosophical doctrines. A Religion of Nature will replace agnostic uncertainty. Evolution and the law of Cycles. Evolution as a series of 'events'. Analogy a guiding rule.

CHAPTER XV

EVOLUTION (continued) 155

The value of Darwin's work; but many of his statements untrue. Apes have some human blood but man not descended from ape. Man the most advanced of living beings. Three succeeding evolutionary waves fully explained in Theosophy, each a fuller type of self-expression for the manifestation of the monadic essence. Evolution is both cyclical and teleologic. Man a composite being. The indrawing of finest energies of man at death and their reawakening after period of rest and entering anew another physical body. The picture of the great Root-Races as given in *The Secret Doctrine*. Root-Races related to geologic periods.

CHAPTER XVI

MAN 169

Man composite, his essential root a monadic center. Period of cosmic manifestation runs into a figure of fifteen digits. Life-cycle of solar system reflects that of Man. The seven substance-principles of Man and Universe explained. Man collectively the handiwork of cosmic spirits. Processes of Death. The 'second death'. The Monad always active, its passage through the higher globes and spheres, and its 'descent' again coincident with awakening of Reincarnating Ego to rebirth. The seven Sacred Planets called so because of intimate evolutionary relation to Earth. Death means freedom. Philosophic rationale of Universal Brotherhood.

CHAPTER XVII

KARMA 185

Karma not Fatalism, essentially a doctrine of Free Will. Family karma. Karma the operations of entities themselves. Universes originate new karmic causes constantly. Everything fundamentally is consciousness. Mâyâ explained. H. P. Blavatsky quoted in *The Secret Doctrine*, "Karma-Nemesis is the creator of nations and mortals . . ." All world religions contain the doctrine of karma. The heart of Nature is Harmony or Love.

CHAPTER XVIII

REINCARNATION AND THE GENERAL DOCTRINE OF REIMBODIMENT 200

Pre-existence, Rebirth, Reimbodiment, Metemsomatosis, Metempsychosis Transmigration, Reincarnation explained. The Cosmic Adventures of Monad and life-atoms; what happens after death? The real meaning of metempsychosis. Seven sacred planets listed and monad's passage through them after death. The Sûtrâtman or Thread-Self. Plato's teaching of *anamnesis* or recollection. Reincarnating Ego returning to incarnation picks up on each plane the life-atoms previously dropped. Man in *essential* respects the personality of his last life, the fruitage of the man that was. Buddhists right in saying man reincarnating is the same yet not the same.

CHAPTER XIX

REINCARNATION AND THE GENERAL DOCTRINE
OF REIMBODIMENT (continued) 216

Origen of Alexandria held belief in Reincarnation. Literary dishonesty of Rufinus quoting Origen. Origen's *First Principles* quoted. Origen initiated in Eleusinian Mysteries. Before 2nd century doctrine of Reincarnation among Christians was secret. Jerome quoted in *Letter to Marcella* re reincarnation. Essenes believed in metempsychosal reincarnation. Philo quoted "On Dreams Being Sent From God". General doctrine of Reincarnation once universal; held by Orphics, Pythagoreans, Platonists, Manichaeans, Cathari. Held by German philosophers, Goethe, Lessing, Bonnet, Herder, and others. Herodotus on Egyptian belief in reincarnation. Misunderstanding of teaching of reincarnation in *Encyclopaedia Britannica* article under Metempsychosis (11th ed.). H. P. Blavatsky did not invent the Theosophical teachings but was the Mouthpiece of others greater than herself; taught men a new meaning of Life.

ADDENDUM

BIOGRAPHICAL SKETCH 238

Preface

That prince of biographers, Plutarch of Chaeroneia, priest of Apollo, philosopher, literary man, historian, and gentleman, writes in the introduction to his *Life of Theseus*, as follows:

In books of geography, Sossius Senecio, the writers put the countries of which they know practically nothing into the farthest margins of their maps, and write upon these margins legends such as the following: 'In this direction there are waterless deserts full of wild beasts,' or 'Here are unexplored swamps,' or 'Here it is as cold as Scythia,' or 'Here is a frozen sea': so I, in my writings on the parallel lives of great men, pass through the period of time where history reposes on the firm basis of facts and can truly say: 'Everything beyond this is full of portents and fables, the land of poets and mythologers, in which there is nothing true or certain.'

We find exactly the same in any attempt to write a true biography of some eminent individual. We know somewhat of the individual whose career it is attempted to portray, the place and date of birth, somewhat of the physical personality, somewhat of the deeds done or left undone, somewhat of the difficulties perhaps that the hero or heroine of whom we are writing had to face and overcome, and other things similar to these, which furnish the so-called facts for the framework of a biographical sketch.

But, as in Plutarch's observation, the moment that we endeavor to pass over into the realm of causes (in other words, into what is unknown or but partly known) and to ascertain the dominating influences which guided our hero or heroine into this or into that path or caused this or caused that action, or to analyze the mysterious profundities of the human soul which built the life, then indeed we enter into those mysterious and wonderful regions of the unknown or of the partly known, of which Plutarch writes, and which, as he says in speaking of geography, the ancient geographers crowded into the margins of their maps; and we find that the work done by every would-be biographer is usually part well-known fact and part myth, some true story and much legendary material.

Probably the real truth regarding any great character has never been adequately written in any biography. And how could it be otherwise? The attempt to enter into the working and secrets of the motives which govern the life and actions of any world-shaking character is always a most difficult attempt, always a hazardous proceeding; and it is for these reasons mainly that we feel that with the exceptions of the well-known facts such as those mentioned above, all that has hitherto been written upon or about the life of H. P. Blavatsky is about as worthless as the paper on which it appears.

It takes great minds to understand great minds. Small men have sketched the memory of great men and belittled that memory through the smallness of their own understanding, and therefore have distorted the lineaments of the individuality of him or of her whom they attempt, however honestly, to portray. Biographies are usually unsatisfactory things, simply because the biographers as a rule have some favorite hobby to ride, and they fasten this hobby upon an imaginary framework of ideals born in their own minds; and how could such a figure be otherwise than a distortion of the truth?

Plutarch was wise. He restricted his discriptions of the lives of the great men who had preceded him to a setting forth of the historical data. But this is a limitation in work which cannot be followed by anyone who desires to give an honest and faithful and more or less complete portrait of such a character as H. P. Blavatsky. How then should such a biography as hers be written?

The eminent Russian, Count Leo Tolstoi, in one of his works complains with great justice of the inadequate manner in which history has been written in the past, and he very truly says that no man can understand world-thought or world-events if his viewpoint of the circumstances be restricted to merely political and social movements. These latter are but the results of viewpoints of certain beings moving in a limited sphere and are bare outlines of events and leave totally untouched the main and dominating powers which produce these facts of history.

What then are these energies or powers controlling and guiding the events of the human story? They rise and spring forth from the workings of human minds and hearts—a subject which few if any historians have done more than point to with wavering and uncertain finger, confessing and properly confessing their ignorance of and incapacity to deal with these causes. And yet, how on earth is it possible to write a history of human events, or the still more important history of a human soul and its work on earth, if we do not know the main motivating causes operating in the mind and thus producing the thought of the world, which reaches its culmination in the events of history?

This is to be a biographical story, and a true one, of the most noteworthy and outstanding figure of nineteenth century philosophy—H. P. Blavatsky, breaker of the molds of mind, mover of the hearts and souls of men, producer of a new system of world-thought—the influence of which is already perceptible by any perspicacious mind in the literature and thoughts of men today. This biographical story it is possible to write with some approach to adequacy and completeness of treatment because of the majestic world-philosophy which H. P. Blavatsky brought anew to man, as the Messenger of great Sages and Seers, forming that brotherhood of illuminated human beings of whom all students of Theosophical literature know somewhat from their reading. It is this philosophy which gives us the key enabling us to unlock the mysteries of the human soul, to penetrate deeper than surface-appearances of mere events and acts and facts, and therefore to see and in seeing to understand and to know the hidden motives and reasons in her life which made her what she really was—not what she was in the eyes of men, who, alas, have misunderstood her sadly, but as she was in fact and in the clear and undimmed light of natural truth.

This Theosophical Religion-Philosophy-Science, which is older than the enduring hills and formulated into systematic shape by the Great Seers just spoken of, explains all things and all human events because it is a system based on the *nature of things as they are*. It is derived from no one's say-so; it is not founded on imagination nor imaginary lessons derived from history, but is founded on Nature itself, the Great Mother. It tells us not merely of man and of his origin and destiny and of his present nature, but it tells us also of the Universal Nature of which man is an inseparable part; and, further, it is founded on the laws which have been deduced from the co-ordinated workings of the energies infilling the universe. To particularize, it tells us what man is, what his inner constitution is, how the latter is held together in a coherent unity, whence it comes, what becomes of its various principles when the great liberator, Death, frees the imprisoned spirit. And telling us all this it teaches us likewise to understand men; and understanding them, this enables us to go behind the veil of outer appearances and under the surface of the seeming into the fields of realities. It teaches us likewise of the nature of civilizations, and how they arise, and what they are based on, and of the working of the energies springing from human hearts and minds, which form civilization. So that it is no vain boast nor is it vainglorious in any sense to say that having this knowledge, the life of H. P. Blavatsky, the Soul-Mover, placed under the illuminating rays of this Ancient Wisdom, can be seen as it really was, and in thus seeing her we can truly describe her and her world-work.

Part I

Mystical and Psychological

All waits or goes by default till a strong being appears;
A strong being is the proof of the race and of the ability of the Universe.
When he or she appears materials are overawed,
The dispute on the soul stops,
The old customs and phrases are confronted, turned back or turned away.

—Walt Whitman: *Leaves of Grass.*

I—A Spiritual-Psychological Mystery

H. P. Blavatsky was a great psychological mystery to the world of average men. She was a great psychological mystery even to her followers; ay, even to those who thought that they knew her best, and who met her daily and worked with her and were taught by her. To them, at least to most of them, she was an astounding paradox of what seemed to be conflicting and confusing traits of character. The intuitions of her followers and pupils told them that they were in the presence of a World-Teacher, the Messenger of other World-Teachers even greater than she was, who had sent her forth to strike the key-notes of a new age; and yet despite all this she puzzled these followers of hers most sadly, as much by those other traits of character which astonished and perplexed them because they had not the vision to expect to find such lofty and almost incomprehensible traits in a spiritual Teacher and Leader of men.

The reason and cause of all this confusion of understanding, it may truthfully be said, lay not in H. P. Blavatsky herself, but in the imperfect vision of those who knew her. They had built up for themselves an idea and an ideal of what a World-Teacher should be. Doubtless they expected to see a wonderful miracle of mere physical beauty. Doubtless they thought to themselves that each day should bring forth some new and amazing demonstration of mystic power, startling, unusual, mysterious. Instead of that, they found themselves in the presence of one whose outer characteristics at least were essentially human: wit, the play of fancy, humor, kindness, indignation; they found themselves in the presence of a penetrating mind before which no shams could stand. They saw themselves laid bare to themselves through the power of a mighty intellect and a spiritual intuition which halted at no barriers and stopped at no frontiers of human personality.

Some of H. P. Blavatsky's students and followers, however, were grateful for this self-revelation. But others were irritated because their minds were small and they lacked understanding; for few are the people who like to see themselves held up to their own inner understanding as they actually are. We are all so prone to excuse our own faults, and call them peccadilloes which amount to but little! None of us likes to feel that the very one whom we revere and look up to, is the one who reveals our own smallness of character to ourselves. Nor could they come to understand, at least in any but a very small degree, the strange double character which they both felt and saw when in the presence of H. P. Blavatsky: a most embarrassing and to them inexplicable union of splendid masculine and feminine characteristics. And just here we lay our finger directly on the key to the mysterious spiritual-psychological riddle that H. P. Blavatsky was for the world.

But if this was the case with her own followers, how much more completely was the great Theosophical Messenger misunderstood by the general public, who had not even that modicum of acquaintance with her which her immediate disciples had. To this public she was not so much a mystery or an unsolved problem as a strange and perplexing study in erratic genius which, because they could not definitely place it and label it in the usual fashion, became to the imagination of these outsiders something to be written about indeed, but with pens dipped in spleen and in anger arising out of the quasi-consciousness of their own inability to understand her.

When one surveys the world as it was when H. P. Blavatsky lived, and realizes the power over human minds which the set and crystallized ideas regarding religious and scientific subjects then had, one can find little heart to blame people who sinned through ignorance rather than through will, and who erred in their judgment from inability to understand rather than because of a desire wilfully to misinterpret. Those were the days when the scientists on the one hand thought that virtually all that was to be known of Nature, as regards fundamentals, had already been discovered and that nothing new of any important character excepting, perhaps, development of what was already supposed to be known, could be wrested from her. On the other hand, religious circles, having with some acerbity settled down to make the best of their defeat at the hands of scientific thinkers, were but the more ready to misjudge and to condemn anyone who was so daring as to do what they durst not do: face the Sir Oracles of science with unparalleled boldness as H. P. Blavatsky did, challenging openly and publicly in her doctrines and public writings the then acceptedly orthodox ideas regarding physical nature.

There was still another class of people, men and women of a more or less mystical bent, yet without the remotest conception withal of what their hearts were really hungering for. Impelled by the energies of their own inner natures to see and to feel that neither popular science nor popular religion supplied them with the pabulum that could feed their souls, they wandered hither and thither in thought, drawn to this and to that new ism or ology, and finding in none of these anything to feed their minds and souls. These were the mystical cranks of various types and kinds who flocked around H. P. Blavatsky much as moths are drawn to a bright light. Probably it was her indomitable courage which first drew them to her, and it was doubtless her magnificent intellectual power which, once attracted to her, held them more or less bound to her. From H. P. Blavatsky's standpoint, however, how on earth could a World-Teacher find in such material as these the proper instruments for disseminating her Message to the world!

If the people to whom science was their god, squirmed in futile indignation at her bold challenge of accepted scientific views; and if the people belonging to the other class of more or less orthodox or religious bent watched her with a mixture of indignation and alarm, this third class it was which by the very fact of their presence around her, and more or less openly-voiced championship of her, told sadly in one sense upon her reputation in the opinion of the general public. This more or less vocal and positive class of people gave to the general public the impression that the Theosophical Leader and many of her followers were, at the very least, a set of mystery-loving cranks; and this phase of public misunderstanding of H. P.

Blavatsky's mission and teachings lasted for a certain time, in the European countries more especially.

It so happened as time went on, that little by little the men and women composing this third class were not encouraged and they dropped out of the ranks of those who looked upon H. P. Blavatsky as a Teacher of philosophical religion and of philosophical science; but the effect of her compassionate interest in these mystical cranks remained for years afterwards. The truth of the matter was that the great heart of H. P. Blavatsky refused to no one entrance into the Theosophical Society, provided there seemed to be the least chance that such admission would benefit them.

This matter is referred to because it does not lack a certain importance in attempting to adjust our present vision to the situation as it then existed, and should be clearly understood if we are to have a true viewpoint of some at least of the difficulties that the great Theosophical Messenger had to face and overcome.

But, after all this is said, the fact remains that one of the most interesting and significant factors in the history of the Theosophical Society during the lifetime of H. P. Blavatsky, was the large number of highly reputable, loftily intellectual, and truly spiritually minded people whom she drew into the membership of the Theosophical Society. They numbered literally thousands in all parts of the world. They included philosophers, scientists, clergymen, statesmen, literary men, men of various other professions, artists, men of wide and successful commercial experience; in fact an actual cross-section, cut through the heart of our Occidental social structure. It is these last who formed the body of devoted, energetic, and highly intelligent members, who supported with all the power at their command, the efforts of H. P. Blavatsky to make her Message to the world a vital power in the hearts and minds of men.

And even among these choice persons, there were very few who had any conception of a clearly defined character of the real nature and mission of H. P. Blavatsky; but these few, these choicest of the choice, intuitive, aspiring, longing for truth, hungering for reality, and who formed a fifth class by themselves—these last were they, we say, who were in the real sense of the phrase her true pupils and who gave to her the most invaluable part of the assistance that she then received in casting her message broadly and deep into men's souls. They were very few indeed, but the Theosophist of today, with the added experience that time has given, can do no otherwise than record his sense of gratitude to them for their utterly true-hearted loyalty to H. P. Blavatsky in the days of her first and perhaps greatest efforts. While even these few did not fully understand their great Teacher, as was only to be expected, yet they understood enough of her to realize that they were in the presence of and working under the inspiration of one of those World-Figures of which history records the appearance among men at cyclic intervals.

We have said that this book is to be a study of a profound spiritual-psychological mystery, and that statement is true. But to lay bare this mystery to the understanding of thoughtful men and women is in itself a task of Herculean proportions. We are going to treat of subjects concerning which the average Occidental has no conception whatsoever; or if, in moments of quiet thought, or under the refining influence of spiritual intuitions, some of the early members of the Theosophical Society may have gained some intimation of the truth, yet in the nature of things, such suggestive intimations must have been but rarely and sporadically recorded. Our task would be quite different, perhaps, were this book written solely for the better class of Orientals who are more or less accustomed to psychological mysteries by training, and whose magnificent religious and philosophical systems have guided them even from childhood to realize that there are in the world subtle and mysterious forces which play through the human psychological mask, in other words, through man's inner constitution, and thus form of one man a sage and saint and of another man a human brute and rogue.

It is precisely on matters dealing with man's inner constitution that we shall treat and thereby solve as far as possible in the compass of a printed volume the amazing riddle of H. P. Blavatsky's character, life, and mission.

H. P. Blavatsky was of course born a woman, but for all that, her character in one direction was at times importantly, intensely, masculine, and the work which she so magnificently performed was essentially a man's work and very largely done after the manner of a man. Can we say that she was but one of those strange and erratic geniuses whose careers have at different times aroused the admiration and astonishment of men? No. That is not our meaning at all. Genius is one thing: it is the efflorescence of the native powers of a normal individual; but the case of H. P. Blavatsky, Soul-Shaker, Breaker of the molds of mind, and Founder of a new and brilliant hope and destiny for mankind, rests on entirely different foundations, foundations which are laid in some of the most mysterious and, to the Occident, utterly unknown secrets of human spiritual-psychological economy.

Yes, H. P. Blavatsky's intermediate or soul-nature at times seemed distinctly that of a man. Yet she was intensely feminine in some respects, as was only natural, and a gentlewoman to her finger-tips, strangely and alertly sensitive, delicately organized, keenly awake in both mind and heart to the noblest human impulses. But behind all this, over-mastering all this, controlling all this, and working through all this, there was the dominating influence of a Master-Intelligence: her own individual, egoic, spiritual part, or center of her inner constitution—the developed Spiritual Soul of her, her Inner Divinity, the monadic essence or root of her being, evolved forth in its transcendent powers into conscious activity on our human plane, as the consequence of many previous reincarnations on earth and imbodiments in the invisible realms of the Universe.

This inner Self of her was one of the Great Ones of the ages, an actual, real, self-consciously energic Individuality or Power, which worked through her and used her both psychologically and physically as the fittest instrument for the saving of the souls of men that the Occidental world has seen in many ages.

Let us anticipate here an important thought which will find

its due place in later chapters, by calling attention to the nature of man's inner constitution as the wonderful Theosophical philosophy sets it forth. This constitution may for easy understanding be divided into three parts—the spiritual-divine part, which is the monadic essence of man's inner being, sometimes called his Inner Spiritual Self; second, the intermediate or psychological part which is the center of the human consciousness *per se* and which actually is the child or outflowing of a part of the spiritual energies from the monadic essence before spoken of; and third, the vital-astral-physical part which makes up the lowest or vehicular part of man.

The monadic essence or Spiritual Soul above spoken of must be understood to be an individuality, an actual, real, living entity having its own sphere of action in its own lofty realms or fields of activity. This acts through the intermediate part which may be called the Reincarnating Ego or, more simply, the higher Human Soul, this being what we ordinarily mean when we speak of the soul of man. It is the personal individuality of the human being, and not only is it the child of the monadic essence or Inner Divinity, but it also partakes of the stream of consciousness, flowing from its parent; and in proportion as it can manifest clearly and undimmed the supernal light and intelligence of this stream of consciousness, is it great and does it partake of the sublimity of its parent. This parent monadic essence is the source of all great human inspiration, and in proportion as the human being can ally himself with this Inner Self he thereby raises himself towards the spiritual stature of the great Seers and Sages who have made such a profound impression on the history of the human race.

The above gives an outline of the case of H. P. Blavatsky, for through long training and initiation under her great Teachers, who were of this Association of great Seers, she had become fitted to become their Messenger and Mouthpiece to the world. The secret key regarding the mystery of H. P. Blavatsky lies in the paragraph which precedes. Intuitions and intimations of the existence in the human being of such transcendent faculties and powers and energies have been had by very many of the Great Mystics of the ages, whatever may have been the race among whom they were born or the time in which they lived; and they have naturally also come into the consciousness of more modern writers, even though they are men of less insight.

Maurice Maeterlinck, the Belgian mystic, in a Preface to a French translation of Emerson's essays, expresses in these words some of the vision which he has had of the deep-lying but wonderfully beautiful faculties in the human being:

> The face of our divine soul smiles at times over the shoulder of her sister, the human soul, bent to the noble needs of thought, and this smile which, as it passes, discovers to us all that is beyond thought, is the only thing of consequence in the works of man. They are not many who have shown that man is greater and profounder than himself, and who have been able to fix some of the eternal suggestions to be met with every instant through life, in a movement, a sign, a look, a word, a silence, in the incidents happening round about us.
>
> The science of human greatness is the greatest of sciences. Not one man is ignorant of it, yet hardly one knows he possesses it. The child who meets me cannot tell his mother what he has seen; and yet as soon as his eye has touched my presence, he knows all that I shall be, as well as my brother, and three times better than myself. . . .
>
> In truth, what is strongest in man is his hidden gravity and wisdom. The most frivolous among us never really laughs, and in spite of his efforts never succeeds in losing a moment, for the human soul is attentive and does nothing that is not useful.
>
> *Ernst ist das Leben.* Life is serious, and in the depths of our being our soul has never yet smiled. On the other side of our involuntary agitations we lead a wonderful existence, passive, very pure, very sure, to which ceaseless allusion is made by hands stretched out, eyes that open, looks that meet. All our organs are mystic accomplices of a superior being, and it is never a man, it is a soul we have known. I did not see that poor man who begged for alms at my doorstep; but I saw something else; in our eyes two selfsame destinies greeted and loved each other, and at the instant he held out his hand, the little door of the house opened for a moment on the sea. . . .
>
> But if it be true that the least of us cannot make the slightest movement without taking account of the soul and the spiritual kingdoms where it reigns, it is also true that the wisest almost never thinks of the infinite displaced by the opening of an eyelid, the bending of a head, or the closing of a hand. We live so far from ourselves that we are ignorant of almost all that takes place on the horizon of our being. We wander aimlessly in the valley, never thinking that all our actions are reproduced and acquire their significance on the summit of the mountain. Someone has to come and say: 'Lift your eyes; see what you

are, see what you are doing; it is not here that we live: we are up there.' That look exchanged in the dark, those words which have no meaning at the base of the hill, see what they grow into and what they signify beyond the snow of the peaks, and how our hands which we think so little and so feeble, touch God everywhere unknowingly....

What Maeterlinck here speaks of as the "face of our divine soul smiling at times over the shoulder of her sister the human soul," expresses in terms different from our Theosophical phraseology, but yet very truly, what the Theosophist means when he refers to the divine-spiritual nature of man, or his Inner Spiritual Self, or, in other words, the monadic essence standing back of and expressing itself through *not* its 'sister, the human soul,' but its child, the intermediate portion of man's constitution.

It is when this intermediate portion, popularly called the human soul, becomes so pellucid, through evolution and initiatory training, that it can manifest the wonderful powers and faculties of its parent-monad, that the human soul becomes the self-conscious center of what we may truly call a divinity—man's own Inner Essential Divinity. The lofty human whose intermediate nature has thus become so pervious in character to the stream of spiritual-divine illumination is spoken of variously in the different races. Among the Buddhists such a human being would be called a Buddha, or Bodhisattva perhaps; among mystical modern Christians reference would be made to the being in man of the immanent Christ or Christos; while the Hindû, the student of the wonderful Theosophy of Brâhmanism as imbodied in the Upanishads of India, would speak of such a case of lofty humanity as one in whom the 'inner Brahman lives and shines.'

Here, then, is the key—the only key thus far—to the spiritual-psychological mystery of H. P. Blavatsky, the key we are going to place in the lock of circumstance and give it a turn, and then another turn, endeavoring to pass over the threshold of what to the public is an unknown land, to the brilliant and amazing scenes of human quasi-divinity.

II—The Threshold of the Mystery

In embarking upon the first stages of the fascinating subject before us, it would probably be impossible to get even the first glimpse of the truth regarding H. P. Blavatsky, unless we have some more or less clear-cut ideas of the nature of man's inner constitution; for there, in actual fact, lies the secret key of the Mystery that she was.

We have spoken of H. P. Blavatsky as a great spiritual-psychological mystery. It must be carefully noted and understood, however, that the use of this word 'mystery' is not the popular one as signifying something which it is impossible to understand, or which natural circumstances or human inability prevent us from understanding. We use the word in much the same sense that the ancient Greeks did, who gave us this term, as signifying something the explanation of which could indeed be readily enough known, but only through and by a course of training and study combined, undertaken and followed out by certain ones who had, however, been chosen, or who had chosen themselves, to pursue such a course. In other words, 'mystery' as here used, signifies not an unsolvable riddle, but an aggregate of little known facts combined with a series of circumstances which requires only elucidation and explanation to become clear.

The 'mystery' spoken of is really a simple one, and there is no reason whatsoever why the average Occidental—or Oriental indeed for that matter— should have any real difficulty in understanding, and greatly profiting by, the explanation which we purpose to set forth.

Those who have read more or less of Theosophical literature of course know that the usual and popular method followed in Theosophical works of showing the nature of man and of the Universe is the outlining of and explanation of the so-called Seven Principles of which man's inner constitution is built as a miniature copy of the sevenfold constitution of the Universe. And this is quite correct and no objection is made to it here. But there is another method, and for our present purpose a simpler method; it is by considering his inner constitution to be built up of three perfectly harmonious, naturally interacting, and correlated divisions: a spiritual nature, a psychological or intermediate nature, and a vital-astral-physical nature. These three obviously include the seven principles of man, and furthermore are at the basis of the usual Christian division of man's being into three—spirit, soul, and body.

In other words, man himself is but a copy in the small of what the Universe is in the great. He is the microcosm of the Macrocosm. His spiritual nature is rooted in and a derivative of the spiritual nature of the Universe, of which he is an organic part. His intermediate or psychological nature is equivalently rooted in the intermediate or psychological portion of the Universe, of which he is an organic part. And his vital-astral-physical portion likewise is derivative, as a composite, from the same composite portion of the Universe, of which he is, vitally, astrally, and physically, an inseparable offspring.

The consequence of all this is, philosophically as well as religiously, and, indeed, scientifically speaking, that whatever is in the Universe — powers, functions, faculties, energies, forces, substances, consciousness, what not — plays and functions through him; because all these play and function in the universe, of the whole of which man is an inseparable part. It is also obvious that as the Universe itself is one consistent and coherent whole, and therefore includes the invisible worlds and spheres, such a universal structure can be builded after only one pattern. That pattern is that of a hierarchical or graded series of planes or stages or worlds, call them what you will, of different degrees of tenuity or ethereality, as regards each other, some being very high in evolution, and others being in an evolutionary period of lower degree.

This basic fact it is which gives a philosophical explanation of the fact that the human host itself is composed or constructed after the same hierachical pattern that exists in the

Parent-Universe. In other words there are very great men; there are men less great; and there are men who are great; and below these are the various stages, from the better to the worse, of average and middling men; and below these again, continuing the hierarchical ladder of human life, there are the different degrees of what we may call inferior men.

It is to the superior men, the men of the first class, we now wish to call particular attention. No one who has read history can be oblivious of the fact that its annals are bright at certain epochs with the amazing splendor of certain human beings, who during the periods of their lifetimes, have swayed the destinies, not merely of nations, but of whole continents. The names of some of these men are household words in all civilized countries, and the most negligent student of history cannot have done otherwise than have stood amazed at the mark that they made in the world, while they lived—yes, and perhaps have left behind them results surpassing in almost immeasurable degree the remarkable achievements of their own respective lifetimes.

A few of these are the Buddha and Śankarâchârya in India; Lao-Tse and Confucius in China; Jesus the great Syrian Sage in his own epoch and land; Apollonius of Tyana, Pythagoras, Orpheus, Olen, Musaeus, Pamphos, and Philammon, in Greece; and many, many more in other lands. Nor is it to be supposed that all these great men were of equal spiritual grandeur, for, as in the other classes of human beings, so do these great men likewise differ among themselves in degrees of evolutionary development.

One point of great importance should be noted: that a careful scrutiny of the teachings of these Great Men, the Seers and Sages of past times, shows us that in the various and varying forms in which their respective Messages were cast, there is always to be found an identical systematized Doctrine, identical in substance in all cases, though frequently varying in outward form: a fact proving the existence all over the world of what Theosophy very rightly points to as the existence of a Universal Religion of mankind—a Religion-Philosophy-Science based on Nature herself, and by no means nor at any time resting solely on the teachings of any one individual, however great he may have been. It is also foolish, downright absurd, for any thoughtful man or woman to deny the existence of these great outstanding figures of world-history, for there they are; and the more we know about them, the more fully do we begin to understand something of their sublime nature and powers.

Do you ask; What on earth have these great world-figures to do with the spiritual-psychological mystery that H. P. Blavatsky was? If so, you have not yet grasped even the first principle of the explanation of H. P. Blavatsky's individual character, and of the Mission which she was sent forth to accomplish. We do not mean to say that H. P. Blavatsky, the Russian noblewoman and much misunderstood philosophic teacher, was in all senses of the word one of these towering World-Figures; although on the other hand we do not mean to say that she was utterly distinct and separate from that class of beings. Our meaning is very plain: It is that for work planned by titanic spiritual wisdom and intellect, a great and powerful individuality is needed in order to carry it out. This alone places H. P. Blavatsky in the ranks of the Great Ones, although, as we have before said, she was also the Messenger and Mouthpiece of others greater than she.

Or again do you ask: Was then H. P. Blavatsky the Messenger of the Buddha, and of Jesus and of Lao-Tse, and of the others of whom you have been speaking? Are they not all dead men, who lived indeed and moved the world at their time indeed, but who are now no more? How can that be? No, that is not our meaning. We instanced these great men in order to illustrate the thesis that the human race has produced these monuments of surpassing genius in the past; and there is not the slightest reasonable or logical argument that could be alleged by anybody in support of the very lame and halting notion that no such men live now, or could live in the future. The burden of all the evidence at hand runs quite to the contrary. It would be a riddle virtually unsolvable, if one were to suppose that because such men have existed in the past, they could not exist again or that—and this comes to the same thing

—what the human race has once produced, it could never again produce.

How does such a fantastic notion harmonize with the unquestioned truth of evolution—in other words, progressive human development? Has the human race at the present time grown so feeble, has it so far degenerated, that genius, and what is more than genius—which these Great Ones showed forth—no more can spring forth from human material? All these questions and comments sufficiently state the case, and we need pause no longer upon that phase of the question.

We do not mean that H. P. Blavatsky was the Messenger and Mouthpiece of men once dead; but we do mean that what has been in the past is but a shadowing forth of what likewise can be and must be at a later date, and, in the course of natural law, will be bound to come forth in the future. She was the Messenger and Mouthpiece of that great Brotherhood of which our Theosophical literature says so much, and which is composed not of the 'spirits of dead men' at all, but of the aggregate of Great Ones living today, similar to those who lived in the past, and who are the successors, and in some instances, doubtless the reincarnations of the Great Ones of former ages.

Thus, then, it may be taken for granted that Nature is neither more inept than she was in former times, nor deprived of the powers that then she manifested. The old question may here arise in the minds of some as to why these Great Ones, if they still exist, do not come forth before the public and show themselves, allow people to touch them and question them: why they do not prove themselves, in other words, to all the doubting Thomases of our more modern time.

This is a question which has been answered fully and adequately in our Theosophical writings. One may, however, ask the questioner a very simple query: Why on earth should they do so, and whose business is it if they do not do so? Why should they come out before a doubting and skeptical public, which would either worship them as gods on the one hand, if they so appeared, or perhaps persecute them and do them to death, if that were possible. If these Great Ones can pursue their surpassingly splendid work better in the silences of retirement, and utterly unknown of ordinary men, or usually unknown of ordinary men, it would be positive folly for them to choose the path of greatest resistance rather than the one which the experience of ages has shown to be in all senses the best. They have no desire to be made social lions in modern drawing-rooms, or to stand in pulpits or on any modern Areopagus, and preach mysteries to a wide-eyed and openmouthed public. That may be all very well for small men; but as anyone who knows the history of those Great Men can see, precisely the opposite course has invariably been chosen, even by those who appear in the world as Messengers from their own great Brotherhood in times of cyclical crisis, when a new keynote is to be sounded in human hearts and minds. Then they appear indeed, but they are wrapped in the garments of mystery—in the Greek sense of the word—and shun, as the average man would a pest, the distracting and corrupting influences of the mob, or the inane and often deadening influence of the drawing-room.

We have moved already a step or two towards the Threshold of the Mystery. Once grant—as reason and history and human experience and our intuitions compel us to grant—that their work is utterly unselfish and loftily humanitarian, a work devoted solely to the spiritual and intellectual benefit of their fellow-men, and the foundations are therein laid in proof of H. P. Blavatsky's Mission, and of the Powers behind her who sent her forth to do it.

No sensible workman, having a task of delicacy and importance to perform, selects imperfect tools, or inadequate instruments to perform the work in hand. On precisely similar lines of common sense and reason do the Masters of Life, those Great Seers and Sages of the ages, select the rare few who are born into the world at different times, as their faithful agents for carrying into that world their Message of Truth for men, and of Light for men, and of Liberation for the human race: a liberation which is in no sense of the word the following of a mere political or social nostrum, but a liberation, above all other things, from the chains of personal selfishness and the thraldom of the lower self.

We have given so far a mere outline of the usual manner of presenting the Mystery which enwraps any such Messenger. But it is more particularly on the least known part of this mystery that we wish to elaborate.

A Russian gentlewoman springing from a stock of high ancestral distinction on both sides, showing even from child-days unwonted abilities and extraordinary capacity and power: yet one who at the same time gave most astounding and perplexing evidences of a loftiness of character which both amazed and sorely puzzled those who thought, and vainly thought, that they knew her best. Such was H. P. Blavatsky. The world stands awed and astounded when an individual of power and genius appears and gives evidence of spiritual and intellectual worth! Such human beings are accepted as real enough, although amazing perhaps; but the idea that some human entity can contain in the compass of its own individuality the most splendid mental and psychological characteristics of both physiological divisions of the human race, arouses not merely the awe, not merely the amaze of the ignorant and the thoughtless, but a feeling somewhat akin to that aroused by the appearance of a startling phenomenon. This feeling arises solely from ignorance of the wide and deep reaches of the latent spiritual and mental powers in man.

There is a delightful and quaint old Zulu tale about a maiden who once upon a time went to sleep in a cave after playing with her attendants, and was awakened by hearing voices. What was her amazement, when her eyes opened, to see standing around her a company of apparently human beings, but who, instead of walking as human beings do, proceeded by leaps and bounds; and she noticed in wide-eyed wonder that these individuals had each but one leg! When this dusky Venus arose from her couch and walked towards them, they fled in utmost consternation, and her best efforts could hardly bring them back into her presence—for she had *two* legs! She understood their language, and she heard one of them say in a voice in which both horror and indignation as well as awe were evident: "It is a pretty thing, but, oh heavens, look at the two legs!"

And indeed most people seem to be just like this one-legged tribe of story, in their judgment of people and of things that they do not understand. We are all so accustomed to taking things that we see around us for granted, as being the inviolable order of Nature, that we fail to realize that what our senses tell us of regarding surrounding appearances and things is merely the world as these very imperfect physical vehicles of report interpret that world to us. It is actually the Theosophical teaching that there are many mysteries even in our own physical world of which ordinary humanity at the present time knows nothing at all, or is just beginning to learn something of; and furthermore, that the vast ranges in the hierarchical structure of the invisible Universe contain not only substances and energies, but beings of all-various kinds and classes, which the far-distant future, through the evolutionary progress of human beings, will begin to make known to them.

Man's own inner constitution, through and on the same grounds of organization as those just set forth, also contains vast and deep mysteries which man himself, in his present imperfect state of evolutionary development, knows almost nothing of; but the knowledge of which indeed is in the guardianship and possession of the Association of great Sages and Seers. These inner mysteries of man of course are straitly involved in any explanation of such a psychological mystery as is offered by the great Sages and Seers, and by their various Messengers, such as H. P. Blavatsky was.

Only real genius—indeed something more than merely human genius—only sublime spiritual and intellectual capacity, native to the constitution of some lofty human being, could explain the reason for the choice of such Messengers. But indeed, this is not saying enough; because in addition to genius and to merely native spiritual and intellectual capacity, such a Messenger must possess through initiatory training the capacity of throwing at will the intermediate or psychological nature into a state of perfect quiescence or receptivity for the stream of divine-spiritual inspiration flowing forth from the Messenger's own Inner Divinity or monadic essence. It is obvious that such a combination of rare and unusual qualities is not often found in human beings, and when found, such a one is fit for the work to be done by such a Messenger of the Association of Great Ones.

We do not mean, as might perhaps be supposed from the foregoing by those who are prone quickly to judge, that H. P. Blavatsky was merely an evolutionary forerunner of a future mankind, who, as an individual, foreshadowed the type of the human race to be in distant aeons of the future. That is not our meaning, although there is a certain amount of truth in such a supposition. All great men and women are in a certain sense forerunners of what is to come in racial development; for, as everyone knows, coming events do verily cast their shadows before—a wonderful suggestion and truthful proverb. Our meaning will become clear as we proceed in our study.

III—Pausing on the Threshold of the Mystery

We have already made clear that both the Universe and Man its child are logically and indeed necessarily divisible into various principles; and special attention is now called to this tripartite character of man's inner constitution. It is a very ancient teaching, one more or less corroborated even by modern psychological thought, that certain of these principles composing man's inner constitution may be separated off, as it were, from the others without causing the dissolution of the human entity.

It is very necessary to keep clearly in mind, however, an understanding of the statement that the human being is composite, that is to say, formed of the 'principles,' so-called, enumerated in the preceding chapter; although these various principles work together and are naturally so correlated that the complete entitative human being is the harmonious interconnection of them all.

Just what the spiritual portion of this constitution may or may not be is in itself extremely important, but not necessary to describe in detail for the purposes of our present study. Much more important is the intermediate or psychological portion of man's constitution; while, as regards the vital-astral-physical elements of the human being, these are sufficiently described by the terms used and need no especial emphasis here.

Looking then at the human entity in this light, it becomes immediately obvious that the spiritual part of his constitution is of an eternal, or rather, perpetually enduring character; the psychological or intermediate portion is descriptive of the human ego, whose destiny it is, as an individualized center, to attain individual perpetuity in time and space, so to say, as the wonderful processes of human evolution perfect it to that end; and, of course, the third or lowest portion of the entitative human being — the vital-astral-physical — is purely mortal.

We have, therefore, before us, first, the picture of the human constitution as composed of an element of perpetual splendor, the product of long past ages of aeonic evolution; second, the picture of the human entity, the intermediate part, likewise the product of past ages of evolution, but still imperfect, and still subject to the play of the various energies resident in ethereal substance. In this intermediate or psychological portion, lie the elements of ordinary human consciousness, pulled this way and that by its own inherent attractions, to things of spirit or of matter, as the case may be, and the destiny of which depends upon the degree in which it receives the inspiring and refining influences of its parent-spirit on the one hand, or, on the other hand falls victim to the strong pull of the material energies which attach it to the lowest part of the human constitution.

Now these three parts are separable in a relative sense, each from the two others, without causing death; but when this separation becomes absolute, the break-up of the constitution of the entitative human being immediately ensues. But note well in this connection the following. When an absolute separation of the lowest portion of the three takes place from the other two, there ensues what is called physical death, and this of course is the destiny of all human beings. When, again, an absolute separation of the highest or the spirit from the intermediate and the vital-astral-physical, which two still then remain in vital union, takes place, then there ensues, as shown in the majestical Theosophical philosophy, the occurrence of a truly dreadful fate for the unified two portions left behind. For this is what is known as the case of a 'lost soul.' This term may not be very accurately descriptive nor very correct in phrase, but it is sufficient enough as a term to set forth the destiny of the bipartite portion of the human entity thus abandoned by its inner divine Essence. Of this exceedingly rare case no more need be said here.

And now we come to the third, and for the purposes of our

present study, the really important matter which we wish to set forth. Ancient legend and story, as well as ancient philosophy and mysticism, combine in the declaration that it is not only possible, but actually not infrequent, for the intermediate or psychological portion of man's constitution, which is usually called the human soul, *temporarily* to undergo a disjunction of incomplete character from the vital-astral-physical vehicle in which it is inshrined, and which in normal human life it regularly works through. The inner divine Essence of course remains in full control of the intermediate portion, which intermediate portion thus temporarily stands apart, so to speak; and this leaves the body still vitalized, still to all appearances a normal, living human entity, still receiving, but in a minor degree, the stream of individuality pouring forth from the two higher portions.

It is most important not to suppose that this disjunction is absolute, for were it so this would be the case of simple physical death. The man lives, so far as physical eyes see him still; he is to all appearances exactly what he was before; the man still thinks, still goes about his work, still persists on all the customary paths of personal activity; but in actual fact is both spiritually and intellectually, for the time being, so to say, a spiritual and psychological cripple.

Now this last state or condition of the intermediate psychological portion of the individual was not the case with H. P. Blavatsky. There is the reverse or opposite state or condition of this intermediate part of man's inner constitution, in which it is highly developed, powerful, positive, but translucent, pellucid, withal, to the inflowing stream of spiritual-divine consciousness from the Spiritual Soul, or active individual part of the monadic essence. In this case the monadic element in man, or the monadic essence, is dominant in the individual, and is neither hindered by the positivity and strength of character of the intermediate portion of the human being, nor colored by the individuality of the latter as the spiritual-divine stream of consciousness flows through it into the personal consciousness of the human being. In this case again the intermediate portion, so to say, by an act of will of the human entity himself or herself, is stilled, or rendered wholly receptive of these inflowing streams and thereby becomes a canal or channel through which these streams of divine-spiritual energy and power and consciousness pass into the normal brain-mind consciousness of the human being.

Let us try to describe this wonderful psychological phenomenon in other words, for in these circumstances lies the foundation of the explanation of the Mystery which we are studying. Perhaps one of the commonest facts of ordinary human life is the influence which one mind exerts over another mind; so that, as the saying might run, we no longer see the man as he is in his own soul-power, but sense instead the will-energy and individuality of the dominating or controlling mind. Such cases in popular language are described when men say: "Why, he is no longer himself; he is the mere shadow or mirror of so-and-so!" This is the case where one human being exercises a powerful psychological influence over another human being, and thus proves the condition of receptivity into which a human psychological apparatus can be thrown, becoming receptive of extraneous influences. This in the Theosophical viewpoint is wholly wrong, inexcusable, immoral, and should under no circumstances be suffered to come to pass.

Instead of an extraneous influence, instead of the will-power and mind-energy of one man passing over to another man, let us replace such a dominating influence with the transcendant and lofty stream of consciousness flowing into such a psychological apparatus or brain-mind from the individual's own spiritual self, or Inner Divinity. This is wholly beautiful; this is sublime; this takes place only in the loftiest and noblest of the human race; and it is the entire procedure of evolution, considered teleologically, to bring about in ever increasing perfection the receptivity of the lower part of man's inner constitution towards his higher part.

When such receptivity is virtually perfect, then we may say: "Behold an incarnate Sage, behold an incarnate Christ!" The entire structure of morals reposes upon this wonderful fact as its basis; and put in very simple language and in plain words, such a sublime human being is one of the great Sages and Seers, one of the Fine Flowers of the human race. These last individuals are they in whom the entire human constitution becomes at-one with the indwelling and inspiring Higher Self or Inner Divinity, and so far as our own Universe is concerned, which includes of course as most important the *invisible* realms of our Universe, such Great Ones may be truly said then to become possessed of omniscience, or quasi-omniscience, for the evident reason that they have become at-one with their own inner divinity, and the individual's consciousness then ranges over Universal fields.

But such Great Ones are necessarily very few and far between in human history, and many are the mysteries that pertain not only to their makeup, constitutionally speaking, but to their lives. Those who are fond of their Christian New Testament doubtless have paused often and long over passages which describe the touching and appealing episode in the Garden of Gethsemane, where Jesus is pictured as saying to his disciples: " 'My soul is exceedingly sorrowful unto death. Tarry ye here and watch with me.' And he went a little farther and fell on his face and prayed, saying: 'Oh my Father, if it be possible, let this cup pass from me; nevertheless not as I will but as thou wilt.' "

The mystic appeal which these pathetic words make to most people is based upon the intuitive recognition of the fact that a human being can become the vehicle or Mediator for the manifestation of the power and work of some lofty spiritual-divine consciousness-energy working in and through him. We see here, in the case of Jesus, the true resignation of the personal will to the will of this dominant spiritual energy; and we have only to turn to the history of many of the great World-Sages in order to realize that very much the same set of circumstances is found in their lives also.

The human nature even of the Great Ones, so it is said, at times feels the burthen of the Kosmic Work which such Great Ones carry. And this human nature, being obviously inferior in evolutionary development to the Higher or Spiritual Self, needs rest and consolation, and occasional surcease from the burthen of such lofty Kosmic Labor. Of course, in this case of the pathetic cry of Jesus, as alleged, in the Garden of Gethsemane, the appeal made is to the dominant influence of the high spiritual-divine Power working through Jesus and not to the intermediate nature; but the case illustrates, nevertheless, the separability of the various principles or portions of man's constitution regarded as the seats of consciousness and energy.

We need not here go into any particular relation of the standing of Jesus, called the Christ, nor of the work that he wrought as the instrument of the sublime spiritual essence working through him, although the case is exactly similar, as regards the psychological mystery of it, to that which takes place or has taken place in the cases of other Great Ones, as before alluded to. Probably no great spiritual and intellectual Movement was ever inaugurated without involving the self-surrender of the Messenger—a self-surrender which in all cases has been a definitely joyful one; for the Messengers have always known what their work was, at least in general outline, and have always known likewise how greatly sublime and how divinely beautiful participation in this work is.

It should now be clear from the foregoing what was meant when it was said that a temporary disjunction or 'absence' of the psychological portion of man's constitution takes place, but always with the individual consent and willing participation in the action on the part of the human being in whom this occurs: an action which happens always in order that the dominant spiritual-divine and noëtic energies of the Higher Self may flow temporarily outwards into the consciousness of the normal human being and uncolored by the intermediate part of the man—in other words, uncolored by his own human egoic center of consciousness.

When this wonderful mystery takes place, then the man is for the time being wholly allied with his Higher or Spiritual Self, and becomes the physical vehicle for the transmission of teachings and precepts regarding the greatest mysteries of Nature, and of the sublimest spiritual truths. During these times the intermediate nature of the individual, his human soul-entity, is completely stilled, so that it may become an organ acting easily and freely and as it were obeying automatically the divine-spiritual energies then flowing through it.

Words almost fail one in an attempt to describe this matter; appeal is made to the intuition of the reader rather than to the ratiocinative activities of his lower human mentality. Yet in truth the idea is not difficult to understand, at least the principles of it which are really simple.

We pause therefore on the threshold of the Mystery—the spiritual-psychological Mystery—of H. P. Blavatsky. She was in all senses a complete entitative human being, unusual, highly developed, alertly sensitive to all spiritual impulses from her own Inner Divinity, delicately organized, devoted to her Teachers, a lover of mankind, utterly self-forgetful, surrendering all her own personal aptitudes to the Great Work which she was sent into the world to accomplish; and for the full accomplishment of which she gave herself, her life—indeed, all that she was. Therein lies perhaps her greatest claim to our reverence and love.

Standing on the Threshold of the Mystery can we now begin to see a little at least of the solution of the great riddle that H. P. Blavatsky has always been to the world? One must indeed be dense who can imagine for a moment that she could have done what she did do, could have given birth to the Movement to which she did give birth, could have moved the minds and hearts of men all over the world as she did move them, could have founded a spiritual-intellectual Movement which has actually shaken to pieces the fabric of the materialism of the world into which she came: could have done all this merely from the innate but uninspired and unaided impulses of her own personal psychological economy, and without the help of, and except through, the inspiration of the lofty spiritual and intellectual energies which played through her at times. And lastly, without the other help so freely and fully given to her by the Great Men whose Messenger to the world she was.

Yes, there is the truth. She was the vehicle of a surpassingly sublime and lofty Master-Intelligence—her own Inner Divinity or Spiritual Self. From that high source she received during those frequent periods when it came to her the inspiration of this inner divinity, and which thus filled her with its own splendor for the time being. Here inspiration of the loftiest type has its place. On a much lower plane, telepathy, as commonly understood today, gives the key to this process in ordinary human affairs. But this word 'telepathy' is not to be used for that which we have just outlined, unless that word be enlarged, and very greatly enlarged, to include not mere thought-transference but also a transference into the ordinary human being, from his own inner divinity, of Consciousness and Will.

In the case of H. P. Blavatsky, there is one extremely important element of the mystery which surrounded her, and the process which took place in her inner constitution, to which we point only and then pass on. It is connected with a Tibetan teaching of the Mahâyâna School, which teaching is called the doctrine of 'Hpho-wa,' and has reference in her case to her intimate spiritual and psychological connection with her Tibetan 'Home,' but is of too sacred and esoteric a character to discuss in a published work. Mere genius does not show in any of its phases the extraordinary attributes of the spiritual and intellectual and psychological nature which H. P. Blavatsky possessed in common with all other World-Teachers. How often has she herself not set on record in her letters and in her writings, her own state of mind with regard to these matters, always expressed by her with the utmost care and prudence, however, and always rather by hint and by allusion than by direct and open speech. Yet no one can collect these scattered references, often humorous, sometimes sad, reminding one of Jesus' cry in the Garden of Gethsemane, without feeling most forcefully that there is behind it all a secret carefully guarded as the most sacred and holiest event in her life. Yes, H. P. Blavatsky was a genius, but she was more; she was a human phenomenon of the most joyful and noblest self-sacrifice that it is possible to conceive of, yet a self-sacrifice withal, which, as she herself taught, brought her a joy and a peace that nothing else in the world ever could have brought to her.

How great her own unaided personal genius was, however, not only her followers and those who loved her best are the first to proclaim, but it was precisely her own unaided native powers, which brought to her the greatest part of the recognition that the world has accorded to her. Her literary ability was not only an outstanding phenomenon but was marvelous. One has but to turn for proof of this to the series of articles, quite apart from her great and definitely Theosophical works: articles, that is, which she wrote for different Russian magazines, therefrom deriving the income from which she lived; for she never took a dollar for her teachings, from anyone, and devoted the income derived from the sale of her Theosophical works to the support of the Society which she founded, and which she loved better than all else.

It was the famous M. N. Katkoff who first induced her to write for his own two Russian periodicals, the *Russkiy Vestnik (Russian Messenger)* and the *Moskovskiya Vedomosti (Moscow Gazette)*, both of Moscow. She wrote for these publications the serial stories: *The Mysterious Tribes of the Blue Hills*, and *From the Caves and Jungles of Hindostan*, which were published during the years of 1879-1886. The pseudonym, or rather the literary name under which she wrote for these Russian papers was Radda Bai, and these products from her ever-busy pen in themselves compose a monument to her extraordinary literary ability.*

But it is sufficient merely to compare these otherwise extremely interesting works with the vast profundity of wisdom and the wide reaches of ancient and modern esoteric knowledge that her Theosophical books contain, such as her *The Secret Doctrine*, in order to see the difference in type and power between the two. Like all authors, H. P. Blavatsky had what may be called a style of greater power, which was reserved for her Theosophical literary productions; and a style couched in a lighter vein when writing the many articles and stories that flowed from her ever-busy mind and pen. These two styles are marked however by a greater degree of difference than pre-

---

*[Only partial English translations of both the "Tribes" and the "Caves and Jungles" have been published. Complete English translations of all the writings of H.P.B. in her native language will be published in forthcoming volumes of her *Collected Writings*, eleven volumes of which are now available.—*Editors*.]

sumably could be found in the writings of others, or at least of most other writers.

Thus, we repeat, we have here the sheer, unvarnished truth—H. P. Blavatsky was one in whom the mere personality was entirely absorbed in the spiritual individuality of her, the mere personality or human aspects being devoted on the altar of truth and to the service of her inner spiritual essence or divinity, and to the sublime work of the Great Sages and Seers who sent her forth as their Messenger among men.

She was indeed their chosen Messenger, and, so far as her Theosophical Message of the Ancient Wisdom went, she was the Mouthpiece, and the only Mouthpiece for the time being, of the Association of Great Sages and Seers. Such a choice in itself places her on the topmost pinnacle of human greatness; for none but great talent and lofty genius could be fit for a work so great and sublime.

We pause on the Threshold of the Mystery, and deep in thought, with our hearts filled with reverence, look across the threshold and contemplate what we see there.

IV—Over the Threshold

Men have their unselfish moods; but even their great purposes are fickle and changing; their aspirations are here today and gone tomorrow. How then could such a one as Helena Petrovna Blavatsky have been understood by her time? The slanders of her enemies are a tribute to her greatness: she will always be a mystery to a world that does not look towards the sources of light. Except to those who have discovered that the worldly life is not the delightful thing it claims to be, who have come to the limit of it and found ambition and selfishness delusions, she will remain forever a mystery.

Those who did understand her must have had that experience. Before they left their bodies in some previous life they must have waked to the unreality and impermanence of the things men mostly set their hearts on; and then they must have waked to the Reality beyond, which demands of us the will to grow and the will to serve; and it was this will, this desire, that drew them to be her pupils. She knew when she came that many would be waiting for her; and her Teacher would have told her and she would have known it for herself—what he told her would have been confirmation of her own knowledge—that of the many who would profess faith and friendship, but few would stand the tests.

Every Teacher has hours of loneliness. With all their knowledge of and love for humanity, and their hopes for the future, there must come to them a sadness and a loneliness at times; because the links in the disciples' hearts with the Teacher are not always strongly forged, and the grand truths are brushed aside for the falsities; and because insincerity and hypocrisy and selfishnes and vice are the powerful agents of today; but most of all the loneliness comes when the disciples fail, and turn and would destroy the work that has helped and sought to save them. With her disciples that sometimes happened, as we know; and she did her utmost always to avert their disaster; and knew in each instance that of her duty to them she had left nothing undone.

There is about H. P. Blavatsky a certain grandeur that impels us towards search for the inner meaning of things and an effort to awaken the deepest part of our nature where all truth abides for us to discover. We have not identified ourselves with her work for our own salvation's sake; our aim is at a mark more unusual: to make mankind happy glimpsing the wonderful hope that we cherish, glimpsing the wonderful truths; to unfold in our lives a divine influence to take out into the world and to give to humanity, that the great heart of Helena Petrovna Blavatsky may be understood; and that the doors of the temple of peace and brotherhood may be opened wider and wider, that we may look out beyond and see other and other portals of other and other temples opening and opening to the utmost heights; and that many may see and come forward who now fall back and die, and must, until the light so shines through their lives that without speech or writing it will make itself known.

This was the light that she brought into the world; it was for these ends she came, and was heroic, and suffered. Therefore if we would pay right tribute to her we must weigh well every word that we utter and protest against the entry into our minds of any single worthless or personal thought. For she offered her life on the altar of truth, and had little to support her but the power of the great doctrines that she brought with her; for the whole world was against her in the beginning. Through every phase and action of her career that superb courage shone which manifests in the world but here and there, in those whom we call the heroes; and then only when their highest motives are dominant in their minds, and some lofty emergency calls into play that which is greater than the normal self. For this kind of courage is spiritual: it is inherent in the Spiritual Will, the noble ruler of the mind; it is a quality that marks the Divine Soul of Man.

Science goes on accepting one after another many of the

great ideas she promulgated, but usually ignores their source; while the more she opposed materialism and labored to bring the supreme religious truth of human brotherhood to the knowledge of mankind, the more she was hunted down by the professed followers of religion.

She saw how humanity had been drifting through the ages unaware of its birthright and unconscious of its dignity; how the indefiniteness of modern ideas had confused the minds of the people and engendered everywhere uncertainty and helpless doubt; how the essential truths of religion had been honeycombed with falsehood by the tortuous forces that retarded the progress of mankind: and she left for posterity a body of teachings with power in them to change the whole world, and as it were to raise from the dead the Immortal Part of man.

To make perfectly clear what we have said before, let us repeat: the case of H. P. Blavatsky was identical with what has taken place at other times, when, for various reasons, a Messenger is sent forth from the glorious Association of the great Sages and Seers, exactly as she was. In all cases of the appearance of these Messengers, their work is based on the combination, briefly speaking, of two facts, or rather the concurrence of two quite distinct and yet closely similar sources of spiritual and intellectual inspiration: first, inspiration from the Messenger's own Spiritual Self or Inner Essential Divinity, and in the manner already outlined, and this is in large part the result of previous initiations which the Messenger has passed through; and second, constant and continuous help in an intellectual and psycho-spiritual way from the Messenger's Teacher or Teachers, who have sent the Messenger forth into the world in order to do the work which the civilization of the time, in its cyclic evolution, has made possible.

It is one of our Theosophical teachings that, as the great Plato put it, human history is composed of periods of spiritual barrenness and periods of spiritual fertility, which succeed each other regularly in time. When the periods of spiritual fertility occur, the streams of natural inspiration and intuitive intellectual action in the leaders of the human race, and of whatever country, are running more or less strong; whereas the periods of spiritual barrenness are marked by times when the evolutionary cycle is running strong in matter and weak in the channels of native spiritual illumination. It is in these latter times, in the times of spiritual barrenness, that the Messengers usually appear among men, and strike the keynote of a new age.

So in the famous Hindû work, the *Bhagavad-Gîtâ*, Krishna refers to the same thought that was in the mind of Plato, and sets forth that, as the Spirit of true illumination, he then incarnates for the destruction of evil, the righting of wrong, and the re-establishment of righteousness upon earth. Plato's idea is a very old one, and in all the great World-Religions and World-Philosophies precisely the same idea occurs and is expressed in a more or less clear manner.

If it were not for the Cimmerian darkness which exists in the minds of Occidentals with regard to what real psychology is, the entire situation which we are attempting to explain as regards H. P. Blavatsky would be so clear that a mere word of allusion to it would be sufficient. But to a people such as Occidentals are, whose ideas regarding the 'soul' are of the vaguest, and who have scarcely any belief that such a superphysical organ as 'the soul' exists, the attempt to explain this Mystery is very difficult indeed and it is necessary once again to remind the reader that if he wishes clearly to understand the problem he must be willing to study it faithfully and to realize that a very cursory reading will not help him very much.

Does what we have before said imply that H. P. Blavatsky was psychologized by her Teacher? Most positively it does not. It does mean, however, that she was a *Mediator*—acquiescent, willing, and fully self-conscious of it—between the Association of the World-Teachers or great Seers and Sages, and ordinary human beings such as men and women usually are. The *Mediator* or *Intermediary* is a highly evolved human entity always possessing a strong and vigorous individuality, and usually a forceful and positive personality, and is the Messenger or Transmitter between others greater than he or than she is, and human beings in general.

The main idea to keep in mind is that the foundation of

H. P. Blavatsky's spiritual and intellectual inspiration lay in the stream of illumination received from her own essential divinity—her own Inner Spiritual Inspirer, and that this was rendered possible by the *complete stilling* of the ever-active and often misleading brain-mind, which in all human beings is an organ that, however useful it may be in daily affairs, is the greatest hindrance, on account of its fevered and fretful activities, to the reception of the calming and refining influences flowing from the monadic essence or spiritual-divine nature within. The idea therefore is most certainly not that the intermediate or psychological nature steps aside or abandons temporarily the constitution, for such an act would have resulted in mere sleep or trance; but that it is trained to be still, to be quiet, to be as pellucid and clear as the waters of a mountain tarn, receiving and mirroring the rays of the golden sun.

The idea is not, again, that this temporary 'absence' or functional 'disjunction' of the intermediate part of H. P. Blavatsky's constitution worked injury, or damage, or degradation, or hurt of any kind, to her or to any part of her constitution. The truth is that the psychological condition which we call by the phrase 'temporary disjunction' or 'absence,' is so expressed in human language only because more accurate and exact terms do not exist in European tongues to describe it with accuracy. It must not be thought that the intermediate or psychological nature is disrupted from the rest of the constitution, but, on the contrary, that it there still remains, but in a state of undisturbed receptivity; and that this condition took place through the exercise of H. P. Blavatsky's own will-power. In fact, this condition is not different, either in fundamentals or in principle, from what occurs in vastly minor degree to every human being almost every day, when he feels himself, as the saying runs, 'in the mood' to receive a new and illuminating idea: beautiful, sublime, inspiring, helpful, uplifting: and makes it a part of his own consciousness and store of rich thoughts.

But in H. P. Blavatsky's case it took place in eminently greater degree, as it did likewise in the cases of all other Messengers or World-Teachers who occupied the same relation to their Teachers on the one hand, and to humanity on the other. Her intermediate or psychological nature was as fully connected by all natural vital bonds with the remaining two portions of her own inner constitution as at any time. We repeat: it was merely that the personal will and brain-mind and psycho-mental apparatus were temporarily perfectly stilled by her own will-power into full psychological quiescence, so that the overshadowing—if we may here use this rather misleading word—or the inflowing thought and will and consciousness of her own Inner Spiritual Essence, the spiritual-divine Individual, or Self, of her, could work through her psychological and vital-astral mechanism undisturbed and with ease and facility of self-expression.

In the ancient literatures often very wonderful and mystic and psychological teachings and most illuminating references are made to what was then spoken of as a man being filled with the glory of his inner divinity. There is nothing strange or supernatural about this. Nothing is so natural, nothing is so holy, nothing is so helpful. The Christian New Testament, in referring to the transfiguration of Jesus, later called the Christ, speaks of the same identical fact of his having been filled with the divine spirit within him, which later ages construed to mean the spirit of the extracosmic Deity which it had become the fashion to believe in.

With reference to the Greek Mysteries, the ancient literatures of Greece and Rome occasionally refer to the fact that in certain stages of the initiatory procedures the initiant or postulant was so filled with the energy and splendor of his own Inner God that his body was clothed with light—'clothed with the sun,' were the words—and that his face shone, so that his whole being was transfigured.

It is therefore abundantly clear that the case of H. P. Blavatsky was not self-hypnotization in any sense of the word, nor psychologization by the will of another, either of which would be utterly against the teachings and rules of the Great Sages; a condition which would have utterly unfitted one to be the disciple, and, *a fortiori*, the Messenger of the Great Sages and Seers.

As we survey H. P. Blavatsky's life from her childhood-days, and mark the different stages of growth of the developed and wonderful nature that was her native heritage, we see not only that growing power that was her own, but also quite clearly the appearance at times—the comings of which the average person could not predict—of what the world, using popular language, would call a genius still greater than hers: the appearance of a mighty and rushing tide of sublime thought, stamped with an individuality distinct from her own ordinary brain-mind thought, and yet obviously working in and through her physical personality.

This subordination of personality to quasi-divinity is one of the most mysterious facts in human history, and is one which has always furnished the greatest problem even to the most intuitive historians. They sense the presence of splendor; they perceive the workings of an illumination which dazzles, in the life and teachings of this or some other World-Figure; and puzzled by the phenomenon, which they fail to understand, they speak of the man or woman whom they are then studying as one of the inexplicable figures of history.

We see H. P. Blavatsky in childhood, surrounded by her family, a child full of mystical thought, tender and loving to those who surrounded her, strangely touched by any story of suffering or pain, living an inner life of her own, which those around her never could understand; we see her in later years traveling from land to land, learning everywhere, gathering knowledge and unusual teaching in unexpected places; we see her arriving at New York in 1873, and gathering around her a devoted body, not merely of friends but of men and women keen to take from her what they felt by a sort of spiritual instinct she had to give to them; we see her in later years leaving for India with Colonel Henry Steel Olcott, and in that far distant peninsula creating a veritable furor of interest and astonishment, gathering around her some of the keenest minds of the keen-minded Hindû peoples. We see her at last beginning to proclaim to the world through the pages of her magazine, *The Theosophist,* and through her letters, written to correspondents all over the world, a philosophy of the Universe and of life generally, at which she had previously but hinted, as in her *Isis Unveiled* for instance.

We see her leaving India at different times for more or less protracted sojourns in European countries, where in 1890, she finally settled in London at 19 Avenue Road, and where she then delivered in literary form the full-grown flowering of her mission to men.

We see her idolized as a woman of sublimely beautiful and wonderful character by her friends; we see her decried and ridiculed by those who had no understanding of her; we see her in her last days, in her loose and comfortable garment, sitting in her arm-chair, writing, writing, writing, every day—until she finally passed away in 1891—an uninterrupted stream of literary productions; and we see her finally, one morning, surrounded by her friends, and in the same arm-chair where she so loved to work, quietly and with scarcely a movement of the muscles of her face, pass on to what she always called 'Home.'

Through all this period of time she was always the same H. P. Blavatsky, firm friend, true and steady counselor, devotion itself to her Mission, a hater of shams, an unfolder of men's hearts and minds, a revealer of their own souls, laying bare the Wisdom-Religion of the ancients to all who would pay attention to what she had to say; and laying the foundations of a new civilization reposing on the everlasting rock of the Archaic Wisdom. She brought peace and solace and wisdom and happiness to men's hearts, and to their minds she brought surcease from sorrow and pain.

How profoundly H. P. Blavatsky's Message has moved the world, and how greatly it has stirred the intuition of all thinking men and women, is abundantly manifest today in the amazing approaches of the various branches of science, through the speculations of the most eminent scientific men, to her teachings, given between 1873 and 1891. Her greatest work, *The Secret Doctrine*, may fitly be said to be filled from cover to cover with an unending series of invaluable hints and allusions to Nature's secrets, and concerning its constitution inner and outer, and therefore also the nature and constitution of man.

Modern chemistry, modern biology, as examples, are beginning to discover, and their foremost exponents are beginning openly to teach, secrets of Nature and philosophical deductions regarding those secrets, that would have brought about the social ostracism of any scientist of H. P. Blavatsky's day, had he dared even to voice his possible intuition of such knowledge.

The unreal and illusory nature of matter; the energic constitution of the physical world; the ultra-modern scientific speculations regarding the nature and constitution of atomic structure; the great changes that have come over men's minds with regard to the real meaning of evolution, and the rapidly progressing rejection of the teachings of Darwinism in favor of a more spiritual and loftier interpretation of the undoubted truth of evolution; the appearance in authoritative scientific works of statements that bear directly on the existence of invisible but discoverable energies working through man and the universe: these and many more such, which have now become the commonplaces of scientific thinking, all exemplify most forcefully the statement just made as to the approach that the greatest men in science are now making, and in larger degree with the passage of every year, to the teachings of Theosophy, the modern presentation of the Wisdom-Religion of the archaic ages.

Science has advanced with strides of seven-league boots since H. P. Blavatsky's time; and in all directions, philosophic as well as technically scientific, it is today giving voice to theories and hypotheses based on the most recent scientific discoveries which corroborate in general and often in particular, statements and doctrines broadcast by H. P. Blavatsky as teachings of the Ancient Wisdom imbodied in her books.

We have but to turn to the revolutionary theories of Dr. Albert Einstein regarding the relativity of natural laws and substances and energies and their phenomena, to see in them, modern scientific formulations of facts in Universal Nature which H. P. Blavatsky, as the Messenger of the Archaic Wisdom, clearly taught and brilliantly elucidated in 1888, as far as it was possible to do so in an age when not even the most intuitive minds understood the ABC of what the coming years were to bring forth. Whatever Dr. Einstein's mathematical demonstrations may prove, and whether these demonstrations at the present time be subject or not to correction, is another matter; we allude solely to his principal thesis of Relativity.

Most recently, indeed [1929], the newspapers have carried reports of another advance made by Einstein regarding the nature of gravitation and its connection, and probable fundamental identity, with cosmic electricity and magnetism. Here again the famous German philosopher and scientist is endeavoring to cover ground that H. P. Blavatsky in 1888 pointedly and definitely called to the attention of the scientific world, and then wrote about, and explained with unparalleled success, to those intuitive minds who were able to grasp her meaning and to follow her reasoning.

Or we may turn to Professor A. S. Eddington, Plumian Professor of Astronomy, Cambridge University, England, a remarkable British philosophical scientist, who amazed his fellow-scientists attending a very recent meeting [1929] of the Royal Society in England, with his championship of the existence of consciousness functioning throughout Nature in individual particulars—in other words, teaching precisely in modern scientific phraseology what H. P. Blavatsky did in 1888 and in previous years regarding the existence of a graded series of consciousnesses throughout Universal Nature; all of which is one way of stating that the universe is but imbodied consciousnesses.

This conception was in the background of the philosophy of archaic times, when the ancients spoke of the Universe as being filled full of gods and *daimones*, etc., in practically infinitely varying grades or stages of evolutionary development, some very high and some very low, with all intermediate degrees.

Professor Eddington's amazingly correct theory, if we have understood aright newspaper-cables carrying the news, is briefly summarized by Professor A. Wolf, professor of Scientific Theory, London University, as follows:

"It is Professor Eddington's theory that they [physical events and phenomena] all partake—everything partakes—of the nature of mental activity, of consciousness, or sub-consciousness, sometimes of a low and sometimes of a higher order, and these mental activities can be described by other and higher minds, but all these have a consciousness of self which is different from their appearance in the consciousness of other minds and from the description. . . . Electrons are to be thought of in terms of rhythm and energy, electric charges, not in terms of infinitely small 'billiard-balls,' etc., etc."

We may likewise instance the forecasting of the discovery of radio-activity in physical nature which H. P. Blavatsky in 1888 likewise clearly outlined, also pointing out that what we now call radio-activity was not merely existent in certain natural provinces, so to say, or in certain physical elements, but was universal; and she then instanced the so-called 'radiant matter' of Professor William Crookes, as being the starting-point of remarkable discoveries to come, regarding the constitution of Nature and its foundation on invisible and inner elements; and this is exactly what has taken place.

Whence did she derive the power to descry, and, descrying, to describe in her great books these things? How was it that she was so truly a prophet as to see so clearly, and to set forth so pointedly, what was to take place within two generations from the time when she wrote? How is it that in *The Secret Doctrine*, published in 1888, she should describe in extraordinarily similar words, as teachings of the Ancient Wisdom, what Sir James H. Jeans today (1929) calls his 'singular points'— points existent in cosmical nebulae, which, according to him, are the open doors, or channels, connecting our physical, visible universe with one which is invisible and non-physical, and which, let it be said in passing, he speaks of as another 'dimension.'

These singular points of Dr. Jeans, H. P. Blavatsky then called 'Laya-Centers,' which she described with the remarkable facility native to her writings, and also pointed out that the ascription to these invisible worlds or spheres of the term 'other dimensions' is entirely wrong; for these invisible spheres are not dimensions of physical matter in any sense, but, exactly speaking, are other worlds having their own natural dimensions, as our physical world has its dimensional series; calling attention at the same time to the fact that while the word 'dimensions' is wrong, it nevertheless did signify an intuition on the part of the writers of her day of the fact that other and more subtil and causal realms were at the basis of the physical universe.

This single instance illustrates what we might fill many pages with by way of proof of the statement that H. P. Blavatsky foresaw scientific discoveries soon thereafter to be made, but in her day unguessed at. As regards Dr. Jeans' 'singular points,' the student who is interested may turn to her *The Secret Doctrine*, Volume I, page 148, and elsewhere.

These questions of priority in scientific and philosophical matters as belonging to H. P. Blavatsky, the historian of the future will certainly have to answer, for they are too important for him ever to be able to leave them unnoticed. Meanwhile, students of the Message which H. P. Blavatsky brought to the world from the Guardians of the Ancient Wisdom, move steadily along in their work of disseminating the age-old Truth wherever it can find even a remote chance to strike its roots deep into human hearts and minds.

V—Approaching the Light

We have opened the doors and have passed the Threshold and now approach the heart of the Mystery. Before us lies what is to the Occidental readers the *terra incognita* of the inner nature of man.

We now turn to a sketch of the other facts and circumstances composing the heart of the Mystery that we are trying to explain: the Light which we are now approaching.

Human beings may be divided into three general Classes, in whom the intermediate or psychological nature is more or less pellucid to the Inner Light: (1) those in whom it is moderately pervious to the Light and Power of the Inner God; (2) those in whom it is pervious in large measure; (3) those in whom it is wholly pervious thereto. These three Classes, beginning with the first, or lowest, we may speak of as: I: Ordinary men; II: Messengers and disciples of the Sages, and the Sages themselves; III: the Avatâras. Moreover, the intermediate or psychological part of man, in addition to the above conditions, is also subject by nature to certain other conditions or states of 'presence' and quasi-'absence,' during life, which states or conditions result in marked psychological phenomena; and, especially as regards our present subject, these states or conditions produce the varying degrees of human greatness. The following will briefly set forth our meaning.

Let us begin with the first Class—a matter which will not require any heavy mental work and which may therefore serve as an easy introduction to understanding the other two Classes more difficult to explain. The quasi-'absence,' or perhaps rather the temporary 'disjunction' of the psychological apparatus of an ordinary man, from the remainder of his inner constitution, is exceedingly common in life, although temporary: so common, indeed, that it is the basis of a body of psychological phenomena which belong to practically everybody: to every human being, normal or abnormal, as the case may be.

We may instance the most common case of all, that is, sleep. In sleep the intermediate or psychological or, as it is commonly called, the 'personal' part of man's constitution is 'absent': in other words, non-manifesting through the physical brain; and, indeed, it is this absence itself, this temporary disjunction of the intermediate or ordinary human nature, which is the ultimate cause of sleep itself. The body sleeps because we, the average personal human beings, are no longer there.

Another case is that of trance, a word which is grossly misunderstood and absurdly used by a number of popular writers on so-called abnormal psychical phenomena. The annals of medicine, as well as the knowledge derived from the practice of every experienced physician, show that trances are as common to human beings as blackberries in season. A man is in a species of trance when he is what is called absent-minded, which exactly describes the situation; for his mind is no longer there, so to say. A man is in a minor trance when he is oblivious of surrounding circumstances or is inwrapped in what is popularly called a brown study.

A man is likewise in a trance when he has foolishly allowed himself to become the victim of the practices of some hypnotist; and anyone who has seen men and women in this state of hypnosis must realize not only how dangerous, how baleful and wrong it is, but also that it exemplifies the trance-state perfectly. The reason is that the intermediate nature, or the psychomental apparatus of the human being, has been displaced from its seat, is disjoined or absent, and there remains but the vitalized human body, with its more or less imperfect functioning of the brain-cells and nervous apparatus. Another case is that comprised in the various degrees of insanity. A man is insane simply because his intermediate or psychological nature is 'absent' in various degrees, or, in cases of violent insanity, has been practically dislocated in permanent or absolute measure. Minor cases of insanity, or periodic mania, are other instances where this disjunction has taken place. So much for Class I.

We come now to Class II, that of the Messengers and the advanced disciples of the Sages, a Class which stands on an entirely different footing. Whereas in Class I the various phenomena appertaining to the 'absence' or disjunction of the intermediate or psychological apparatus is mostly involuntary, and beyond ordinary control, and in its evil and vicious ranges is a great and positive affliction, in this Second Class the 'absence' or disjunction is an exceedingly rare phenomenon, is entirely under the control of the individual, is voluntary, and takes place only when and if and as the individual so desires it, and its results are always sane and healthful.

The differences between Classes I and II are enormous. In Class I the intermediate part or nature is imperfectly evolved, is only moderately pervious to the supernal light and energy of the divine-spiritual Soul or Inner Essential Self, and is subject to consequent disturbances and distortions of function which still more largely interrupt the spiritual stream of consciousness from the monadic essence or Inner Essential Self.

In Class II, on the contrary, the intermediate part is highly evolved, trained to respond to the stream of inspiration, and through training and initiation has become both positive and powerful. Thus the Spiritual Will and Consciousness are able to function easily and freely, and, whenever necessary, can so control and govern the intermediate part as to set it aside temporarily, so to say, in order that the consciousness-stream flowing forth from the Monad or Inner Spiritual Self may pass directly into the ordinary human or brain-mind consciousness.

This last condition opens the path to the highest spiritual inspiration uncolored by the personalized individuality of the intermediate nature of the inner constitution of the man. When this occurs the man becomes in consciousness and power virtually an incarnate god. His consciousness is, for the time being, of universal range and vision, and this therefore includes what may be called temporary omniscience — so far as our own Home-Universe is concerned. A man in this condition is, for the time being, a Buddha, a Christ. Buddhists could speak of this condition as that of the 'inner Buddha'; Christian mystics could speak of it as that of the 'immanent Christ' in manifestation; the Hindû might speak of it as the 'splendor of the Brahman in the heart.'

Into the condition of the intermediate nature thus temporarily created, there flows, then, for the time being, the Will and Thought and Consciousness of the Inner Essential Self or monadic essence, for whom the Sage or Messenger or disciple has thus prepared the personal lower vehicle; and through it performs the work or gives the sublime teachings of Reality kept in mind to do and to give.

It should be emphasized here again that such temporary filling of the self-conscious mind with the spiritual essence in no sense, as is obvious, injures that mind, or the body that it functions in, or degrades it, or renders it less fit when the normal state or condition is resumed. On the contrary, all the results or consequences are greatly for betterment. It must be obvious that if the ordinary human being could feel his brain and psychological and emotional apparatus inspired and filled full with the presence of a divinity, it would be incomparably good for him, and would strengthen him, in all higher senses of the word, in an incomparable degree; and exactly the same applies to one possessing what we may call quasi-divinity.

All this may seem to be very strange to the average Occidental, because he knows nothing about these marvelous mysteries in Psychology—the *real* Psychology that Theosophy, which is the Ancient Wisdom, teaches of. But in actual fact, could he penetrate behind the veils enshrouding the Great Ones of history, the towering monuments of spiritual and intellectual capacity, as expressed in and through these World-Teachers, he would immediately see that the condition or state that we have briefly described is, in those cases, one of the most usual of the psychological phenomena belonging to them. Probably every World-Teacher, or Founder of religion, in history, has been spoken of by his followers or disciples as having been at times *illuminated;* or it has been said of them that they were infilled with a glory; or it has been recorded of them that the face and the body of them shone; and indeed the ancient Greeks, to take an instance, have left it on record in much of their religious and mystical philosophical literature, that such appearances of divinities or quasi-divine Beings—the inner spiritual Self or Monad—manifesting through the body of some chosen one, was a well-known fact of archaic Wisdom and Knowledge, certainly so in the cases of initiation.

Usually this illumination or filling with glory came from the man's own Inner Spiritual Essence or Self; but sometimes it occurred because some great and lofty human being—of Class II above described—became the vehicle or channel for the temporary manifestation of some Celestial Power, so called.

Here then, in these paragraphs, we have briefly laid bare the solution of the spiritual-psychological Mystery that H. P. Blavatsky presented to the world.

Now, it should not be supposed that these pages are an attempt to lay bare, for the first time in the world, secrets of the Esoteric Wisdom which heretofore have never been divulged. No such claim is made, and certainly it would be both improper and unwise to burden the mind and thought with subjects which require not only deep and conscientious thinking, but, for a more or less complete understanding of them, years of preparation and honestly impersonal study. This entire subject is a very holy one, and we have endeavored to write of it as such, appealing to the intuition and heart to understand, and, in understanding, to feel somewhat of the mighty power which came into the world and worked in it for the world's own and sole benefit through H. P. Blavatsky, the Messenger and Co-Laborer of the noblest and holiest of Men.

Class III are the Avatâras. This Class is again quite different, so far as the details of the mechanism of the psychological mystery is concerned; but nevertheless this third Class of Men, all supremely holy Men—very few indeed as they are—falls within the general psycho-spiritual subject which we have been studying; because, *in addition to* other spiritual and psychological mysteries appertaining to them, there is a Mystery closely similar to that of the psychological matters of which we have been writing.

The great difference between the Avatâras and Class II, and Class I, lies in this fact: in the case of the Avatâras, there is an absence of a karmically *natural* personal intermediate or psychological vehicle from the very beginning of their physical existence; indeed, from a period of time even before the birth of the physical body. Their intermediate part, forming the psychological link between Spirit and physical body, comes to them from elsewhere; so that in one sense of the word, and in a very mystical sense—one extremely difficult to explain to European and American students or readers—the absence of a *naturally* personal psychological intermediary may be called absolute and complete, for it certainly lasts from birth until those Avatâras disappear from among men.

This entire Class of Men, the Avatâras, have a history so marvelous, so different from anything that ordinary human beings know anything about, that without years of study it is almost hopeless to give a satisfying explanation of it, and yet we cannot leave this third class out of our category without justly incurring the charge of presenting an incomplete outline of the subject under discussion.

Here once more we are deeply sensible of embarrassment in pointing to subjects, and only briefly touching upon them, which are so difficult and abstruse. And yet what can be done? Once an explanation of H. P. Blavatsky's mission and work in the world is attempted it is obvious that something has to be said. Indeed much has to be said, and little known mysteries of the inner life of human beings have to be sketched. But, on the other hand, were these matters to be fully developed, not merely one volume but many would be required. Our hope is that hints have been given which will appeal to the intuition and will encourage students to find by their own study of the majestical system of the ancient Wisdom-Religion today called Theosophy, treasures of unspeakable worth, both for mind and heart. Of themselves they must dig into these mines of ancient wisdom; and the value of so doing on their own account is that they will inevitably light upon and take unto themselves those more especial treasures which each will instinctively feel to be most native to his own character.

The word *Avatâra* is a Sanskrit compound, and may be translated as 'passing down,' and signifies the passing down of a celestial Energy or, what comes to the same thing, of an individualized complex of celestial energies, which is equivalent to saying a celestial being, in order to overshadow and illuminate some human being—but a human being which at the time of such connection of 'heaven and earth', of divinity with matter, possesses no karmically intermediate or connecting link between the overshadowing entity and the physical body: in other words, no human soul karmically destined to be the inner master of the body thus born.

What, then, is it which furnishes this absolutely necessary intermediate link of the chain of man's inner constitution, so that the human being to be may have the human intermediate or psychological apparatus fit to express the invisible splendor of this celestial descent? This intermediate or psychological link in these cases is supplied by the deliberate and voluntary entrance into the unborn child — and coincidently with the overshadowing of the celestial power—of the psychological or intermediate principle of one of the Greater Ones, who thus completes what is to be the pure and lofty human channel through which the 'descending' divinity may manifest, finding in this high psychological part a properly evolved link enabling that divinity to express itself in human form upon earth.

The important, the main, point about the Avatâra is this: the Avatâra is karma-less. The spiritual-divine part, or the celestial descent, has of course no karma, individual, national, or racial, attracting it into our sphere; and his descent, if governed by karma at all, is controlled by karma of a cosmic character.

Now, although it may not be immediately evident, there is more similarity between the characteristics pertaining to the Avatâra-Class and those of the Second Class than one may off-hand suppose. Consequently, therefore, H. P. Blavatsky, who belongs to the Second Class, in a certain particular sense may be looked upon as having belonged to the Class of minor Avatâras; and the same observation would apply to any other member of the Second Class.

These three Classes of course are obviously divisible, each one, into various grades or stages, from the less great to the greatest. Thus in ordinary humanity of the First Class, we have in the lower ranks, the inferior men, running up to the highest stage of that First Class, whom we may call men of genius and quasi-Great Men.

So, also, in the Second Class we have the Messengers and disciples belonging to various grades, from the lowest, or the neophyte in Esoteric Wisdom and training, to the great Sages and Seers themselves.

Thus, also in the Third or Avatâra-Class, although this Class contains very few examples—very few indeed—in human history, yet, as already hinted, the Avatâras are not of precisely equal spiritual rank and grandeur.

It may be of interest to illustrate the point if we cite two, and perhaps three, examples of Avatâric lives. The first one was a true Avatâra, Śankarâchârya of India, who lived some few generations after the date of the passing of Gautama, the Buddha. He was born in Southern India, and from earliest childhood, to the day of his death, he manifested transcendent capacity. He was the reformer of much of the then current and orthodox Indian philosophy, and may be regarded as the founder of the great Adwaita-School of the Vedânta which flourishes even to this day, and perhaps may be called the most widely disseminated and popular School of modern philosophical Hindûism—and perhaps the noblest also. There is a great deal of mystery connected with the life of Śankarâchârya, and many legends, doubtless having some foundation of fact, are still current regarding his existence.

The second instance which may be illustrated is that of Jesus, the great Syrian Sage, who was another Avatâra, and like all of his Class, had no merely human karma. This was what we had in mind when earlier reference was made to the mystical episode in the Garden of Gethsemane, and to the exclamation there alleged to have been made: "Let this cup pass from me; nevertheless not my will, but Thine be done!"

It should be said in passing that the entire story of the Christian Gospels is a mystery-tale, and represents various episodes of the Initiation-Cycle as these episodes were understood and followed in Asia Minor; and such a mystery-tale is as applicable to any great World-Teacher as it was to Jesus, around whom this particular mystery-tale was builded as a type. To this of course no Theosophist has any reasonable objection, although he does object to the taking of the beautiful New Testament story as a unique instance of quasi-human divinity in the spiritual history of the world, and consequently to the considering of Jesus, the Christos, as the unique and unparalleled World-Teacher.

Deeper knowledge of that sublime personage and of his exalted and lofty character ought to be, and undoubtedly will be, welcomed by every thoughtful mind, and nothing we here say should be construed as derogatory of that sublime character or intended to diminish the respect and reverence which his figure holds in Occidental hearts. We feel, however, that the truth about him is far more wonderful in every respect than what tradition or story has ever yet told; and having this in mind we feel also that greater knowledge of him, as the Ancient Wisdom teaches it, can bring only an added respect. Looking upon Jesus the Christos as one of the long line of World-Teachers, and seeing what he was both humanly and psychologically, brings him closer to the hearts of men. Truth, for all harmoniously developed minds, never, under any circumstances, is something to fear.

We may add further that our esoteric doctrines show us that the psychological part of Jesus the Avatâra was almost certainly the same psychological entity or psychological individuality which had furnished the intermediate or psychological human vehicle in the preceding Avatâra, Śankarâchârya; and that this same intermediate psychological entity acting in both cases is closely connected, in esoteric history, with the noblest Sage and Seer that history has record of—Gautama the Buddha.

In a closely similar sense also, although in a far larger sense than applies to the Wonder-Woman H. P. Blavatsky, Gautama the Buddha may be called an Avatâra—but, we repeat it, in a certain sense only; and the same remark regarding H. P. Blavatsky may be made with regard to Apollonius of Tyana.

It is thus evident that the position herein assigned H. P. Blavatsky as regards spiritual and intellectual and psychological capacities, is incomparably superior to that which she has hitherto been supposed to hold, either by her warmest friends and followers, or by those who were keen enough to recognize in her a spiritual energy of paramount importance in religious and philosophical history. Woman, saint, sage, martyr: the judgment of the world of the future will place her on the high vantagepoint of wisdom and moral splendor where she rightly belongs.

VI—Clothed With the Light. The Inner God

Perhaps the noblest detail of the wonderful doctrines which H. P. Blavatsky, as Messenger of her Great Teachers, brought to the Western World, is the one which recalls to the consciousness of modern man the age-old truth of the living reality of one's own essential divinity, the existence in every normal human being of his own inner god. There is not a great World-Religion, there is not a great World-Philosophy, existing in the past or still existent in the present, which does not teach this same fundamental truth of human existence. Indeed, it may be called the very foundation-stone on which were builded the great systems of religious and philosophical thinking of the past; and rightly so, because it is founded on Nature herself.

The inner god in man, man's own inner, essential divinity, is the root of him, whence flow forth in inspiring streams into the psychological apparatus of his constitution, all the inspirations of genius, all the urgings to betterment. All powers, all faculties, all characteristics of individuality which blossom through evolution into individual manifestations, are the fruitage of the working in man's constitution of those life-giving and inspiring streams of spiritual energy. It is they which furnish the urge behind all evolutionary progress. It is they which in their intricate and complex connections and workings in the material substances of which man's constitution is composed, not only build that constitution itself into individual form, but lead it on to develop or throw forth into manifestation the innate or rather the inherent characteristics composing it. It is thus that personality is born, and out of personality through evolution, combined with the luminous stream above spoken of, arises, phoenix-like, the glorious individuality in genius and in impersonal power that mankind of the future is destined to manifest, and which even man today manifests in some degree.

It is no wonder, then, that those ancient World-Religions and World-Philosophies are based upon this fact of man's essential divinity. It was this natural fact which took form in those different systems of thinking as a doctrine; which brought also into being the many and various schools of religious development existing at different times throughout the ages; and it was a more or less distorted vision of this great truth which led many individuals of either sex to seek the monastic life, thinking that by so doing, they could have better chances for cultivating the divine consciousness and super-normal faculties belonging to this highest essential nature of man. This natural fact formulated into doctrine, furthermore, is at the back of all the systems of mystic training pursued in various lands and in various ages, by both individuals and schools; while it is a matter of common knowledge that the mystics of all the ages have united in teaching the existence and ever-present power of the inner god in man as the first principle governing the progress of man out of material life into the spiritual.

Nevertheless, while the main idea has been invariably clear from remotest times, an accurately reasoned formulation of the dotrine, and clear-cut proofs of its philosophical sufficiency, as shown and demonstrated by human beings who already have attained in some degree union with their inner god, was utterly unknown to the Occident until H. P. Blavatsky appeared in 1875 as the Voice and Expositor of the wonderful teachings of the archaic Wisdom-Religion. Thereafter, for all who were hungering for truth, and were willing to set aside personal or philosophical or religious predilections or prejudices in favor of a provable system of doctrine, the doors were opened, the path shown, and the Light, towards which this path led, was clearly designated and logically proved.

The fact alone that H. P. Blavatsky recalled to the consciousness of Western men and women the existence of the Association of these great Sages and Seers, awakened anew in Western minds their sleeping intuitions, and thenceforward they could for themselves not merely see but also understand that those great Seers and Sages were the evolutionary manifestation of the transcendent powers of the inner god in man, and that, as such, they proved what all men could attain to, if they but *willed* to do so.

She pointed likewise to the existence of the great geniuses of the world, and argued with irresistible logic and force of illustration that it would be imbecile to suppose that such examples of human greatness existed by chance, or could be otherwise than the manifestations or effects of causes of a spiritual and intellectual nature working in the human constitution, and bringing forth these fine Flowers of the human race as the necessary evolutionary fruitage of the invisible powers and potencies working in man's inner economy. Further, once grant the existence of these great geniuses and Great Men in human history, and it would be absurd to say that as the human race had already attained in such beings a certain high level of capacity and ability and spiritual power, men could go no higher; or, equivalently, that no greater men than those already known to history ever existed or could in the future ever exist.

The argument was irresistible, the illustrations were appealing, the call to the understanding was both immediate and fruitful. It became at once apparent to every thoughtful man that the existence of the great Seers and Sages of the world, as taught by H. P. Blavatsky, was not only a necessary result of human evolution, but a logically necessary result from the premises which it was impossible to avoid accepting.

No human mind could admit that there was a path which abruptly stopped at some halfway period, or at some one-third-way period, marked by the examples of human genius thus far known; and that thereafter this path was mysteriously and ineluctably broken. This curious supposition needs only to be stated in plain words, in order to ensure its immediate rejection.

What Nature has once done, she almost invariably will do again. What she has once brought forth, is necessarily a promise of what she will again bring to birth; and as no two men are identical, any more than two leaves on the millions of trees in the forests of the world are identical; and as also no two human beings stand in perfectly identical stages or degrees of human evolution—for if they did they would be the same person—therefore it is impossible to call a halt anywhere, or to fix boundaries anywhere, or to say that here and no farther extend the powers of Nature.

The example of King Knut (Canute), as legend tells the story, who set his arm-chair on the strand washed by the waves of the North Sea, and said: "Thus far, O sea, and no farther!" is one which the wiseacres and know-everythings of history have always been prone to follow; but Nature has little patience with the egoisms of human limitations, and seems to take delight in destroying human illusions of this type.

Oh! if men and women of the Occident could only get the conviction of the existence within themselves of the individual's living god as the fountain of his noblest parts, what a revolution in human thinking it would bring about! If they could only get the conviction, as they will in time most assuredly, that at the core of each one of them, at the heart of the heart of each one of them, is this glorious Sun of consciousness: then indeed not only would their lives change immensely for the better, not only would human relations be softened and refined, not only would the horrors attending our present civilization disappear as do the mists before the morning sunlight, but to the individual himself there would come inspiration, a sense of high human dignity, a sense of well-being, and of undeveloped power—which both intuition and instinct would then tell them could only be developed through altruistic use. And could this idea become the conviction of their minds and the persuasion of their hearts, then indeed should we be members of a new race, enlightened with an all-embracing and high racial consciousness, and the Theosophical ideal of Universal Brotherhood would follow fully and in completeness as a necessary sequence. Our fellow human beings would act, think and dwell among each other almost as a race of incarnate gods—for that in the name of holy Truth is just what we human beings are.

It has been nobly said by some Western thinker that when he laid his hand on a fellow human being he did so with awe, because he felt that he was touching the garment of divinity;

and this, in very truth, is the case. It is but the imperfection of our present understanding which blinds our eyes and which causes us to dwell, through selfish fear, in our own small spheres of petty interests, and cuts us off from the heart-elevating influences which we otherwise should receive in full flood from the hearts of our fellows.

The human race at the present time is passing through only one of the phases of its long evolutionary journey back to divinity; and it is ignorance of this fact that has produced the hard and harsh outlines of human thinking today, which in its turn is the imperfect mother of the imperfect civilization of which we boast.

It is to be the destiny of the human race, through slow degrees of evolutionary progress, to transfer the seat of the individual-personal consciousness upwards from the brain-mind, and out of it and up from it, into a nearer approach to the noëtic or spiritual-intellectual part. And this transferring of the seat of individual-personal consciousness, will of course be attended with an equivalent ennobling and betterment of human thinking, and therefore also, of human civilization; until finally in the far distant aeons of the future the reunion will be made with the god within—the ever-living inner Spirit—by the upward evolving personal consciousness of the human being. Then there will occur that at-one-ment of which the great Seers of all the ages have taught us.

Meanwhile it is these great Seers and Sages themselves who have outrun the army of the human host in evolutionary development, and who therefore now live among us as exemplars of what the remainder of the human race will be in the distant future. They are the forerunners, and being ahead and higher than we, they see more and farther than we. They are the Prophets and the Seers and the Sages and the Illuminated Ones and the Wise Ones merely because they are in closer and straiter union with their own inner god. In very truth they may be said to be 'clothed with the Sun,' that inner sun of essential divinity existent in the core of the human being, which, as the Christian New Testament puts it, lights every man that cometh into the world.

Plato has a very telling description of men as they now are: beings living in the deep recesses of the cave of material existence, almost unconscious of the sunlight streaming in in feeble rays from without. They see the dancing of shadows on the walls, mistake them for realities; and only when they learn more and turn their faces towards the light with will and objective purpose do they see the pathway outwards towards the outer splendor.

So it is with us today. Most see these dancing shadows of consciousness and circumstance, mistaking them for ultimate realities. So firmly convinced are they that what they see is true and that the shadows are real, that their minds are crystallized in that conviction and they deny the very existence of the inner sun, of which the shadows are but the deceptive illusions of the human brain-consciousness.

The Divine Fire which moves through Universal Nature is the source of the individualized Divine Fire in man, man's inner god. And as Universal Nature manifests in all-various and bewilderingly diverse forms and shapes and powers and energies and substances—the effects of the working in itself of the Cosmic Fire—just so is man himself the effectual result, the phenomenal product in his own multiform and manifold characteristics and diversities as between individuals, of the working in each one of us of each individual's own central Divine Fire—his own inner god.

All through the ages the truth of the actual existence of the inner god in human lives has been voiced and exemplified in the teachings and lives of the great World-Figures and Sages, and their teaching is always one in fundamentals, ever varied though it may be through the necessities of circumstance, such as language, or type of civilization, or manner of presentation.

But fundamentally that truth is always the same: Come up higher, ye children of men, look within, leave the valley of shadows for the sunlighted peaks of wisdom and illumination. There is no other pathway for you individually than the pathway leading ever inwards towards your own inner god. The pathway of another is the same pathway for that other; but it is not your pathway, because your pathway is your Self, as it is for that other one his Self. All tread the same pathway, but each man must tread it himself, and no one can tread it for another; and this pathway leads to unutterable splendor and expansion of consciousness, to unthinkable bliss, to perfect peace, for it is the pathway of evolution in the Theosophical sense: the unrolling, the unfolding, the unwrapping, the coming forth into manifestation, of the powers, faculties, energies, substances, lying dormant or partly dormant, or latent or partly latent, into consciously realized activity—consciously realized in and by the individual who experiences it.

Within you lie all the mysteries of the Universe, for any human individual is the Microcosm of the Macrocosm, the Little World of the Great World, and all truth and wisdom and power for the individual, are rooted in his own inner god, in his own spiritual heart of hearts, in the core of his own being.

This is the pathway of evolution. This is the way to freedom for men; the way to light for men; and there is no other way. And all the Sages of all the ages have taught nothing but this: Be one with your own inner god. The pathway is difficult to follow in the beginning, but only in the beginning, because the difficulties arise in the individual himself or herself, and are utterly non-existent outside of the individual. It is his own nature that he must master and control and direct. Man must direct his own evolution, self-chosen, self-followed, for we can progress and grow only through self-directed evolution.

O you men and women of the race, do your hearts yearn for better things? Do your minds aspire towards a larger light? Do you wish to become more truly yourselves, your better selves? Do you wish to feel growing within your souls an ever-expanding consciousness of spiritual and intellectual strength and power and capacity? Do your hearts yearn to help your fellow-men on the difficult pathway of self-conquest? If so, open your hearts and minds to the message of Theosophy, the Wisdom-Religion of archaic ages. Hearken to its message, and become brothers and co-workers in their labor of love with these great Sages and Seers who, having become cognizant in themselves of the actual ever-presence in them of the god within, have taught the everlasting truth. This message is as religious as it is truly philosophical, and as scientific as it is religious. There is nothing of worth that can be said against it. There is everything of worth that can be said for it. It is not imaginary, because these great Seers and Sages have lived, and have themselves proved by their own lives and spiritual powers what they taught, and they have moved the world with their teachings; and while you aspire as you do, and yearn as you do, to be more and to do better, do not turn deaf ears to the lessons of their teaching.

Turn then your eyes to the unspeakably beautiful Power within yourself, realizing at the same time that it is the same unspeakable glory in essence which illuminates the core of the being of all your fellows. Wisdom without bounds will in time be yours; knowledge solving the most wonderful problems of the universe and of man will in time be yours. Love without bounds, all encompassing, all-embracing, will fill your hearts in time; and together with these blessings you will attain a joy and a peace impossible to decribe in words.

Part II

Philosophic and Scientific

VII—The Great Sages and Seers

In considering a universal view of the great world of beings which surrounds us, one is struck with a very interesting fact, which is, that if we place Man as being the highest known entity on earth—highest, that is, with regard to faculty and the use of faculty and the self-conscious perception and enjoyment of faculty—we find that as our survey leaves him and travels backwards along the descending scale of evolutionary development, our attention is caught away from the individual and particular towards composites. It has been said, and probably said with perfect truth, that no two leaves in a forest are exactly the same; for if they were, they would not be two leaves but the same leaf. With how much greater force can this be said of so highly individualized a being as Man! And, despite the formal individualities even of the leaves in a forest of trees, they are as a single entity when compared with the marvelous development of what is popularly called individuality as found in Man.

It would seem as if the whole purpose of Nature, or the whole trend of development, were the bringing out, the rolling forth (which is of course the etymological meaning of the word 'evolution'), or the unfolding, of characteristics lying latent in the invisible, as well as visible, fabric of living beings. An English scientific writer, Bateson, some years ago expressed this very neatly when he spoke of the "unpacking of an original complex" as representing the evolutionary process. We must regard the evolutionary processes working in Nature as being the effects of a concatenation of causes working in living beings, and leading such beings into constantly extending paths of individual development. This is the 'tendency' in the living things of Nature to advance towards individuality and away from the perfect communism of the lowest forms of animal life, and from the simple unism of the rocks.

But this is looking at the matter on its merely material side. How our ideas expand as we study the *mental* and *spiritual* activities of mankind! Here we observe the 'struggle' to reconcile duty with desire; right with justice. In employing the word 'struggle' here, we are using the ordinary phraseology of modern quasi-philosophical biology in order to be understood easily; but actually the struggle is purely imaginary, for the entire field of human effort is in the individual himself, and only relatively and in small degree does any such imaginary struggle along these lines arise from man's relations with the surrounding sphere of circumstance, or with his fellows. The so-called 'struggle' is simply the conflict in man's own mind; and as all men have this conflict, they imagine that it exists outside of themselves. Once the realization comes home to him that all Nature is a unity, and that he himself forms but one small wheel in the cosmic macrocosm, directed and inspired by a unifying spiritual force, man finds his freedom, sees his so-called 'struggle' to be what it is, his own illusion, and attains peace and liberation from the bonds of desire arising out of the thraldom of the personal self to the desires which that personal self gives birth to.

One of the great virtues of the teachings which H. P. Blavatsky brought anew to the western world lies in grasping this idea, for she showed to Occidentals the pathway out of this stifling morass of personality into the golden sunlight of spiritual freedom. In doing so she merely put in philosophic and religious form the teachings of the Sages of all the ages, that true and real freedom lies in abandoning the thraldom of selfish personal desires, and in realizing one's absolute fundamental oneness with the great motivating and causal impulses of Universal Nature which thrill through us and really make us what we are.

These great motivating energies in Nature show to any observant eye what is popularly called the evolutionary 'tendency' in man; and this tendency, at man's present stage of development—a tendency which will grow constantly in strength—is to re-combine, to reunite with his fellows, and to see and to find in them other parts of himself, as it were. All the foundations of morals repose on this so-called 'tendency.' We instinctively know a man from his thoughts and acts, in other words from his character, from the workings in him of those forces which predominate over other forces; for in all human beings certain psycho-mental energies are dominant over others, which latter are recessive; and it is these dominant energies of a psycho-mental type, which show forth in man's character.

Indeed, when we say 'good' man, we mean one conscious of duties to other beings, who carries these duties out regardless of any temporary loss to himself, if such take place. This is, of course, a declaration of the fundamental or spiritual unity of all beings; of what Theosophists so truly but inadequately express when they speak of Universal Brotherhood as a fact in Nature.

What man can fail to see the difference which exists between a man and a tiger, for instance, or between a man and a fish? Or between these, and the unself-conscious existence of the stone? And yet all these beings, and all the multitudinous hosts of beings existing in all-various grades of development which are both invisible and visible, all are offsprings of the same fundamental spiritual-divine Source; all are beings working their various ways upwards, each along the particular path outlined for it by its own impelling energies of higher consciousness, and some of which beings are far along the path of evolution, while others have as yet hardly done more than begin their journey. What man is rash enough to say that these entities are separate in origin, separate in being, separate in destiny? We have the contrary proved to us by every glance of our eyes, by every object that our eyes rest upon; for all Nature proclaims the coherent aggregate of beings as indissolubly interrelated and interlocked both in activity and in destiny. Yet how enormous are the differences that separate the highest from the lowest, the Man from the Stone, or the Man from the Fish, or from the Tiger. We see everywhere stirring around us in the lives, in the emotions, in the instincts, and impulses, of the humbler things that environ us the same forces that stir in our own breasts: love, affection, fear, passion, sympathy, remembrance, hatreds, and many more. Still, Man stands supreme over all that are beneath him. He has attained a post whence he surveys the beings below him with fascinated interest; and he turns his eyes in the other direction, and he is subtilly conscious that farther along the way and ahead of him, there must be beings greater than he, beings in comparison with whom he is as are the animals now to him, beings who in ages, aeons long since past, were in their turn where he now stands.

Man's logical sense obliges him to accept this graduated scale of beings in evolutionary development; for he is utterly incapable of pointing to a beginning or of finding an end. Such imaginary breaks are obviously mere fantasies of the imagination.

An important point here is not merely that beings superior to men exist—for rigid logic compels us to admit their existence—but that if such beings ahead of man do not exist, the anomaly of the graduated scale of beings beneath man would require an explanation that no one yet has succeeded in giving.

Following the teachings of the great Sages and Seers of the ages, brought anew to the Western World by H. P. Blavatsky, we are enabled for purposes of convenient illustration, to divide this graduated scale into seven (or even into ten) stages of evolution, somewhat after the following fashion:

a First Elemental Kingdom—
Fluidic in type, with unmanifest and unindividualized monadic corpuscles posessing a common vital organic existence.

b Second Elemental Kingdom—
Separation into droplets, so to say, of quasi-particularized entities held together by the same vital wave.

c Third Elemental Kingdom—
More highly particularized beings, although still bound together by, and functioning in, a common vital organic existence.

1. The Mineral Kingdom—
   Quasi-individualized corpuscles, or particulars, functioning in organic unity. Simple unism.

2. Vegetable Kingdom—
   Simple communism. The pressure towards individualism increases.

3. The Beast Kingdom—
   Dawning of individualized existence.

4. The Human Kingdom—
   Efflorescence of individuality. Dawning of a common or general consciousness.

5. The Great Ones—
   Full grown individuality. Self-conscious realization of a unifying general consciousness.

6. Quasi-Divine Beings or Lower Gods—
   Perfected individuality merging, without diminution, into a general consciousness. Dawning of cosmical consciousness.

7. Gods—
   Emergence into conscious realization of cosmical consciousness, without loss of a perfected impersonal individuality.

The mind pauses in wonder and awe in contemplation of the utterly sublime reaches of self-conscious existences thus spread out before the inner eye. It would indeed be an anomaly in Nature if Man were the highest possible reach of consciousness in the Universal Life! Great as he is, nothing shows his greatness more than the ability to recognize greatness elsewhere; and how clearly has H. P. Blavatsky not shown forth and proved with inimitable philosophical logic this fact!

As we ponder over the spectacle that our mind spreads befor us, we realize at length that the essential difference between Man and the beings beneath him in evolutionary development lies in his self-conscious mind. Here also we have the link binding us to the higher realms of being, the bridge over which the consciousness passes to and fro between Matter and

Spirit, one the pole of the other; and as we study the lower beings, we also realize the fact that they too have minds of their own, of their own type and kind belonging to their own respective classes: centers of consciousness, in other words, but not of reflective or indirect consciousness, such as man has.

Here, then, in Man it is that we perceive the union *of another and higher* plane of being with *this* plane of being. The spiritual and the material have, so to say, effected a union; or perhaps it would be better to say that in man's case the sensitive and the psychological and the spiritual have united; and the product of this union is seven-principled Man. Heaven and earth have kissed, as the quaint ancient saying has it, and their offspring is the human race.

No one is blind enough not to see the enormous, indeed apparently almost impassable, gulf which separates the self-conscious mind of Man from the direct sensitive mind of the lower creatures. Man may truly be called a god inshrined within a tabernacle—the psycho-material framework of his lower nature. It is the destiny of the god within him to raise up to its own level of power, beauty, wisdom, and strength, the struggling, falling, aspiring center which man usually calls himself. This is achieved through evolution, which we must always keep in mind is evolution in the Theosophical sense, of the flowing outwards into ever-increasing and more perfect manifestation of the inlocked, infolded, or in other words, the native capacities, abilities, powers, faculties, of the inner god.

As man grows towards a fuller union with his inner god, *pari passu* he grows into greatness of understanding and sympathy with all that is. He realizes with ever-enlarging comprehension his essential oneness with the Universal Nature from which he sprang in the beginning of this period of Cosmic Evolution and towards which he is now again journeying. He left it in 'eternities' past, an unself-conscious god-spark, and he shall in a future aeon rebecome one with it again, but as a fully self-conscious divinity. The cycle of evolution, of development, shall have then closed for him until he again begins another and a new pilgrimage in the cosmic spaces, both invisible and visible, but on heights at present inconceivable to the human soul.

The lesson that we learn from all this is the lesson of fundamental unity, of inseparable interests, and of unbreakable bonds between all that is, and everything that is. We begin to understand why all the greatest figures that the human race has ever produced, the Master-Minds of the ages, the great Sages and Seers, have taught one Truth, one fundamental Reality, one Universal Life, of which we all—human beings and those below us, and those above us—are, as it were, the sparks; and this Essential Reality, the Universal Life, underlies all the manifold Mysteries of Being.

It should be amply clear from what we have said that the existence and living reality of the perfected Men whom Theosophists commonly call Teachers, Elder Brothers, Masters, Sages, Seers, Mahâtmas, is founded on no vague and imaginary hypothesis, but conversely, that their existence is imperatively called for by the rigid logic and the inescapable deductions that flow from our study of Nature itself. These observations lay the foundation for what we may call our argument—in Nature itself. On no other grounds of reality is the existence of such perfected men properly to be proved. They are, as much as anything else is, the Children of the Universal Life; they are men, just as we are men; born of human mothers by wholly natural and usual methods; they think as we think, they breathe, smile, walk, speak in human tongues, and are as other men are—except (and this exception is of course a great difference between them and other men) that they are greater in all things than average men are.

It is of the utmost importance to have this statement of their human and yet sublimely human nature and characteristics clear in the mind, because those great-souled beings—'Great Soul' or 'Great Self' is the Sanskrit meaning of the Word 'Mahâtma'—are sometimes spoken of, by those who do not understand anything of them, as quasi-'supernatural,' 'superhuman,' 'gods,' or, most foolishly, as 'returning spirits,' and what not. They are not 'supernatural' because there is no such thing as the 'supernatural.' Nothing can be outside of or above Nature, the Universal Mother, the Universal Origin; and what most people ignorantly mean when they use this term is what we Theosophists express by such words as 'inner,' 'occult,' 'hid forces of Nature,' etc., etc. We attach no sensible meaning whatsoever to the word 'supernatural,' if used in any other signification. Our souls, our spirits, the invisible and unknown forces and energies and substances of Nature, the Heaven-Worlds—planes or spheres of being wholly outside of our physical ken and belonging to what is popularly called 'the Spiritual World'—all these and much more are included in what the Theosophist means when he uses the word 'Nature' without accompanying qualification.

The idea that Nature is merely our gross, visible, physical world, and that all that is outside of it (and the marvelous and daily growing achievements of modern science have taught us to realize that what is hid and invisible is incomparably vaster and greater than what is visible) is 'supernatural,' with the implied idea of something contrary to Nature is the result of centuries of miseducation with regard to the Mysteries of Being.

We Theosophists do not recognize the 'supernatural' in the popular sense, as having any existence at all. Like the posibility of 'miracles,' if by this word we mean the working of marvels contrary to natural law, or by the suspension of natural law, we reject it as unphilosophical, unnatural, and therefore unscientific, as well as irreligious, and as springing from ignorance of the inner constitution of the interlocking, interrelated, and interblending worlds of Spirit and of Matter.

Of course we not only recognize but emphatically teach— and in all this we follow strictly and faithfully the tenets of the Ancient Wisdom, the Wisdom-Religion of the archaic ages as brought anew to the Western world by H. P. Blavatsky— the existence of hid mysteries in Nature, of little known and of as yet entirely unknown forces in Nature; that these mysteries and forces nevertheless have been known in past ages and are known today by these perfected Men themselves. They know of them not through favor or by chance, but because they are beyond us in evolutionary development and therefore naturally know more than we do of Nature's mystic and wonderful secrets. This is why these Teachers seem 'mysterious' to many.

Precisely so does the chemist, expert in his science, know vastly more about certain of Nature's secrets than the unlettered savage, and is therefore able to work with a knowledge of Nature's laws which enables him to produce what seem to be 'miracles' to the simple-minded wild man. Does the astronomer work 'miracles' when he predicts eclipses? Does the geometer work 'miracles' when he tells the wild man the exact height of a pole or of a cliff by taking the measure of the distance from the foot of the pole or of the cliff, to a designated spot, and the tangent of the angle between the horizontal and the line joining the eye with the top of the pole or cliff? Does not the phonograph appear to be a 'miracle' to the mind of the unlettered barbarian, when he hears his chief's voice reproduced with fidelity and recognizes the very words spoken into the record?

A most stupid impression existed, and still exists, that the work of the Great Teachers and the powers they manifest have wholly to do with what is called the supernatural. It was indeed thought that the Theosophical Movement was founded upon what people call 'phenomena', and that the main objective of the Theosophical Movement was, during H. P. Blavatsky's lifetime, and more or less still is, to found societies for occult or magical practices, or for the working of phenomenal wonders. No idea could be more grotesque. No idea could wander farther from the truth. It is the philosophy of the great Sages and Seers which H. P. Blavatsky brought anew to the Western world which forms the totality of her teachings, and which it was and still is the objective of the Theosophical Movement to disseminate among men.

In fact, so far were 'phenomena' so called from having anything to do with the Theosophical Movement *per se*, that in the very beginning Theosophical students were repeatedly warned, and with unceasing reiteration, that the founding of a nucleus of a Universal Brotherhood of mankind, combined with the dissemination of the archaic Wisdom-Religion, were the aims of the modern Theosophical Movement, and that for such purposes alone had it been founded.

This the world in general found it difficult to believe. The movement was launched in an intensely materialistic age, and as was only natural, in one sense, that which was *a priori* denied as possible, and which was falsely supposed to be proclaimed by the Theosophical Leaders as their purpose, aroused both the interest and the antagonism of most people of a conservative bent of mind.

Now, these Great Men, these Sages and Seers, possess knowledge of the laws of Being because such knowledge, first of all, springs up readily and wholly naturally in them, from experience gained and stored in the mystic volume of Memory in past lives (for reincarnation, or repeated imbodiment in bodies of human flesh, is the manner after which and according to which natural evolutionary law works upon the human species in urging the latter towards perfection).

Second, they owe their wisdom and knowledge also to the fact that, composing a Society, an Order, or Brotherhood among themselves from immemorial time, they possess the means and the power not only to aid the development of wisdom and knowledge in themselves by association with their fellow Great Ones, but also to assist the growth of wisdom and knowledge in such men as they have found to be fit and worthy recipients of such aid.

We have already given answer to the question: Why do not these Great Teachers come openly before the world and declare themselves? And we repeat: Why should they? Of what benefit would it be, either to the human race or to themselves, for the work in which they are engaged, to do so? Obviously it can be argued with telling logic that if they could work with larger results and more easily behind the veil of invisibility, so to say, and unknown to the multitude — and this is just what is claimed — of what possible benefit either to themselves or to others would it be to come out publicly and preach? It would surely be folly to cripple their efforts by a concentration of attention on purely personal and unimportant details which would assuredly follow from such action.

The truth is that these Great Teachers are just as much subject to the laws that govern Universal Nature, as is the humblest animate thing that is, except that their vast knowledge of Nature and of her laws and processes and secrets, and their relatively perfect self-identity with those laws, give them powers and faculties undreamed of by the average human being. But it should be noted also in passing, that knowledge carries with it responsibilities of the loftiest moral character in the hearts of these Great Ones. Furthermore, were they to come out and stand before the public, that public would probably straightway begin to worship them as gods—or, indeed, that public would persecute them, if it were possible, in the usual spirit of distrust that average men always show to what they do not understand, and therefore fear.

However, it is a matter of historical fact, that at certain critical periods in world-history, one or more of these Great Teachers, either themselves come out from their seclusion, and teach more or less publicly, or send a Messenger to do so; and the latter was the case of H. P. Blavatsky.

Realizing, therefore, that these Teachers or Mahâtmas are human beings like other men, except that they are farther advanced along the path of evolution than the majority, it is easy enough to begin to understand something of their nature as individuals, and as a corporate body, and of their capacities, and of their vast knowledge of Nature. It is perfectly true that they possess knowledge of Nature's secret processes and of hid mysteries which to the average man may seem to be little short of the marvelous; but after all, this mere fact is of relatively small importance in comparison with the far greater and more profoundly moving aspects of their nature and life-work. It is more important to realize that their knowledge of the spiritual side of Universal Nature and of human life is the foundation for the reverence that unspoiled human hearts and unprejudiced minds instinctively give to these Superior Men.

It is because of this spiritual knowledge which they possess, and on account of their highly developed spiritual and intellectual power, that they are so often called in the Orient by the term Mahâtmas. They are also called Elder Brothers, because they are older in experience than the average of men; because they are of ripe understanding, perfected through lives of labor and self-conquest in past ages, and because they stand in much the same relation to the majority of men that an elder brother does to his younger brothers.

Especially are they called Teachers because they are occupied in the noble duty of instructing mankind in inspiring elevating thoughts, and in instilling impulses of forgetfulness of self into the hearts of man. Also are they sometimes called the Guardians, because they are, in very truth, the Guardians of the Race and of the records—natural, racial, national—of past ages, portions of which they give out from time to time as fragments of a long-forgotten Wisdom, when the world is ready to listen to them; and they do this in order to advance the Cause of Truth and of Civilization.

It must be apparent also that there must exist different grades of these relatively perfected men, different stages of advancement as among themselves. This is what Theosophy teaches as a matter of natural necessity and law. Nothing can be more accordant with what we already know of the varying grades in natural existence; and a moment's consideration will at once show that, granted the existence of these Great Men, differences of degree in evolutionary advancement among them are inevitable.

The more we penetrate in our study into the natural procedures of the Environing Life, the greater is the degree of individuality found in the beings occupying the innumerable steps of Nature's scale the higher those beings stand thereon. In other words, the farther the being has progressed, the greater is his individuality; but we also see that the higher the degree of development, the greater is the sense of unity among the beings occupying these higher stages; but this is *conscious* unity, the spiritual and intellectual *realization* of the oneness with all that is.

Starting on its evolutionary journey, the Monad or spiritual Spark through its radiant Light by almost incredibly slow stages creeps out of the stone into the plant, and from plant into the beast, and from the beast it yearns upwards to higher things, until finally the urging spirit within the evolving entity has brought it to the point where it is enabled to understand self-consciously its fundamental unity with the universe—the Environing Life—and here the human, Man, appears, child of heaven and of earth in very truth, with the lower nature brought under ever-increasing control.

This is a very old teaching: the doctrine of the slowly developing powers and faculties of the evolving entity by reason of the invigorating and inspiring urge of the Monad or spiritual Spark or consciousness-Center working outwards and upwards, into continuously more perfected self-expressions of its native or innate powers and faculties. It is an evolution beginning in the darkest or most material portion of the evolving entity's cyclic journey, until it is self-consciously united with its inner god. This teaching lies at the bottom of all the great philosophies and religions of the archaic world.

The astonishing spread of the evolutionary *idea* fired the minds and imagination of men in Europe. Men like Lamarck and Darwin and their followers caught from the invisble thought-reservoir of the planet the *idea* of a progressive growth, however imperfectly and materialistically they may have taught. This in itself was a proof of the appeal that the *idea* of evolution *per se* can make to man. Not that we Theosophists accept either Lamarckism or Darwinism as being identical with the teachings of Theosophy as regards evolution; for we do not, and this for the reason that both of these schemes are incomplete in conception and largely wrong in detail; but we do most decidedly accept and teach the general doctrine of a slow and steady evolutionary growth *from within outwards,* or, as it would probably be phrased today, from pre-existent faculty to subsequent organ.

We also teach that this steady evolutionary process consists in bringing out, through what we may call self-expression, the intrinsic, native, latent, dormant powers or faculties inherent in and urging on the evolving entity; and, furthermore, that this process is at certain cyclic intervals marked by noteworthy spurts or increases of evolutionary intensity, followed as surely by periods of quiescence or dormancy, and even occasionally by apparent, but not real, retrogression. Such periods are, respectively, the epoch of racial manifestation in civilization reaching a culmination of power and brilliance, and then sinking back into barbarism: the evolutionary height reached in the one case, and the following depth of retrogression in the other case, varying with many other factors contained in the problem.

This remarkable system is sketched with masterly hand, in all its main features, in the books written by H. P. Blavatsky, and especially in *The Secret Doctrine*. And if she had done nothing more than this, had given nothing more to the world than this outline of a scheme of spiritual, intellectual, psychological, and astral-vital evolution, she would have merited the gratitude of all thoughtful men.

VIII—The Great Sages and Seers
(Continued)

So far as our own earth is concerned, Man stands at the midway point of the evolutionary ladder. Below him are the hosts of beings less than he is; above him are other hosts greater than he is only because older in experience, riper in wisdom, stronger in spiritual and in intellectual fiber and power; because of greater evolutionary unfoldment of their inherent faculties and powers immanent in the individuality of the inner god —the ever-living, inner, individualized spirit.

As man is to the creatures below him, so are other beings in Nature unto man. As man himself is split up into different stages of progress, or, to put it in another way, as the human race is composed of families differing among themselves in mental, psychical, and spiritual power, even so do we find the same wonderful phenomenon of diversity among the creatures lower than man. Even so our majestic Theosophical doctrines tell us, may we also find the beings above man different among themselves in power, wisdom, and expansion of consciousness.

Is not all this just as it should be and just as it must be in Nature's wondrous fields, bringing individualized experience? Do we find anywhere in Nature a dreary uniformity of universal sameness, arid and uninspiring identity among the beings that are? Nowhere indeed; but everywhere we see diversity, change, movement, progress, with all that the word implies as regards scale and difference and growth.

Of course all this manifold diversity, springing from the hierarchical unity of Nature herself, makes for, and actually is, the explanation of the fascination of the study of Nature, including under that word, as we must do, *all that is;* for as the Theosophist always implies, when he uses the word Nature without qualification, he means not merely the gross, physical nature which our imperfect senses of report tell us of, but more particularly inner and invisible Nature, and especially the invisible and spiritual realms which verily are the Heart of Nature.

Who can deny these obvious truths? Who even would wish to deny them? Yet if you do not deny them, you tacitly admit all of the argument, and you need only to follow the logical sequence of your admission to see, ay, and to accept on your own initiative, all that our Theosophical doctrines set forth regarding the existence and nature and powers and faculties of the Order of Perfected Men already spoken of, who are the great Teachers of mankind.

There is an absurd, logical dilemma in which anyone must necessarily entangle himself who should attempt to deny what is so obviously true, so transparently logical. Men do or they do not differ among themselves in body, psychological power, intellect, consciousness, and moral sense. Now, we know that they do. No fact is of more universal acceptance; and this being so, common knowledge of mankind likewise recognizes that these differences are of many kinds. They exist not only in such obvious instances as in the complexion of the skin, or in the muscular proportions of the body, or in the shape of the head; but also in the mental, psychological, and moral factors of his being. And it is these very factors which most remarkably distingiush the different families of men from each other.

If men therefore differ among themselves as they do, as regards racial families or so-called racial stocks, probably few students of Ethnology and of Anthropology—indeed, no really observing eye—can fail to note that men as individuals vary far more widely than do the families of men one from another. The evolutionary differences among men are vastly more profound and of greater psychological reach than the differences between races, as for instance, the differences as regards a Homer, a Dante, a Goethe, a Shakespeare. Such men stand head and shoulders, in their own particular line, above the average of the race, for it is readily seen that no race of Homers, of Dantes, of Goethes, of Shakespeares, is known on the globe. Such men are geniuses, and so are other men whose natural aptitudes pursue other lines of activity, such as an Edison, a Tesla, a Marconi. And yet these geniuses stand in evolutionary development as children to Others far greater than they.

These Others of course are the great World-Teachers, men whose names are household words, at least in most instances, in every home that is above the level of the savage's hut; and it is these other and greater men who have sent forth into the world Messengers of such power and spiritual vitality that their Messages persist, even though stifled, as the ages pass, under the cloaks and by the gags of fear, superstition, and hatred. These Other Men are in very truth, the Fine Flowers of the human race. So great are they, that succeeding generations of men invented marvelous tales concerning them, sometimes founded upon more or less of truth and fact, but often the mere products of pious and reverent fantasy. They were given a divine birth, a divine origin, 'miracles,' so called, attended their steps in life, and sometimes they were worshiped by the unthinking as incarnate gods, which, indeed, considered merely as a fact, they were in more senses than one; but not in the sense that unguided reverence and unilluminated piety have felt.

Such legends also tell us that celestial spirits or angels, or the inferior gods, according to the race in which they appeared, announced their conception or their birth, or that swans sang a dulcet melody, that all Nature trembled in joy at their coming, while the Great Mother of Men herself, the mighty Earth, moved with feeling. During their lives they were also sometimes said to have been tempted by evil powers, and to have conquered them. They passed their existence on earth in works of benevolence and labors of compassion, teaching their fellow-men a lofty doctrine, and in anticipation of their death training disciples to spread abroad the glad tidings.

Legends also tell us sometimes how they 'raised the dead,' healed the sick, comforted the afflicted and heartbroken, and stayed the hand of vengeance and cruelty; and finally how they passed out of this life in different ways, but usually in a so-called 'miraculous' manner. The legends tell us in some cases that at their respective deaths Nature again was in travail.

Perhaps it was the sun which was shorn of its light, so that darkness fell upon all the earth; or there was a mighty earthquake; or the sheeted dead walked the streets; indeed, many are the various phenomena of wonderment that have been believed in.

One need not accept any of these legends; the thoughtful and reverent mind has no need of them in order to understand the greatness of the Great Men in whose honor simple piety and unthinking worship gave birth to 'miracle.' Indeed, to the reverent mind, such things often work a detriment, and distract the thought away from the essentials of the life and of the teachings of these Great Ones. Still, it is perhaps only fair to say that probably most of these legendary tales have some basis of distorted natural fact in them, some misunderstood or half-forgotten memory of incidents which have been warped by later minds out of any accurate semblance to the reality.

The only real value of these legends lies in the testimony that they bear to the lofty spiritual and intellectual stature of the Great Men who have lived. This it is which it is desirable here to bring sharply to the reader's attention, brushing aside once for all, all the glittering fabric of imagery that faith, unguided by knowledge, has woven around these sublimely beautiful Flowers of Mankind.

We must realize more clearly that only titanic genius, indeed titanic capacity immeasurably over-topping mere genius, could have so stupendously affected the minds of the generations in which the Great Men appeared, and the numerous generations of men who followed them in time. Such men of titanic capacity stand like gigantic figures before the mind's eye, their proportions striking us properly only as we note the environing circumstances. Probably not one of them was welcomed by his fellows when openly and deliberately he came into the world in order to guide them and to teach. Virtually always we find the same tale of bitter opposition, and sometimes of bitterer hatred on the part of those whose interests seemed—and only seemed—to be menaced. So true is this that it has become a proverbial saying that a true prophet is not honored in his own time or country.

However much myth, legend, worship, and pious, reverent fancy, may have inwrapped them in the garments of fantasy; however much their true lineaments may be thus hid from our scrutiny, so that in trying to observe the truth clearly about them, we seem to be walking in enchanted realms of romance and of faery, yet behind it all we sense their presence, and know them to some extent for what they really were—Great Souls, titanic figures, truly Masters of their ages, Teachers, Leaders and Guides, Elder Brothers of the humanity among whom they appeared.

No capable student of history, indeed no sane man, doubts this fact; no capable reasoner has two thoughts about it, whatever he may think of the later accretions of story and of song that have almost hid their real figures from our gaze. This fact admits virtually all that we Theosophists claim; only we go logically to the end, and point out that what has once been can again be, indeed must again be: and, as the race moves farther onwards towards the distant but splendid goals of the future, such figures must reappear more frequently than before, due to the ever enlarging perfection of faculty and understanding appearing in and through all manifested beings, and in the human race in particular. The same figures reappear except that the ranks of them are growing in number as others at one time less developed evolve into the spiritual and intellectual stature of their former teachers.

Is not this, then, a noble teaching? Does it not appeal with wonderful force to every faculty in us? Is it not consistent with all the facts of Nature as we know them, and furthermore does it not offer the best, the most reasonable, explanation of the facts of Nature and of human history as far as these latter are known?

These Great Men differ among themselves; yet they can in perfect truth be called an Order of Perfected Men, using the word 'perfected' in a relative sense, because there is no such thing as absolute perfection, and the sooner this is realized the better. Absolute perfection would mean a stopping, a ceasing, of all possible growth and future development; and the idea is truly an untrue and idiotic one. There are no limits placed for advancing souls, no barriers beyond which they cannot or may not pass; but instead there is constant growth in an ever-widening consciousness and in an ever-deepening love.

Do these Great Souls spend a single earth-life among their fellows, thereafter to evanish away forever into other spheres? How can that be? Our Theosophical doctrine of Karma, old as thinking humanity, the doctrine of 'consequences' as it may rightly be called, of 'cause and effect' as it is usually called, steps here into the argument and shows us that even as they came among us *because* they were men, so must they continue to incarnate again and again and again and again, as long as the present cycle of manifestation lasts. In each life they set in motion karmic causes (although these karmic causes are of a far higher and more subtil kind than is the karmic chain of causation working in ordinary men), because they live to benefit mankind, and thus of their own choice deliberately incur these bonds and relations of karmic destiny. In other words, they make new chains of causation, while working out those of other lives, albeit this is done for the sole benefit of their fellow-men; and as one short human life is obviously insufficient for the full evolution of all the effects necessarily flowing forth from these precedent causes, therefore must they return to the sphere—our Earth—where those precedent causes were initiated and set in movement along the courses of destiny. Doubtless the greater they are the more subtil become the karmic links of causation, but such links connecting them with human life there must be, for otherwise never would they reappear among us, as Leaders, Teachers, and Guides.

This noble doctrine of Karma declares, further, that there comes a time in the evolution of man wherein he reaches such a point of moral strength, and will-power, and understanding, and of universal sympathy also, that he becomes not indeed superior to death (which is inevitable sooner or later to all composite beings and things), but that he becomes able to control the forces of Nature to some extent as he pleases; so that he can, within certain defined limits, stave off the time of physical dissolution, thus attaining twice or thrice the normal length of life in one physical human body that the ordinary man can attain. The cases of unusual longevity known among ourselves support this as showing that there is nothing of the 'miraculous' in it, but that human flesh, under certain circumstances, can last in health and strength beyond the common bounds of human life. Yet this is, relatively speaking, a very small thing. Far greater in fact is the power which these progressed men have of leaving at will one worn-out body, and of entering another fresh and strong from Nature's hands, to carry on with scarcely a break in consciousness the Sublime Work to which their lives are wholly consecrated.

Never—such is the teaching—since the human race first attained self-consciousness, has this Order or Association or Brotherhood of Exalted Men been without its representatives on our earth; and further, it is increasing in numbers constantly, as new recruits become ready, by inner growth, to share the high duties and responsibilities of their former Teachers, and although this increase is necessarily slow, first, because such men are of necessity the rare Flowers of the Race, few and far between, and second, because it also happens that the time comes when some who have been members of this Order are called upon to take up loftier duties elsewhere than on this earth; yet the number of them is, for all that, slowly but steadily growing.

It is for good reasons that these Great Men have been called the 'Guardian-Wall,' for they form in fact a living, spiritual and intellectual, wall of protection around mankind, guarding it against whatever evils these men are unable to neutralize, in view of the dominant Karma of humanity; for against this, the racial Karma, they can no more work than against any one, or against all, of the other 'laws' of Nature. They help, they inspire, they protect, they succor, whenever they can, and in such fashion as their profound knowledge of the karmic chain of cause and effect permits them to do, the humanity over which they stand as Elder Brothers and Guides. This is their Great Work; this is their sublime duty.

Where do they live, it may be asked? The answer is simple, for the teaching about them in this respect is that they live wherever they please; but that when not actually mixing with men—a rare occurrence—and unknown as a general rule to these latter, they find it best and most convenient and in harmonious accord with their duties, to select spots on certain lands of the earth which are usually far away from the hurly-burly of human activities such as our great cities are, or the thickly inhabited lands. There are associations of them in Asia Minor and in Egypt, in America, and elsewhere; but the chief Seat, it is said, of the greatest among them, is in a certain district of the less known part and least inhabited portion of Tibet. There, far from the stifling atmosphere and the bustle of the heavy material life of our cities and thickly populated districts, they live, when not in actual physical intercourse with other men, for the working out of their sublime and self-appointed task.

This task is the teaching of their fellows in an unceasing and never interrupted effort to raise the level of humanity constantly higher; and secondarily to take unto themselves as disciples for direct instruction and training the noblest individuals chosen from out the vast multitude of the human host.

Few doctrines have ever been taught which are so pregnant with thought and suggestion as this of the existence and living reality of these great Seers and Sages; none perhaps which appeals more to the reflective mind. It is so consistent with what we know of ourselves and of our aspirations, with what we know of Nature herself and with the lessons of history, that the man must indeed be dull of wit and slow of understanding and without the fire of spiritual imagination who does not feel its force and sense the appealing charm that it holds.

Yet we should emphasize again that we Theosophists have no dogmas 'necessary to salvation' in our Society; no man among us is called upon to sign a formal creed or a creed of any kind, or to accept any merely authoritative exposition of belief. Our doctrines, when once understood, are seen to be as certain and sure in fundamentals as are the principles of mathematics; so that one is led on by trains of thought from one to another, just as in the latter science; they are wholly self-consistent, and their proofs are found in themselves.

As this is equivalent to saying *found in Nature,* it is therefore readily perceived that Theosophy is in fact 'ordered knowledge,' in other words, science *per se*, and we frequently speak of it as 'the synthesis of Science, Religion, and Philosophy.' It merits well that definition.

This is also the definition that H. P. Blavatsky printed on the title-page of her greatest work, *The Secret Doctrine;* and it is what may be called a popular definition rather than a technical one. The meaning which she tried here to set forth was not that Theosophy, as a system, was a mere syncretism or collection of various religious and philosophic and scientific ideas gathered in many or several quarters and more or less successfully woven into a consistent whole; but, on the contrary, that Theosophy was that single system or systematic formulation of the facts of visible and invisible Nature, which, as expressed through the human mind, takes the apparently separate forms of science and of philosophy and of religion.

Our meaning should be clear. These three departments of human thought are not naturally separate things, but merely three forms by which the human mind aspires to attain an understanding of invisible and visible Nature, and the methods by which human reasoning follows those three forms. Religion, Philosophy, and Science, are but three sides of the triangle of Truth; and in the Theosophical view, it is as impossible to separate one from the other two, as it would be to separate away one of the three sides of a triangle and to claim that the two remaining sides form the Euclidian figure called a triangle.

Human religion is the expression of that aspect of man's consciousness which is intuitional, aspirational, and mystical. Philosophy is that aspect of the human consciousness which is correlative, and which seeks the bonds of union among things, and exposes them, when found, as existing in the manifold and diverse forms of natural processes and so-called laws which demonstrate their existence; while Science, the third aspect of human thinking, is the activity of the mentality in its inquisitive, researching, and classifying, functions.

Man's consciousness is the root of all three, and this conception alone does infinite credit to the penetrating power of H. P. Blavatsky's strength of intellect. It is at once seen, then, that the notion that there could be a conflict between Science and Religion, or between Science and Philosophy, or between Religion and Philosophy, is absurd on the face of it; and any such apparent conflict arises solely out of the untoward and wholly mistaken idea that the so-called 'soul' of man is a radically separate function, or is a radically different thing from that of his philosophic intellect, or of his researching and ratiocinative brain-mind mentality.

Any outline-sketch of the facts and laws of Being, or any formulated system of thinking which departs in any degree from this essential truth of the fundamental unity of all things and faculties, is, *de facto*, an imperfect and therefore in proportionate measure, a false system. No system can be true which does not take in the entirety of *things as they are*, and of all planes of interpretative human consciousness. Now, this universality of conception and exposition is precisely what characterizes Theosophy, and for this reason the Theosophist so frequently speaks of the Ancient Wisdom as wholly based on Nature — using the word Nature in the sense that has hereinbefore been set forth as including not merely physical nature which is but the outward shell of things, but all that is visible and invisible, past, present, and future.

In his moments of quiet reflection it must have struck every thoughtful individual that the rigidly co-ordinated phenomena of Nature *must* be subject to a thoroughly logical and wholly inclusive explanation of what things are — in other words, of what *life is*. Things are, and this is only saying that there is an explanation of them, and of all other phenomena, could we grasp it; and this all-inclusive explanation is what is claimed for Theosophy.

Those people, relatively few in number nowadays but in H. P. Blavatsky's time more numerous than now they are, who proclaim as a discovery of their own that 'Theosophy is nothing new,' are simply, but unconsciously to themselves, telling the holy truth, and are but showing what we Theosophists have been voicing from the housetops ever since the foundation of the Theosophical Society in 1875. Indeed, most emphatically it is not new; it is the oldest human system of thinking on earth;

it has existed in all lands and in all times; and its Guardians are those Great Men of whom we have spoken.

In Theosophy we have no dogmas whatsoever. Should anybody honestly refuse to accept a part, or, indeed, the whole, of our teachings, that is his own affair; nevertheless—and we say this as a matter of simple information, and as a matter of justice—those of us who have been in the work of the Theosophical Movement for many years, and who have spent our lives—some of us— in the study of these grand verities, know that the man who thus refuses or rejects, because of ingrown personal predilections, any part of our teachings, thereby amputates from his own consciousness, intuitions which we may truly call 'keys' to the various mysteries of Nature, both cosmic and human. These mysteries would become clear to him, and open up for him vast fields of fascinating thought, did he but open his mind to receive these intuitions, or keys, or did he but realize that truth, if anything, must be one unitary whole: not diverse, nor builded of conflicting parts, nor mingled with error.

Thus we see that the Theosophist is at once the most truly religious, scientific, and philosophic, as well as the freestthinking type of mind, probably, that could be found anywhere. He stands for law and order without reserve, on the one hand; but is at all times searching to improve himself and all his faculties, and this, on the other hand, makes him as powerful and energetic a supporter of progress as it would be possible to find in any civilized land. He derides the religion of no man, but as one of the main objects of our Society is the study of ancient and modern religions, arts, sciences, and philosophies, he retains his right as an individual to subject to the most rigid criticism and searching investigation any form of belief that may interest him, and, of course, to publish the results of his study if such seems desirable and wise.

Truth is what he is searching for, the goal upon which his eyes are fixed, and the ideal to which he has given his heart; and he considers nothing of greater value than an increase in human knowledge and wisdom, which is Light, and the resurrection in the human heart of those divine impulses of self-forgetfulness which spring from that fountain of truth within us, one's own inner god.

The radiant light which streams forth from that immortal center or core of our inmost being, which we have called our inner god, lightens the pathway of each one of us. It is from this light that we obtain ideal conceptions; and it is by this radiant light in our hearts that we can guide our feet towards an ever larger fulfilling in daily life of the beautiful conceptions which we dimly perceive.

But a man is not great merely because he thinks lofty thoughts, or has sublime ideas, or is a preacher of beautiful phrases. He is great only in proportion as these, through his own deliberate will, show themselves in his life. The greatest claim that the Seers and Sages of the ages have upon our gratitude is not that they have been merely Teachers of men, but that they have been Teachers and Ennoblers of men's souls; and they are Ennoblers because they are Doers, because they put into example—themselves first of all—the sublime spiritual ethic which is at the heart of their Message.

And this is precisely what H. P. Blavatsky, the Messenger in our age of the Great Ones, did. History, far better than the present time, will unveil in even larger degree the record of her uninterrupted life of work, of doing practical occultism. She never faltered, and therefore she never failed; she never stopped working, and therefore she accomplished; she never stopped teaching and proving her teachings by her own life, and therefore she gathered around her the large body of earnest men and women who, after she passed, have kept burning the light that she brought to men.

IX—The Great Sages and Seers
(Continued)

It is perhaps one of the saddest reflections that the philosophical historian draws from his studies of men's minds and temperaments, as expressed in the past, that all great men, whatever may be their stage of evolutionary development, are invariably misunderstood at first, often violently persecuted, usually derided and scorned, and occasionally even made victims of the public's hatred of innovations. How often has this already happened in history is a question which contains its own answer.

Further, that same public, after having done away with some great man, as a certain few instances of history show, after the passage of a few years begins to elevate him to the rank of the deities, to worship him perhaps, or to bow down to him as a god; in doing so usually losing sight of the noble Message that he brought to the world. Such is the fervor of personal adoration, and most assuredly this is not what the Great Teachers desire.

They come, as just said, at certain cyclical periods, when the currents of the spiritual life are running low, and usually when a wave of materialism is threatening to ingulf men's spiritual intuitions and to stifle the cry for help and light uttered by wounded human hearts. At such periods, publicly appear they must and do, if they are to strike successfully the new keynote, successfully to set the new currents of spiritual aspiration and thought in action, and successfully to direct the thoughts of men towards higher goals.

Consider for a moment two bright stars of life and thought which appeared at an interval of half a millennium or so: the great Śâkyamuni, Gautama-Buddha; and the great Syrian Sage called Jesus by his later followers. In the latter case his devotees have actually turned their noble Master not only into a god, but into the actual figure of the second person of their Trinity; and even in the former case, that of Gautama the Buddha, although due to the majestic intellect and wisdom of the Buddha in stating his doctrine and wonderful ethics no such extraordinary apotheosis has taken place, yet even he is regarded in some, but not in all, parts of the world which recognize him as their Master, with a fervor of devotion which, while perhaps ennobling in the self-forgetfulness that it evokes, must yet be by no means fully in line with the goal which the great Indian had in mind when, leaving the Bodhi-tree, he began to preach his sublime doctrine of *self-control, duty,* and *universal love.*

These two examples, when reflected upon are alone sufficient to provide all the explanation that critics seem to think is needed, as regards the attitude of Theosophists towards this fact of the great Sages and Seers. No, merely personal devotion and personal fervor directed to a human personality, however noble and great, are not what are wanted. As a dog will follow his master to the ends of the earth with a self-abnegation that lacks something of the divine only because so limited to one object, and not universal, so men have a quite similar way of devoting themselves to and loving only that one of the world's Great Teachers in whose family, so to say, they happen to be born.

If anything, the Theosophist learns universality, and this comes only when a man learns of his own essential divinity and tries to follow its mandates. Theosophy teaches us that while we should certainly do our whole duty all the time by those nearest to us, and do what we have to do as it comes to hand, yet we should strive continually to increase the sphere of our sympathies, to enlarge the scope of our hearts and of our minds; and in religious matters to learn to respect, ay, even to love, the greatness of soul that exists in other places among other men and which has existed in other times.

We should know from our studies, as well as from the intuitions of our hearts, that the different Messages brought to mankind by all the great World-Teachers, whether we belong to their time or not, and whether we belong to their race or not, have a profound meaning *for us also* (because these Messages are of universal import), which is ours by our human birthright, and that we greatly lose by not knowing it and accepting it as our own common human heritage.

What horrible and needless wars might have been prevented had this noble teaching of universality of thought and endeavor and aspiration and sympathy, always been followed! What pitiful suffering and mental and physical agony might have been avoided had men known better, and knowing better, had acted more wisely!

Then again, how can one whose ideas of religion and of human brotherhood are limited by racial bonds, or by merely artificial geographical frontiers, know the mighty surge of sympathy, the warm flow of pity and compassion, the keen intellectual delights and strengthening of mental and moral fiber, that accrue to him whose mind reaches out eagerly towards other human minds and souls now living in other parts of the world, or who have lived and have left us the fine flowers of their lives? It is this universality of sympathy with other human beings all over the world and with those who have lived in previous ages, which is one of the greatest blessings which Theosophy brings to us. Such an understanding of the powers and innate beauty of the human soul which this sympathetic outlook on life gives to us, is in itself a potent factor in the process of evolutionary development.

Human minds and hearts are usually conceived as being very soft and plastic things; but actually there is probably nothing in the universe that is so steely hard at times, so adamantine and inflexible in substance. It is a mere truism to say that men detest renouncing their pet prejudices or beloved predilections in favor of established custom or familiar views for something new and strange, however noble the new may be. And this observation applies very forcibly in questions of philosophical outlook or of religious belief. In these fields men's minds and hearts are at times almost immovable; and, paradoxically enough, this is likewise the case when philosophical opinions and religious beliefs are outworn and outlived, leaving behind little except an aching void and the brain-mind egoism which prefers the aching void to the entrance of a new truth.

It is in these well-known facts that we see the reason for the disinclination of a people, among whom a Messenger may appear, to receive the Message thus brought to them. Human nature is a curious mass of contradictions. It calls eagerly for more light, but it must have the light shaped after its own pattern, and the pattern is its own prejudices and predilections. It calls for help, but it insults and rejects the helper when he comes, unless the aid be extended after the manner that is considered customary in substance or in form. The progress of civilization is but a series of conquests over obstacles needlessly thrown in the way of human advancement. It is but a succession of truths rejected in the first instance almost invariably, and later recovered and taken to heart as being the lessons of the gods.

Every great Sage and Seer that has appeared among men in order to help them: every great Messenger sent out from the Association of Sages and Seers when the cyclic period calls for such sending, all, we say, meet with the same difficulties in helping those whom they came to help. They will not be heard; they will not be received; they are mocked at; they are derided; they are scorned; they are persecuted often; and in certain rare cases attempts have even been made to do them foully to death.

Of course it is also quite true that this indisposition to receive new thoughts and new ideas has, in a certain sense, a distinct value, because it prevents the too ready reception of impostors, and the too easy acceptance of what the impostors may say; and to certain degree this instinctive prudence or caution on the part of those to whom the true Teachers may come, is a good thing. It is a knowledge of this fact which has unquestionably worked very largely in governing the form and method of presentation of the Message brought at different times by these Seers to the world. They are, all of them, peerless psychologists, and undoubtedly know beforehand, in general if not in fullest detail, just about what they will have to meet, and what will be the reception accorded to them when once they begin to deliver their Message to the usually unwilling ears of men.

It is evident enough, of course, that these reflections in themselves constitute a perfectly sufficient and telling answer to the criticism that might be made by some, in saying that the reception accorded to H. P. Blavatsky when she came as the Messenger of the Great Ones was a proof (proof forsooth!) that she was not what Theosophists claim her to have been. For if she had been the Messenger of such great Sages and Seers, this foolish argument runs, then she would have appeared in the midst of wonders and marvels: she would have shaken established institutions to their foundations with the splendor of what she said, and perhaps with the mighty power accompanying her; and this argument has been accompanied with a raised finger pointing with a gesture of significant emphasis to other great World-Figures who have appeared, and of whom legend records a working of marvels and the exercising of mighty spiritual powers, such as those of the Buddha and of Jesus. These critics are wise in their own generation, but only in their own generation! Their criticism shows them as believing more in the legends which they themselves repudiate, than as having the instinctive spiritual intuition of what constitutes the individuality and work of a World-Teacher. They set themselves up as judges and jury at the same time, and seeing things as their prejudices and predilections urge them to see, they judge the case without giving the unfortunate accused even an opportunity of an impartial hearing. All this is absurd.

Is it not a truth that every great man who has appeared in the world with a new Message to mankind has had to face ridicule; hatred on the part of the upholders and supporters of established institutions; persecution also at the hands of those to whom he came? And when his Message has been given, and the tremendous power of his character has broken through the stone walls of human prejudice and ignorance, and he has disappeared from among men, then ensues the second phase, like the first arising out of human ignorance and stupidity: he is usually worshiped!

Right here the question could well be asked: Did the work of the Great Sages and Seers die with their disappearance? The answer is obviously No. Further, having given to the world their message, did these Great Ones then cease forever to exist? The Buddha, Jesus, Lao-Tse, Pythagoras, Plato, Orpheus, Olen, Musaeus, Apollonius of Tyana, Krishna, Confucius, and all the other brilliant Stars of human spiritual and intellectual power that shone so brightly in the firmament of our spiritual, moral, and intellectual life—are they no more? With their withdrawal or physical disappearance has life and activity and their spiritual influence ceased? The critic might well concede their onetime physical existence; but the claim that they are still alive today he would be inclined to deny. Very well then, where, pray, are these Great Men? In 'heaven' forsooth? The Theosophist has as much right to deny that (because it is a mere hypothesis), and indeed more right, than the critic has to deny a doctrine which is based on sound philosophical and scientific grounds. The theory of 'heaven,' or again, the other theory of non-entity (that of the pure materialists), are both of them theories without other basis of fact than what value one may choose to place upon his ignorance of the nature of life, human and cosmic.

In our general Theosophical literature, any such captious critic will find an abundance of detailed reasoning set forth, with the following object in view: to show the philosophically and scientifically necessary grounds on which the Theosophical teachings repose, and this particular one among them. After all is said, what is really wonderful is not that a man once existing shall exist again, but if he never shall exist again, that he existed at all!

To conjure such a complex and wonderful entity as one of these Great Men, or, indeed, an ordinary man, out of nothingness, throw him into the midst of a world whose every movement proclaims an endless and inescapable chain of cause and effect, then launch him loose from this chain of causes in order to cast him again into a supposititious nothingness, or into an inadequate and irresponsive 'heaven'—this theory or complex of theories (and it is nothing else) makes such an immense demand upon one's belief and upon one's sense of logical consequence and of natural law, that it exceeds the capacity of a man of averagely developed mentality to accept it.

The Theosophical teachings state that man is bound into this endless chain of causes and effects because he himself in fact is intrinsically a part of that chain of living events, and that there is just precisely one thing he cannot do, and that is to go out of it. Nor is man the only one who is bound into this chain of causation, which is the work of his own individuality, the fruitage of his own thoughts and emotions and actions, the consequence, in other words, of what he has thought and done. But it may be said that the highest god in highest heaven, to use a rather vague phrase, is as much bound by the karma or chain of causation appropriate to that sphere of being, as is the humble ant climbing up a sand-bank very laboriously, only to go tumbling down again. Nor is this pessimism in any sense. It is simply an expression of the fact that the Universe is either consistent with itself — that is to say, that it is what is called governed by law and order—or else it is lawless, a helter-skelter universe without sequence in action, causative continuity in being, or consistency in natural character; and this is just what Theosophy, as well as the common knowledge of intuitive mankind, knows the universe not to be.

So there the matter lies, the argument being, as every open-minded searcher for truth may see, entirely for the Theosophical view, which is that of law, orderliness, consistency, universal harmony, and causation, which is but another way of saying inevitable consequence. The argument therefore is obviously admitted; for if the Universe is what Theosophy proclaims it to be anywhere, it must be so in every smallest part.

Let us ask a frank and honest question: What is there about this Theosophical doctrine of the living reality of these great Sages and Seers, as composing an Association existing from immemorial time and also in the present, which is repugnant either to common sense or to historical records, or to the intuitions of the human heart, or to the reasonings of the human intellect? Is there any sensible argument that can be urged against it, whether they be many or one; or is there in fact none? And the answer comes back: None. It is simply the molds of our minds, set and crystallized, which prevent the acceptance of so reasonable a doctrine, one of such intrinsic beauty and containing such high hope.

Let us remember that the Seers and Sages are what they are because they have more or less come into self-conscious union with the inner divinity. This self-conscious union, temporary or of longer duration, with one's own inner god, lies at the back of one of the most sublime initiatory phases of the Ancient Mysteries.

During those initiatory periods the initiant became, as it were, transfigured, translated out of the common life into self-conscious understanding of a reality surpassing ordinary human imagination. Mystic records which the ancient Greeks, for instance, have left us in certain portion of their literature enable the student very easily to get some more or less clear idea of what took place at such times. It was said of those who succeeded in passing the severe tests which were imposed upon all aspirants, that the face shone with supernal light, that the body was surrounded with a halo of glory, and that, for the time being, the man was so suffused with the inner splendor that, as the ancient expression ran, he was 'clothed with the sun.'

The great Seers and Sages are, then, simply they who have been through this experience, at least once, and who have 'kept the link unbroken,' although perhaps manifesting in less power and with less transcendency in daily life—kept the link unbroken, we say, with the god within. There, in that supreme fountain of our being, lie all wisdom and knowledge and faculty and power; and the Great Ones in proportion as they are evolved, draw upon this Source as they may, and more or less when they will.

X—The Hierarchical Constitution of Nature

It is the teachings of H. P. Blavatsky which clearly are the keys of the Mystery which she was to the world, and of the still greater Mystery behind her—the real character and nature of the Great Ones who sent her forth. In elucidating these very wonderful teachings, therefore, we bring the real nature of the Great Theosophist more clearly to the understanding of modern men.

Now, one of the noblest of these teachings, and one of the most far-reaching in its import, is that of the hierarchical constitution of Universal Nature. This hierarchical structure of Nature is so fundamental, so basic, that it may be truly called the structural framework of being. Either we must look upon Nature as an incomprehensible agglomerate of totally unrelated and incoherent parts most strangely and mysteriously and inexplicably interworking among themselves and producing the marvelous natural phenomena which we all see, or we must look upon Nature as a vast Organism of which every part is interrelated and interlocked and interblended and interworking with every other part, thus forming the framework or structure of the Kosmos, guided by a Universal Reason, and inspired by a Consciousness superior to its component portions. (In order to confine our reasoning within understandable limit, we here refer only to our own Home Universe, which is all that is within the encircling zone of the Milky Way.)

The least thoughtful mind must have realized that the part cannot contain more than the Whole contains. Now, Man, as such an inferior part of the vast Organism of the Universe, has consciousness, and will and reason, and feeling, and emotions, and all the other various energies and faculties which in their aggregate compose him; and it stands to simple reason, therefore, that as man is an inseparable part of the cosmic

Whole, he merely reflects in him what that cosmic Whole contains. This statement alone is enough to show the reality of the invisible workings of the cosmic consciousnesses energizing the Universe and working behind the veils of the outward seeming: in other words, the real existence of the living noumena behind the illusory phantasmagoria which the physical universe is.

Our most advanced scientists today openly proclaim the illusory nature of the physical universe, and place the causes of its being in cosmic energies; which is precisely what the Theosophist does. But in doing this, the scientist grants the whole argument for the Theosophist, because consciousness is but the finest and purest form of energy; and, furthermore, the energies that we see working in the cosmic structure are but the most material expressions of the hosts of cosmic beings which infill the invisible universe.

Of course it should be said in passing that the Theosophist very much prefers putting the consciousness-side of Universal Nature as the first or originating cause, and from it he derives all the lower Hierarchies of consciousnesses which stream forth from this consciousness-energy side, and manifest in the universe of physical existence which these Hierarchies themselves compose—in other words, they live in themselves.

How plain, therefore, becomes the statement, as H. P. Blavatsky so masterly portrayed it in her great books, especially in her *The Secret Doctrine*, that the Universe is but a vast Organism, or, in other words, an aggregate, cosmically speaking, of innumerable Hierarchies of more or less conscious and developed entities all working together, all springing of course from a common source, and thus producing the universe of which our poor and imperfect physical senses, our only physical channels of report, tell us something. We quote her own words. "The Universe," she writes in *The Secret Doctrine* (I, 274-5):

is worked and *guided* from *within outwards*. As above so it is below, as in heaven so on earth; and man—the microcosm and miniature copy of the macrocosm—is the living witness to this Universal Law and to the mode of its action. We see that every *external* motion, act, gesture, whether voluntary or mechanical, organic or mental, is produced and preceded by *internal* feeling or emotion, will or volition, and thought or mind. As no outward motion or change, when normal, in man's external body can take place unless provoked by an inward impulse, given through one of the three functions named, so with the external or manifested Universe. The whole Kosmos is guided, controlled and animated by almost endless series of Hierarchies of sentient Beings, each having a mission to perform, and who—whether we give to them one name or another, and call them Dhyân-Chohans or Angels —are 'messengers' in the sense only that they are the agents of Karmic and Cosmic Laws. They vary infinitely in their respective degrees of consciousness and intelligence; and to call them all pure spirits without any of the earthly alloy "which time is wont to prey upon" is only to indulge in poetical fancy. For each of these Beings either *was*, or prepares to become, a man, if not in the present, then in a past or a coming cycle (Manvantara). They are *perfected*, when not *incipient*, men; and differ morally from the terrestrial human beings on their higher (less material) spheres, only in that they are devoid of the feeling of personality and of the *human* emotional nature—two purely earthly characteristics.

Use has frequently been made, in the course of writing this book, of the expression 'Chain of Causation.' But under no circumstances, if the reader please, should this phrase be taken in the sense of the old physical determinism belonging to a science now outlived and outworn. That physical determinism was practically naught but a wholly unfounded idea that the Universe lacked entirely any background having a reality in consciousness, and therefore that, reduced to the last analysis, the Universe was but a helter-skelter arrangement of fortuitously driven and lifeless atoms without internal guidance, and utterly devoid of any roots striking deep into the fabric of conscious being.

The 'Chain of Causation,' as this phrase is used by the Theosophist, imbodies an entirely different conception; it is not merely founded in the interlocking and interblending consciousnesses of Universal Nature, but actually represents the manifold and indescribable operations of these Hierarchies of consciousnesses in the universe. This Theosophical teaching of the Chain of Causation, or, as it might otherwise be phrased, the Chain of Consequences, therefore, is the polar antithesis of the physical determinism belonging to the old-fashioned and now moribund materialism.

It is impossible for any Theosophical writer to place too much emphasis upon this distinction, for it goes to the root of things, and it is impossible to understand the Theosophical viewpoint without having this first principle of natural being clearly outlined in our minds. We say that the Universe is imbodied in consciousness, flows forth from consciousness, and is wholly built around, upon, and in consciousnesses—coming now to the particular view. This is a theme, however, which will be dealt with at greater length in the chapter on Karma.

Nature therefore works after the hierarchical manner, because it is hierarchical in structure. Nature is but a complexity of interblending hierarchical structures which in their aggregate form the Universe as it is; and therefore an understanding of this structure enables us to understand the nature of *things as they are.* Diversity exists everywhere—one of the commonest known facts of human experience; and we must say either that this universal diversity arises in and out of nothingness, and has no meaning at all: or we must realize that it is simply representative of Nature's hierarchical constitution. There is something wonderfully fascinating about this conception of the innumerable hosts of entities existing in countless Hierarchies, which in their totality are Nature itself.

This picture shows us clearly the pathway of the evolutionary progress of the Eternal Pilgrim, that entitative being to whom we give the name, the Monad. There are no limits in any direction where evolution can be said to begin or where we can conceive of it as ending, for evolution in the Theosophical conception is but the process followed by these centers of consciousness as they pass from eternity to eternity in a beginningless and endless course of unceasing growth.

Growth—here is the key to the real meaning of the Theosophical teaching of evolution, for growth is but the expression in detail of the general process of the unfolding of faculty and organ, which the usual word 'evolution' includes. The only difference between 'evolution' and 'growth' is that the former is a general term in the Theosophical conception, and the latter is a specific and particular phase of this procedure of Nature: in other words, as the mathematicians would say, growth is the particular instance of the general rule called Evolution; but they are essentially the same.

The human seed of microscopic size grows into a six-foot man, and in doing so throws outward into physical manifestation the energies and powers and faculties pertaining to the individual consciousness therein working, and does so wholly along the lines of a causative chain of consequences. And what is this but the evolution of the inlocked and infolded powers resident in that human seed from the beginning, and merely awaiting fit opportunity of time and circumstance to blossom forth into manifestation? Obviously this is growth, and also obviously it is evolution.

Growth, therefore, is not a phase only of evolution, or the mere consequence of evolutionary activity alone, but is, in fact, a demonstration of how evolution itself works. Our meaning is, or should be, very clear, for it is simply that evolution and growth are actually the same thing, whatever modern evolutionists or Darwinists may have to say about the matter. Their opinions they are as much entitled to as other people are to theirs. But there is no need for anyone to accept theoretical speculations concerning the nature and manner of the working of evolution if he has sufficient insight of his own to see that those opinions are personal to those who enunciate them.

Growth is not merely the increase from the small to the large as popularly supposed, as we see it in the case of the growth of the physical body in mere size; but it is, more truly speaking, the throwing out or self-expression in all the varied multiplicity of type and form, of shape and characteristic, of faculty and hitherto latent energy now coming forth into kinetic manifestation, of an entity behind the scenes, or dwelling within—and above—the visibly evolving or growing being.

The identity of evolution and growth would seem to be so perfectly self-evident that one may pause a moment and wonder and question oneself why this obvious identity has not been noted before, and due recognition as a fact of Nature given to it. Probably the reason is simply that growth is such a familiar thing, as we humans see it to be, and evolution as a theory is so surrounded with misty and unnecessary attributes of speculation, that people unconsciously think that the two must be different.

It is again to H. P. Blavatsky that is due the original work in our age of calling attention to the above obvious fact. It would probably be quite impossible to understand the real nature and the real operation and the perfect interblending and intercohering nature of the Hierarchies which infill the universe, and, indeed, make that universe as well as infill it, if another proposition of philosophy and of natural law which H. P. Blavatsky called the attention of thinking people to, is not taken into due consideration. It is this: Fundamentally, as even modern science is now openly preaching, matter in all its various ranges, and energy in all its various activities, are but two forms or aspects of an underlying Reality, both being aspects or forms possessing an entirely illusory character. People have been so accustomed for many hundreds of years to think of energy and matter as radically different things, that it is somewhat difficult to realize that neither has an essential reality of its own, but that both matter and energy are the two phases or 'events' which the Reality behind both imbodies itself in as a consequence of the Chain of Consequences before spoken of, and to which this Reality is itself subject, because this Reality is itself the originating cause.

This may sound rather philosophically abstract, but the meaning is simply that the causative energy, which is this Reality, works after certain manners, and in so working, must necessarily follow the laws of its own being, in other words, its own karmic Chain of Causation or of Consequences; and therefore it is involved or inwrapped into the web of its own self-expressions. The case is precisely similar with man, who, acting through his consciousness, and motivated by impulses of his own being, inwraps or involves himself in a web or a network of destiny, which, as just said, originated in his own essence, in his own will and intelligence; and of necessity therefore he must undergo to the bitter end the fruitage of the causes he himself has set in motion.

This Reality behind, or more accurately speaking, within,

THE HIERARCHICAL CONSTITUTION OF NATURE

all things, is Consciousness. And to be even more particularly definite, we should unquestioningly say *consciousnesses*.

We Occidentals are entirely too apt to deal in glittering generalities and satisfy our minds with more or less vague, generalizing expressions as signifying concrete facts. Of course the aggregate of consciousnesses is totalized in the expression 'consciousness,' just as other abstracts, such as 'length' and 'breadth' and 'width' and 'depth' are merely generalizing expressions, all referring, however, when they have any definite meaning, to particular things, which are long, and broad, and wide, and deep. There is no such thing as length and breadth and width and depth existing apart from things which are long and broad and wide and deep; and so therefore do we insist that while consciousness or any other similar generalizing term is convenient enough as an expression, it means nothing at all unless we mean it only as an abstract way of referring to aggregates of particular things which are individual consciousnesses.

In exactly the same way, when we speak of matter, and energy or force, or when we speak of spirit and substance, of which matter and energy are the physicalized expressions, we must remember that all these terms are abstractions, generalized expressions for certain entities manifesting aggregatively. Spirit, for instance, is not different from matter; it is only relatively so, or evolutionally so. The difference lies not in the roots of these two, where they become one in the underlying Consciousness-Reality, but in their character as two evolutional forms of manifestation of that underlying Reality. In other words, to use the terminology of modern scientific philosophy, spirit and matter are each of them respectively an 'event' as the underlying Reality passes through eternal duration.

Particularizing, therefore, what men call Spirit is the summit or acme or root or seed or beginning or noumenon—call it by any name you may wish—of any particular Hierarchy existing in the innumerable hosts of the Cosmic Hierarchies, all of which are inextricably interblended and interworking.

Now, what men call Matter or Substance, is in one sense the most developed, or in another sense the most evolved form of expression of this same Spirit in any one such particular Hierarchy. And this is but another way of saying that matter is but inherent energies or inherent powers or inherent faculties of that same Spirit unfolded, rolled out, and self-expressed. It is the nether pole of what the original and originating spirit is; for spirit is the primal or original pole of the evolutionary activity which brought forth through its own inherent energies the appearance or manifestation in the cosmic spaces of such a Hierarchy. Between the originant or spirit and the resultant or matter, there is all the infinite range of hierarchical stages or steps, thus forming the Ladder of Life or the Ladder of Being of any one such Hierarchy.

In common with most, and probably all, the great religions and philosophies of the archaic ages, these intermediary spaces or degrees of the hierarchical ladder—and we are speaking at the present moment of any one particular Hierarchy as illustrating the general rule—are seven in number; or, looking at the matter from another viewpoint, these intermediary stages or grades or degrees or rungs of the cosmic Ladder of Life or Being may be enumerated as ten in number. Both methods of enumeration are correct. The difference in figure lies only in the following fact: the septenary or sevenfold Hierarchy is all of the Hierarchy that pertains to the world of manifestation ranging from the spiritual to the ultra-material of any Hierarchy; while the tenfold system of counting includes not only the sevenfold manifested worlds, but also three others of an ultra-spiritual nature and character. These three others we can call the Divine.

Now, conceive to yourself not any one such particular Hierarchy, no matter how great or how small it may be in cosmic space, but numberless hosts of such Hierarchies existent in and infilling and actually composing the fields of boundless infinitude, in other words, the spaces of Space; and all these interlocked and interworking and interrelated and interblended: and you have before you what may be called a thumbnail sketch of the hierarchical structure of the Universe.

Many philosophers and indeed theologians in Occidental countries have wondered whence arose in the minds of the ancients their conception of the hierarchical classes of the gods. How was it that all over the world and in all the ages and in many parts of the world even today, the theogonical construction of the universe, as a philosophical and religious scheme, came into the minds of these ancients?

The question is, in truth, a very pertinent one, because, according to Theosophy, the Theogony of the ancients and their more abstract and refined philosophizing are based on the hierarchical structure of the Universe as we have outlined it. How did they acquire this knowledge? Whence did they derive it unless from the exercise of the same inner faculties of vision and from the keen powers of observation that we know they possessed? We go further, however, and say that their knowledge of these things came to them from the same source whence H. P. Blavatsky derived it: from the Association of great Sages and Seers who are the Guardians of the mystic, archaic Wisdom-Religion.

Mighty men indeed were some of those ancients, men whose names today even are revered; yet it had been customary in Occidental countries during the small period of time of fifteen hundred years or more last past, to speak of them as being men whose untutored faculties and aspiring but more or less ignorant understanding, brought forth these marvels of religious and philosophical 'ingenuity.' How sensible men have ever been able to reconcile an imbecile theory such as this last with the known intuitional power and strength of intellect that the greatest men among the ancients had, is something which must cause thoughtful men to pause in amaze. But the explanation is simple enough. During the last fifteen hundred years or so there was practically no knowledge of Nature whatsoever, except the small portion that came over to the Dark Ages from those ancient nations surrounding the Mediterranean Sea; and consequently men in our early European history were so self-sufficient in their satisfaction with their own particular form of religion that they failed to see into what an extravagant logical *impasse* they had brought themselves.

Growing knowledge of Nature, in other words, the advancing science of European civilization, in time broke down this egoism of our forefathers of the Dark and Medieval periods; and there then succeeded the equivalently self-sufficient egoism of the new-born science. Scientific thinkers and speculators were so desperately afraid of dropping back into the old ruts of scholastic thinking that they blinded themselves to the deductions which they ought of necessity to have drawn from the facts of Nature even then discovered.

But truth is mighty and will prevail, says the old proverb, and this aforetime self-sufficiency has utterly gone to pieces with the new insights into Nature that more recent natural research has given to us, and with the marvelous philosophical deductions that our brightest and best minds have drawn from these latest advances in scientific discovery. So true is this, that the Theosophical student and thinker finds himself obliged to be ever on the alert in order merely to keep abreast with the amazing rapidity with which new discoveries are made and new deductions are drawn from them, as concerns the universe surrounding us; in practically all instances, every new discovery, we find, corroborates and strengthens the Theosophical position, and proves as true the marvelous doctrines of our Theosophical philosophy, which H. P. Blavatsky, brought again to the Western World.

Our greatest scientific luminaries today are becoming mystics indeed, and they have but to follow to the logical end the lines of thought that today are already laid in scientific theory and speculation in order to come into full concord and scientific and philosophical union with the Theosophical standpoints or viewpoints respecting not merely matters touched on in this chapter, but other natural facts as well.

We have great men in science today, for instance, openly teaching ideas regarding the fundamental identity of matter and energy. The amazing theories of men like Dr. Albert Einstein and Dr. Robert A. Millikan, just to mention two names, stand forth on all fours, so far as principles go, with the Theosophical teachings regarding the same fields of thought. Our greatest scientists today are beginning to tell us, as Professor A. S. Eddington of Cambridge Univerity (England) has done early this year [1929] that all Nature is but imbodied consciousness, or, as we Theosophists would say, imbodied consciousnesses. Declarations such as this last are now listened to not merely with patience by the rank and file of the other scientists, but are eagerly read, thought about, and speculated upon by the man in the street.

It is the immense diversity existing throughout manifested Nature which offers a problem inexplicable both from the standpoint of mere logic and from that of even current philosophical and scientific theory—and, let us add, inexplicable by current religious ideas—unless the roots of this bewildering diversity of things and natural beings are laid squarely in the foundations of the hierarchical structure of the Universe—in other words, in the vast complexity of interlocking and interworking and interblending Hierarchies of the cosmos.

These Hierarchies do not exist merely *in* the cosmos, nor in any sense do they exist *apart from* the cosmos; nor are they *different from* the cosmos; nor are they merely *expressions of* the cosmos; nor are they in any other sense or in any other manner, or after any other wise, separate or distinct from the cosmos: but are in very fact the cosmos itself, because not only do they infill it and inform it, but what the cosmos or universe is, it is, because it is they. They are the bone of the bone and the blood of the blood, as well as the form of the form, of the cosmos. It is they that make the bewildering diversity which surrounds us, even in this cross-section of the Universe which we call our physical sphere; for this physical sphere is what we Theosophists call a 'world' or 'plane' of the Boundless All; and these worlds or planes are practically infinite in number and exist in all-various degrees or stages of ethereality or materiality.

There are other cross-sections or worlds, or planes, which are purely spiritual, so far as our own particular Home-Hierarchy is concerned; and on the other hand this same Home-Hierarchy of ours contains other worlds or planes or spheres much more material than is our own especial or particular cross-section of the All which we call our physical sphere. All these: the spiritual and the material, and all intermediate planes or spheres, are infilled, filled full, replete with, living entities, entities in all-various grades or degrees of evolutionary advancement as regards consciousness, and therefore of faculty, and therefore of energy, and therefore of substance, because all these are fundamentally one. And all this vast and bewilderingly incomputable aggregate of hosts of entities in all-various degrees of consciousness, are in themselves not only the informing spirits thereof, but are the very fabric and framework in which they themselves live and work, much as man's spirit-soul is the origin even of his own physical body, as well as of all the other elements of his inner constitution, and at the same time is his inspiring and inspiriting Genius—'genius' in the old Latin sense of the word.

XI—The Hierarchical Constitution of Nature
(Continued)

As H. P. Blavatsky says so truly in *The Secret Doctrine* (I, 274), quoted in our last chapter, "the Universe is worked and guided from within outwards." This of course must be obviously true to anyone who understands the first principles of the doctrine of Evolution, or Unfolding, as it is taught in Theosophy, and as this operation of Nature is becoming more clearly understood by our modern thinkers. It is the Hierarchies of Nature which lie in what we may popularly call the invisible worlds, which furnish the urging impulses which are manifest in this our physical world, and which we human beings sense more or less clearly. Because the roots of our physical being are in those invisible worlds, therefore do they express here on our plane in our sphere the operations of the causative chain of events which originate in those invisible spheres.

It should not be thought for a moment that these invisible worlds or spheres or planes are essentially different from our own, for the exact contrary is the case. The old Hermetic axiom is a very true one, and it voices not only the consensus of opinion of the greatest minds all over the world in ancient days, but also the instinctive sense of harmony and proportion which any unbiased mind actually has. This Hermetic axiom is usually quoted as follows: "What is below is as what is above; and what is above is as what is below."

The idea is not that the physical world is a photographic copy, so to say, in every minutest detail, or in every particular of shape, nor in all the minutiae of operation, which characterize the invisible worlds, but that this world is the general reflection, the mirroring on broad lines, of what the invisible worlds or spheres or planes contain. It does not mean, for instance, that there is a United States of America, as existent in this world, somewhere in the invisible worlds, with every exact detail of coastal outline, or of mountain range, or of every particular atom in any particular portion of the rocky sphere of this part of the New World; but it does mean that the United States of America as existent in this world, is a reflection or copy *in the general* of some equivalent continental body existent in the world next superior to ours.

All these invisible worlds have each one its own congeries of what we may call the physical characteristics of that world: mountains, lakes, oceans, winds; therefore an atmosphere, stars, and what-not. All these are, relatively speaking, as solid and substantial to the inhabitants of any such sphere as our own are to us. It would be incomprehensible if throughout the boundless ranges of the Universe, invisible and visible, things were utterly different, from what they are here, or that the working energies and conscious entities should be utterly contrary to and different here from what they are in other, and to us, invisible worlds and spheres and planes. Nature does not work in that way. She always follows lines of least resistance in her growth and in her building of things; and the line of least resistance is always that of the Chain of Causation as hereinbefore described, which in its workings we call Evolution.

We now turn to a somewhat different aspect of our subject, but one which is, nevertheless, extremely important, and which will make a direct appeal to most thinking men. It can be encompassed in the following question: What relation do these invisible worlds have to man before birth and after death? This includes a subject which will be developed more fully later. For the purpose of rounding out our present theme, however, we introduce it in passing in order to give a general view of the subject to which this and the previous chapters have been devoted.

The truth is that man, like every other entity or thing, is a child of the Universe in which he lives: he springs from it, he lives in it, and he returns into the deep and mystic recesses of the arcana of its bosom when he passes away to his adventures after death, or, what comes to the same thing, the adventures that he undergoes before reincarnation into a new physical body. These thoughts form a subject as fascinating as it is both suggestive and instructive.

Man, then, like everything else—entity or what is called 'thing'—is, to use the modern terminology of philosophical scientists, an 'event', that is to say, the expression of a central consciousness-center or Monad passing through one or another particular phase of its long, long pilgrimage over and through infinity, and through eternity. This, therefore, is the reason why the Theosophist often speaks of the Monadic consciousness-center as the Pilgrim of Eternity. Any one phase that this monadic center may itself bring to pass, or, in other words, manifest in, we may call an 'event'. The human being on this earth in any one incarnation, therefore, is an 'event' in this sense, a passing or temporary expression of the energies and substances flowing forth from the monadic consciousness-center at the core of his being.

Today's scientific thinkers have grasped this essential idea of the ancients. We quote from an article in *The Observer*, of London, England, issue of January 27, 1929, and written by Professor A. Wolf, Professor of Scientific Theory in London University:

> One of the commonest words in everyday use is the word 'thing,' or its equivalent. Whatever part of the real world one refers to, one is prone to describe it as a 'thing', having certain qualities, standing in various relations, doing certain functions, and so on. The 'thing,' whatever it may be, is commonly regarded as a permanent pivot supporting changing qualities, relations, functions, etc. And throughout the history of science, thinkers have grappled with the problem as to the nature of 'things.' In the domain of physical science, this problem is generally referred to as the problem of the constitution of matter. Many theories have been put forward; and the electric theory of matter is the latest of such theories. What I want to explain now is how the electric theory of matter, coupled with the theory of relativity, is tending to change our deep-rooted mental habit of regarding reality as made up of 'things.'
> The oldest and most familiar theory of the constitution of matter is that known as the atomic theory. According to it all 'things' are composed of certain indivisible particles called atoms (or 'indivisibles'). In recent times, some ninety different kinds of atoms were assumed to exist, and all material things were supposed to consist of such atoms in all sorts of combinations and permutations. The changes visible in

all things were regarded as due to changes in the arrangements of the atoms, not to changes in the atoms themselves, which were believed to be immutable. But this view was found to be erroneous, and has now been replaced by the theory that atoms are not such ultimate immutable 'things,' but charges of positive and negative electricity (protons and electrons) of varying degrees of complexity.

Now a charge of electricity is a form of influence, and is not comparable to the diminutive billiard-balls or pebbles, after the likeness of which the atoms used to be conceived. The theory of relativity, moreover, attributes supreme importance to the *relations* rather than to the 'stuff' of reality. This means that the old habit of referring to 'things' needs reconsideration, for the 'things' have turned out to be 'events,' and if we continue to speak of 'things,' we can only do so for the sake of convenience, just as we continue to speak of the 'rising' and the 'setting' of the sun, though we know better.

The outlook may be difficult for many people. We are so used to thinking of 'things' that we commonly refer to even a ray of light as a 'thing,' as though it were comparable in some way with 'the everlasting hills.' Now we have to reverse our comparison, and think of the everlasting hills as events comparable with the vibration of light-waves though enormously slower. To think of events without permanent material pivots may cause the same feeling of amazement that Alice in Wonderland felt when the Cheshire Cat vanished, leaving nothing but a grin. A cat without a grin, yes; but a grin without a cat! We seem to pass from solid earth to unstable water or tenuous air. Yet old mental habits may be wrong. And the thought that some twenty-four centuries ago already the Greek Heraclitus thought of the world as an incessant flux of events . . . may serve as a stimulus to a new orientation. . . .

Even the electric theory of matter, of course, is not entirely free from mystery, for nobody professes to know what an electric charge is in itself, apart from those metrical values with which alone the physicist is concerned. Hence the ease with which some people think of the electric charges composing the atom as a kind of dummy pivot supporting the metrical values in question. Hence also Professor Eddington's revival of the 'mind-stuff' theory, which makes matter intrinsically of the same nature as consciousness.

This shows at once the illusory nature of the Universe in any one—and indeed in all—of its manifestations, whether they be spiritual or physical or intermediate, and particularly so as regards the physical universe.

Not only man, therefore, but the Universe in which he lives, may be, and properly is, to be looked upon as an 'event.' This is the core of the meaning of the teachings of the ancient Hindû mystics, such as Patañjali in his *Yoga Aphorisms,* where he sets forth the true teaching that the Universe may be said to exist for the purposes of the Self, meaning not merely the self of man—nor the self of any other particular entity—but the Self of the Universe first of all, including therefore the numberless Selves which that Universe comprises.

Professor Wolf, furthermore, in a subsequent issue of *The Observer* of February 3, 1929, has the following to say about the changing views of Science, and therefore the changing outlook of man upon the Universe in which he lives, and consequently man himself:

In view of what I said last time about the electric constitution of matter, and the present tendency to think of reality in terms of 'events' rather than 'things,' it should not altogether surprise the reader to be told that there is a marked tendency to think of reality, not as consisting of matter, which fills space, and endures in time, but rather as composed of quanta of actions.*

The substitution of one kind of quantum of action for some ninety different kinds of atoms of matter, is clearly a vast gain in simplification and unification. Moreover, the old conception of matter as essentially inert and dead, is got rid of once for all, and thereby the way is prepared to bridge the traditional chasm between the living and the lifeless.

... But most important of all, perhaps, is the fact that the quantum-theory, by helping to discredit the old classical mechanics, has also helped to discredit the fatalistic determinism that was wont to go hand in hand with it. This is something of first-rate importance. ...
It should go a long way to set the world free for the pursuit of ideals,

---

*Professor Wolf defines a quantum in the following manner:

"The expression 'quantum' means, with reference to physical 'action' very much the same that *atom* means, or used to mean, with reference to 'matter.' An *atom* was believed to be an invisible particle of matter; a *quantum* means an indivisible quantity of 'action.' ('Action' here means energy multiplied by time. The importance of taking time into account when estimating any exercise of energy, will be clear on grounds of commonsense.) Now, according to the quantum-theory, action is not something that flows continuously, so to say, and is capable of being taken in any quantity you like. No. There is an indivisible unit of action. You can have a whole unit (called h), or a number of such whole units; but you cannot have a fraction of one. An atom, for instance, when it radiates light, does not do so continuously, but intermittently—in pulses, so to say. A beam of light, it is true, seems continuous, not intermittent; but that is only because there are innumerable atoms taking part in its production."

when economists, academic and realistic, see their ideal shattered, and grasp the incongruity of making human science deterministic in imitation of a discredited mechanics.

From these quotes can the reader have any grounds for doubt as to the marvelous advance made by scientific research and deduction towards a union with the logical Theosophical Philosophy brought anew to the Western World by H. P. Blavatsky? There are, however, certain passages in Professor Wolf's remarks, before which the Theosophist must pause long, and in one or two cases these remarks contain ideas or conceptions or conclusions or deductions, which he cannot accept.

One of these last is Professor Wolf's reference to the so-called traditional chasm 'between the living and the lifeless.' The Theosophist admits no such distinction as 'living' and 'lifeless,' and he feels that such a distinction is entirely arbitrary as well as illogical, because he cannot see how life, which is the very root of the universe, and incessantly flowing forth as indeed an integral part of consciousness, can exist separate and apart from other portions or divisions or 'events' of the Universe, which are arbitrarily called 'lifeless.'

Another point, however, upon which the Theosophist is in profound agreement with modern thinking as expressed by Professor Wolf, is in the latter's reference to "events without *permanent* material pivots." Now the Theosophist has always pointed to the obvious philosophical fact that to talk of a permanent material center or entity is like talking of changeless change or some other particularly confusing contradiction in terms. The entire hierarchical construction of the Universe is impermanent when considered either in the vast aggregate, or in any one of its details, because that hierarchical construction itself is but a cosmic 'event' in the sense hereinbefore outlined; and therefore, being entirely impermanent, wholly changeable, however lasting and durable particular phases of it may be, this shows that it is illusory in the Theosophical and archaic sense of the word; in other words, that it is not everlasting, eternal, or permanently enduring, as consciousness itself is, consciousness *per se*.

If we, then, look upon the hierarchical structure or constitution of the Universe as reducible to two main ranges of operation—spiritual and material—governed, at least in our own physical realms by two main systems so called, that is to say, the electro-magnetic system and the gravitational system; and if we further are able to reduce these two main systems to one, as Dr. Albert Einstein has apparently recently succeeded in doing mathematically in his paper presented to the Prussian Academy of Science on January 30, 1929—and which, so reports say, contains barely six pages of text!—we come to another fundamental teaching of the Ancient Wisdom. It is this: all cosmical manifestation in the last analysis is the expression of a unitary cosmic consciousness-energy, in other words, the Pythagorean cosmic Monad—a very fundamental Theosophical Teaching. The entire Universe therefore is the product or self-expression or the flowing forth of energies and faculties inherent in what we may call the one and sole fundamental and essential Cosmic Energy-Substance—which is the operation in its phenomenal aspect of the Cosmic Consciousness. We refer here only to our own Home-Universe, which, includes all within the encircling zone of our Milky Way, so far as our physical universe is concerned. That Home-Universe of physical conformation and with all its inhering energies, is, we should remember, only a cross-section, so to speak, of the spaces of Space in which we live, in other words, of the Kosmic Hierarchy of which our physical universe is but one of the planes or worlds or spheres of expression.

We repeat: things and entities are in this, our own physical Home-Universe, what they are and as they are because all of them whatsoever are but reflections or mirrorings of what exists in the invisible spaces of Space, of which our inner consciousness knows much, but of which our brain-mind knows but little. The entities and beings and things inhabiting or existing in those other worlds or planes or spheres are as real as those which exist in our own physical universe—in fact, more so. They have their own sequences of time and of space, and their own sequences of consciousness, all adapted to the respective spheres in which they inhere and which they verily themselves compose.

H. P. Blavatsky sets the matter forth very beautifully in *The Secret Doctrine* (I, 605):

> For example, the Doctrine refuses (as Science does, in one sense) to use the words 'above' and 'below,' 'higher' and 'lower,' in reference to *invisible* spheres, as being without meaning. Even the terms 'East' and 'West' are merely conventional, necessary only to aid our human perceptions. For, though the Earth has its two fixed points in the poles, North and South, yet both East and West are variable relatively to our own position on the Earth's surface, and in consequence of its rotation from West to East. Hence, when *'other'* worlds' are mentioned—whether better or worse, more spiritual or still more material, though both invisible—the Occultist does not locate *these spheres* either *outside* or *inside* our Earth, as the theologians and the poets do; for their location is nowhere in the space *known* to, and conceived by, the profane. They are, as it were, blended with our world—interpenetrating it and interpenetrated by it. There are millions and millions of worlds and firmaments visible to us; there are still greater numbers beyond those visible to the telescopes, and many of the latter kind do not belong to our *objective* sphere of existence. Although as invisible as if they were millions of miles beyond our solar system, they are yet with us, near us, *within* our own world, as objective and material to their respective inhabitants as ours is to us. But, again, the relation of these worlds to ours is not that of a series of egg-shaped boxes enclosed one within the other, like the toys called Chinese nests; each is entirely under its own special laws and conditions, having no direct relation to our sphere. The inhabitants of these, as already said, may be, for all we know, or feel, passing *through* and *around* us as if through empty space, their very habitations and countries being interblended with ours, though not disturbing our vision, because we have not yet the faculties necessary for discerning them. Yet by their spiritual sight the Adepts, and even some seers and sensitives, are always able to discern, whether in a greater or smaller degree, the presence and close proximity to us of Beings pertaining to other spheres of life.

There is among all these various worlds or spheres or planes an unceasing and uninterrupted intercommunication of energies and forces and of substances passing from the ethereal into what we would call the physical and returning again into the ethereal realms. And this intercommunication we call the Circulations of the Universe. These Circulations of the Universe may be figured perhaps by the circulation of the blood in the human physical body, making its rounds every few moments or so, or perhaps more accurately, by the nervous aura or nervous energy, which operates in a similar way. Transfer this idea, then, or perhaps re-form it, and make these

Circulations pass from spirit through many intermediate degrees down into physical matter, and after operating in this lowest stage of the Hierarchy, returning again unto its primordial spiritual source; and the idea is all before you in a thumb-nail sketch.

Now, what is it that composes these circulations of the Kosmos? First, as regards the pathways along which the streams of entities and things pass, they are what we may call the lines of least resistance followed by the rivers of evolving entities. They take place through and by means of certain 'critical points,' which H. P. Blavatsky, using a Sanskrit word, calls Laya-Centers. The Laya-Centers we may translate otherwise as 'dissolving points,' or points where spirit enters a lower sphere, becoming the primordial matter thereof; or, inversely, where the highest matter of any one of these spheres rises and disappears through these Laya-Centers into the superior sphere or world.

Sir James H. Jeans, in *Astronomy and Cosmogony*, approaches extremely close to this doctrine of the Archaic Wisdom in what he calls his 'singular points.' He writes:

> The type of picture which presents itself, somewhat insistently, is that the centers of the nebulae are of the nature of 'singular points,' at which matter is poured into our universe from some other, and entirely extraneous, spacial dimension, so that, to the denizen of our universe they appear as points at which matter is being continually created.

This hypothesis of Sir James Jeans is a most notable scientific corroboration of the accuracy of H. P. Blavatsky's foresight and vision of coming scientific discovery, although the Theosophist would reject the use of the term 'dimensions,' and would substitute therefor the expressions 'other spheres' or 'other worlds' or 'other planes,' or some other phrase of equivalent import.

The Universe, like everything else, is a creature of habit. There is no reason why men should have habits, or the beasts, or the trees, if the Universe has not. What we call 'habits' are but the expression in human conduct of what has become *customary* through reiterated operations; and so it is as regards the Universe also. Evolution itself is but a Habit of Nature, and therefore of individual entities and beings and things working along what have become customary lines of action, so far as evolution is to be looked upon as a method; although of course Evolution as a thing in itself is more truly the unrolling or unfolding, or bringing out, or self-manifestation, of energies, forces, powers, faculties, forming part of the essential nature of each and of every evolving thing or entity.

It should be perfectly apparent from what we have already stated that the hierarchical structure of the Universe is but the self-expression of the unfolding or of the rolling out or evolving of the aggregate hosts of monadic consciousness-centers which are the fundamentals of all that is.

The German philosopher, Baron Gottfried von Leibniz, had a curiously clear and suggestive intuition of this fact, and of these Monads, as he has outlined it in his *Monadologie*. To him the Universe was composed, so far as ultimates are concerned, of literally numberless hosts of Monads, each one a mirror of the Universe and therefore reflecting the nature and activities of every other Monad, and yet existing unto itself as an eternally enduring consciousness-substance-center.

The Theosophical Religion-Philosophy-Science may be called in modern philosophical terminology an Objective Idealism, for while the principles of the Theosophical philosophy are idealistic in ultimates, nevertheless we do not deny the transitory objective reality of entities and things, whether we call them 'events,' after the manner of modern science, or whether we call them the transitory and passing self-expressions of the monadic essence existing in such or other phases of the Monad's eternal pilgrimage. Thus when the Theosophist says that the physical matter of the Mineral Kingdom is composite of Monads, he does not mean that these spiritual consciousness-centers are radically mineral things, or in essence mineral, because the mineral is only a passing or transitory phase through which the Monad is passing; but he says that the Mineral Kingdom — or, indeed, any other Kingdom visible or invisible — is the self-expression of a particular host of monadic essences traversing or passing through that phase of its cosmic pilgrimage.

It would be entirely wrong to imagine the Monad of a Newton or of an Einstein, for instance, having at some remote period in its past been but a speck of mineral substance with no previous spiritual history behind it, and which slowly through the evolving aeons grew to humanhood, according to the ideas of the old fatalistic determinism. On the contrary, the Monad is a consciousness-center and by reason of its karma rolls out from itself the all-various energies and faculties which are essentially its own, and which, during such evolutionary journey, spring forth naturally from its own core. Thus a seed put into the ground brings forth the plant which is potentially inwrapped or involved in the seed's essence; but such seed was neither newly created as a mere physical seed without anything of a spiritual nature within it, nor only a complex of physical elements themselves composed of dead and inert physical atoms.

Here, then, we see just what produced the hierarchical structure or constitution of the Universe. It is all a self-expression of the hosts of evolving Monads which not merely inform it, but which actually are it.

XII—Worlds Invisible and Visible: The Heaven-Worlds and the Hell-Worlds

There is not a great religion or great philosophy of the past, or indeed of the present, which does not contain definite teachings with regard to the existence of superior worlds or spheres or planes, popularly called the 'heavens,' and usually spoken of as 'spiritual'; and of another series of spheres or worlds or planes usually supposed to be 'beneath' our own physical globe, and usually spoken of as the 'hells' or, in the Christian scheme, as 'Hell,' with various chambers or departments appropriate, each one, to some specific or particular type of post-mortem penal purgation.

Dante's *Divina Commedia* illustrates this last idea, in the great Italian poet's hierarchical constitution of the Infernal Regions, as the Middle Ages and his own time conceived them to be, and also his hierarchical constitution of the superior regions or Heavens, as likewise they were supposed to be in medieval European times. But the different circles or concentric rings which Dante imagined, to the number of nine, or, indeed, of ten, in his heaven- and hell-worlds respectively, are of course but an echo, more or less distorted, of the teachings held by the ancient European peoples inhabiting the countries surrounding the Inland Sea.

Now, while the Theosophist does by no means accept the exoteric or popular teaching regarding the Heavens and the Hells as popularly taught and outlined in the various ancient religions or philosophies, he nevertheless realizes clearly that all such religious or philosophical doctrines are based on a fact of Universal Nature — in other words, on the hierarchical structure or constitution of Universal Being. Obviously in any such hierarchical scheme, there must be 'high' as well as 'low' ranges or degrees or stages or steps or rungs on the Ladder of

Life. It is the superior or more ethereal of these worlds which furnish the basis for the doctrinal teachings concerning the Heavens in ancient thought; and it is the inferior or more material degrees of Nature's hierarchical constitution, which form the basis for the ancient teachings regarding the various Hell-Worlds.

As H. P. Blavatsky shows so clearly in her great works, the Theosophist does not look upon these so-called Heaven-Worlds as places or states of eternal bliss; nor does he look upon the grosser and more material spheres and worlds of the hierarchical ladder of Nature as places or states of everlasting torment, or even of perpetual penal purgation. In the Theosophical philosophy, both the Heaven-Worlds and the Hell-Worlds, however long they may individually endure in time, are but transitory or passing 'events,' when we compare them with Eternal Duration: mere flashes of evolutionary vital activity, although, by contrast with man's own short span of existence on this his present physical earth, their periods of manifestation are in some cases exceedingly long; and how could it be otherwise?

Clear then away entirely from the mind two misleading ideas: first, that the Heavens are eternal in duration and are places or states of never-ending bliss; and secondly, that the Hells equivalently are places or states lasting throughout eternity, wherein the follies and failures and the so-called 'sins' and evil-doing of men on earth, bring eternal pain upon the perpetrators of them. Nothing of this kind does Theosophy teach. The so-called Heaven-Worlds and Hell-Worlds are places of purgation, it is true, but so, in fact, is our own physical earth a place of purgation. Purgation means cleansing, purifying, through and by the lessons of experience.

We have already briefly referred to what are called the Circulations of the Cosmos, and it is in this fact that lies the key to an understanding of the real nature of the invisible worlds. Each is as fully inhabited as is our own physical sphere, with all-various classes of animate entities, and with entities similar to what it is popular to call inanimate nature in our own physical sphere.

These animate beings, and the Monads composing the inanimate nature of any sphere whatsoever in the Boundless All, are all units in the Rivers of Life — drops, as it were, of the streaming flow of these Circulations of the Universe; and all entities and things, in the Theosophical philosophy, move in cyclical periods. The Evolutionary Wave—which is but another way of saying the passage through time and space of these rivers of living beings — begins in any one period of cosmic existence at and from the highest point of any Kosmic Hierarchy, and with the passage of time passes through all intermediate degrees, following the Circulations of the Universe down to the lowest or most material sphere of any such Hierarchy, remaining for a greater or lesser length of time in all these different stages or states or worlds or spheres or planes. Then, making the turn on such lowest point of the hierarchical Scale of Being, the River of Life, or the Evolutionary Wave, or that particular Circulation of the Cosmos, begins its ascent again towards the higher realms, steadily working 'upwards,' back to the original Source or Cause of all, carrying with it, however, all results in the shape of experience or evolved faculty or developed power, which in the Chain of Consequences have been gained on the Cosmic Pilgrimage.

There, then, for a vastly long period of time in these highest or spiritual realms the Evolutionary Wave ceases its pulsing life for a time. The entities and beings of all-various classes composing such wave, re-enter into the invisible mystery of the Divine, where they take their rest and repose, and assimilate and build into the fabric of their monadic essence, the fruitage of the evolutionary experience gained in the period of cosmic manifestation just spoken of.

When the cosmic clock again points its hand to the time for a new evolutionary period of manifestation, then this same cosmic wave composed of these incomputable hosts of beings, begins a new evolutionary course, but on planes and in spheres higher or superior to those of the preceding Life-Period through which the Evolutionary Wave had passed.

The above, in brief, gives the outlines of the flowing activities in Nature's hierarchical structure, and also shows us that this structure itself is builded on the very essence and substance of the evolving Life-Wave. They are as necessary in the Universe, these various worlds and spheres and planes, as is man's own particular constitution, inner and outer; in order that the evolving Monad—or hosts of Monads—may experience the phases of life belonging to the wider ranges of cosmic being. The Monad must enter those wider ranges of cosmic being, therein building for itself various temporary vehicles or temples in which it enshrines itself, and through and by which it learns. It is these various temporary vehicles or bodies which in their incomprehensible aggregate form the interblending Hierarchies of the Universe.

Probably no other phase of thought offers so easy an example of the manner in which religions and philosophies degenerate from the teachings promulgated by the original founder of each such system, than does the subject of the present chapter: the existence and nature of the Heaven-Worlds and Hell-Worlds. Later generations of men, willingly but foolishly embroidering the pure teachings of the original promulgator, have covered the body of those teachings with religious and philosophical decorations arising out of pious fancy and imagination, so that the higher spheres or planes of Nature's hierarchical structure have become in these religions and philosophies 'heavens' or Heaven-Worlds; and the more material worlds or spheres of Nature's hierarchical construction have become therein the 'hells' or the Hell-Worlds.

It is perfectly true, of course, that a man or a woman who lives a noble life on earth: one who has passed a long lifetime in high thinking and splendid striving for betterment: who has lived self-forgetfully, aspiring to ally himself or herself with the intuitions flowing into the brain-mind from the inner diviner Self, the god within each: it is true, we say, that the highest part of such an individual ascends to the superior worlds or planes of Nature after death has released the imprisoned spirit-soul. And equivalently the human being who has lived a selfish and degraded life, whose thoughts have been of matter and who has built up longings for things of matter, and who has thereby in actual fact built into the fabric of his being attractions and magnetic pulls to the material spheres, goes to those material spheres by the natural attraction of magnetic sympathy for them, when death releases his imbodied spirit-soul. But in the former case, as well as in the latter, the sojourn in these worlds or spheres, be they high or low, is temporary in every instance.

When the causes or energies released here on earth have run their respective courses in the realms to which the entity has departed, when the attractions have been satisfied or equilibrated, there then sets in, as it were, a magnetic repulsion for the spheres in which the entity thus temporarily finds itself. New factors come into play, factors inherent in the character of the evolving entity, which thus immediately begins another course in the direction to which the newly awakened impulses propel him, or magnetically draw him.

This teaching, it should be emphasized, never reduces man, or, indeed, any other entity whatsoever, to the condition of a hapless and helpless Consciousness-Center driven hither and thither, *nolens volens*, by the winds of circumstance or so-called 'Fate.' What governs the destiny of each and every entity, and governs it continuously from the beginning of any one period of cosmic manifestation to the end thereof, is the inherent consciousness and will of the monadic center itself. It alone creates its own destiny; it alone makes what all its future vehicles or bodies are to be. It alone carves its own pathway in time and space; it alone is responsible for what it alone has done, and will do, and does.

The Monad, with its enclosing veils or garments or bodies or vehicles—call them what you will—passes through the spheres not merely because it is native to all of them, and is therefore drawn to them by its own magnetic impulses, but because it itself wills to do so. Free Will, in other words, is an inherent attribute of itself, although this Free Will may be more or less imperfectly mirrored or reflected in any one of the living quasi-conscious vehicles or garments in which it enshrouds itself. Free Will is a godlike attribute, and Man, as well as every other entity or thing in the Boundless All, has it and has it in ever greater degree as he the more fully self-expresses his own higher parts; and he has it, moreover, because in the inmost of his inmost, in the core of the core of his being, he is a part, a spark as it were, a ray as it were, of the Cosmic Consciousness.

H. P. Blavatsky not infrequently points out in indirect fashion in her great works the real reason why teachings such as this do not meet with immediate acceptance on the part of averagely intelligent men. This reason is a simple one. Men simply won't believe, paradoxical as it may sound, that they themselves are what they are in their highest part, so great and so grand; they simply will not believe in their own spiritual and divine attributes, and not believing they reject. But all men are not blinded by miseducation and prejudice after this manner. The human race contains a relatively large number of men and women whose strong intuitional power enables them, at least partially, to see through the veils and clouds built up around their consciousness by prejudice and miseducation, and therefore to see or to glimpse the Glorious Vision. These latter are the ones whom we call 'born Theosophists,' for the Theosophist is by no means merely one who signs an application-blank entitling him to membership in the Theosophical Movement; nor one who has merely a more or less formal intellectual acquaintance with the Theosophical teachings; but the true Theosophist is, above everything else, one who has to some extent the inner vision, and having the inner vision, 'lives the life.'

It is to the Heaven-Worlds or to the Hell-Worlds respectively that so many passages in the ancient literatures refer regarding the 'paths' to the 'gods' or to the 'demons,' for naturally the literatures imbodying the teachings of these old religions or philosophies use the terms or phrases which were popular when such literatures were composed. Even their great authors naturally had to take account of the lack of capacity and the prejudices of the peoples among whom they came and speak a familiar tongue in order to be understood.

Thus in the *Mahâbhârata*, XII, 525, there is the following expression:

> Two paths are known: one leads to the gods; and one leads to the fathers.

And also in the same work, XIII, 1082:

> The sun is said to be the gate of the paths which lead to the gods; and the moon is said to be the gate of the paths which lead to the fathers.

The expressions 'gods' and 'fathers' are technical terms and belong to the religion of ancient Hindostan. 'Fathers' signifies what the Christian has much less clearly called 'departed spirits,' while the 'gods' refer to the same thing that the ancient Greeks and Romans meant when they spoke of the divinities, many of whom were 'men made perfect'—divine beings who have long since passed through the human stage and have gained divinity, become at one with their own inner god.

The higher worlds or the 'Heaven-Worlds' are the regions of the gods; the lower worlds are the domains or regions of the 'demons' so-called—in other words, of entities whose Karma or destiny has led them into spheres and planes more grossly material than even our earth.

The Ancient Mysteries, such as those of Greece, of course contained teachings identical with what we have been elucidating. The whole attempt in these ancient initiatory rites and ceremonies was the bringing of the human consciousness into a recognition of its inseparable oneness with Universal Nature, and of man's kinship with the gods. "The purpose and objective of all initiation," said Sallust, the Neo-Platonic philosopher, in chapter four of his book *On the Gods and the World*, "is to bring man into conscious realization of his inseparable unity with the order of the Universe and with the gods". Proclus, another Neo-Platonic philosopher, in his *Commentary on the Timaeus* of Plato, says in substance practically the same thing: "Who does not know that the Mysteries and all initiations have for their sole object the withdrawing of our souls from material and mortal life, in order to unite us with the gods and to dissipate the darkness in the soul by spreading the divine light of Truth therein."

These ancient Greek teachings and initiatory methods were identical with the systems practiced in the Far East. The phraseology of course differed in different countries, but the root-thought was always the same, and the objective was always the same. The pathway to the 'gods' or the pathway to the 'fathers,' of which the Hindû speaks, are but a manner of phrasing the activities of the evolving human soul, throwing it on the one hand into the pathway leading to the gods or the superior spheres; and on the other hand, into the pathway leading to the inferior realms. These pathways are the same as the Circulations of the Universe.

There is method in Nature's workings; there is no helter-skelter or haphazard operation in her at all. Everything is regular, orderly, consistent, and coherent with every other thing. Man himself, as a child of Nature, therefore is as much an inhabitant of these other and invisible realms, as he is of this earth, for he is here but as a pilgrim spending a day-night in this our sphere. And what has just been said of men applies equally to every other monadic center whatsoever, which is simply saying, to every other entity or thing.

These superior and inferior worlds, as we have already made clear, have their own inhabitants, their own countries, and, as we would say on earth, their own respective firmaments, in which move the celestial bodies appropriate thereto, even as all this occurs among us.

With no uncertain voice did the old Hermetic philosophy of Greece and Egypt teach that "What is above is as what is below; and what is below is as what is above"; for every part of Nature mirrors, as best it can, and after its own possibilities, all other aspects of Nature which are above such a part; and this mirroring is the stronger and the more definitely and clearly outlined, the nearer the invisible realm is to the world or sphere or plane into which it reflects or mirrors itself. The universe is one vast Organism, an Organic Entity. But Boundless Space, or rather the spaces of Boundless Space, contain many such Universes, a fact which even our modern scientists are beginning to have some intuition of when they speak of Island-Universes lying without the boundaries of our own Home-Universe, the Milky Way. Each one such universe is an organism within a greater organism; and the greater organism is contained in an organic entity still more vast; and so on indefinitely.

Paul of the Christians merely echoed the Wisdom of all the archaic ages when he said: "In It we live and move and have our being." Each one such organic entity or organism is a Hierarchy in the sense which we have set forth.

What a wondrous field of thought this opens to the reflective mind! When man feels himself thus at-one with all that is: when he feels that the consciousness which he calls his own is but a god-spark, so to say, of some vaster consciousness in which he lives and moves and has his being, and that the very atoms which compose his body are builded of infinitesimal lives which infill those atoms and make them what they are: when he feels that he can pass along the pathways of his own spirit ever more and more inwards into a closer and straiter union with some self-conscious entity still more sublime than his own highest: then he feels not only a keen sense of his own high human dignity, but he looks out upon the universe around him, and his heart broadens and his mind expands, in sympathy, love, and benevolence towards all other entities and things. Vast ranges of consciousness open up for him as his own future; duty takes on a new and gloriously bright aspect; right becomes the law of his living, and ethics no longer are a more or less tiresome code of abstract teachings, but very living and vital maxims of conduct; for he instinctively knows that by living in harmony with Nature's Harmony, he becomes self-consciously ever more at-one with it.

Even as the infinitesimal lives which compose his body live in him and in him have their being, so he is one of the infinitesimal lives of some Entity of whose existence he can vaguely sense the reality; and he ever more aspires to become in ever larger degree more fully one with it.

The world as yet recognizes but slightly the debt that it owes to H. P. Blavatsky, but the time is most assuredly coming when these her teachings shall be developed by the greatest minds among men, who then will recognize, and recognizing will show, what her real work was, and how great she was in herself, to have been chosen for the dissemination of what we may truly call a body of teachings based on Cosmic Realities.

The advances that our Occidental world has made in mystical thought since H. P. Blavatsky passed on to her beloved 'Home' are amazing, and indeed greater than most Theosophists would have thought possible when she herself lived. Where there was one scholar in her day sincerely interested in the religious and philosophical thought of other ages, and of lands foreign to his own, there are now a score; and scarcely a day passes without some new and interesting and often scholarly work seeing the light, and introducing us to some often fascinatingly interesting work of philosophical or religious type, belonging to the thought-world of other peoples.

Probably men in all past European history have never been so deeply interested in questions of religious and philosophical import as they are today; and this is one of the best possible signs of the efflorescence of one phase of the human spirit, which we may call, in a sense, a divine hunger for more light. Not all the books so produced are such as a Theosophist could honestly recommend as being along Theosophical lines; and this is something which was only to be expected; but occasionally some work is printed which is of real value and deals more or less with the same subjects of mystical and philosophical import, to which this book is devoted.

Of course modern scholars, outside of what they may have imbibed from reading our Theosophical literature, have no real guiding light by which they may judge of what is true and what is distorted, in the thinking of olden times; and this fact accounts for the rather heterogeneous collection of speculations that translations of such ancient works are usually accompanied by.

A manner of presenting the Hierarchies of the Invisible Worlds may be found by the student in the various branches of the Brâhmanical thought of Hindostan, such as the *Vishnu-Purâna,* of which a translation in five volumes by Wilson exists in English. Here the Invisible Worlds are divided into fourteen *lokas,* of which seven belong to the superior class or range, and seven to the inferior. Another name for the seven inferior worlds is *talas;* and in this scheme of enumeration the earth is taken as the midway-point, and is reckoned as the first in the ascending scale, and also the first in the descending scale.

There are other methods of placing our own world in the hierarchical succession of steps or stages, but the enumeration that is almost always found is either seven of each range or class, or nine, or ten, the difference depending upon the manner of viewing the hierarchical succession, and therefore of enumerating them as ascending or descending.

There is one important point, however, which we should bear in mind: the Theosophist does not accept in any sense of the word the existence of the so-called 'heavens' or of the so-called 'hells' as the popular religions or popular mythology describe them in detail, although of course he most positively does accept the existence, in seven or nine or ten stages, of this hierarchical succession of worlds or planes or spheres. The Theosophical philosophy voices the Wisdom-Religion of Antiquity, which is in the guardianship of the great Sages and Seers, and this is equivalent to saying that the Theosophist looks upon the superior worlds not as 'heavens,' but as ranges of cosmic space, which to us are invisible, and which represent the ascending stages in the pathways of the Circulations of the Cosmos. This also is the same as saying the ascending evolutionary River of Life, or the ascending Evolutionary Wave.

Equivalently, the Theosophical philosophy of the archaic Wisdom-Religion knows of no 'hells' whatsoever in the popular sense of the word; but it does most certainly recognize the inferior or descending series of hierarchical worlds or planes or spheres, which are simply cosmic spaces invisible to us humans, and of a more material character than our own physical sphere.

Our meaning is plain. The 'hells' merely mean spheres or worlds or planes of a material character; and the 'heavens' merely means worlds or spheres or planes of a spiritual character. Consequently, any physically cosmical body falls under the designation of one of the worlds of a material character, and therefore is technically a 'Hell,' and our earth **is one** such; and herein is the secret meaning of the Tibetan word *Myalba*, which H. P. Blavatsky uses in her devotional work, *The Voice of the Silence*, as a name of our earth. A 'hell' is only a sphere of purgation, where the karmic consequences or web of destiny in which evolving souls have involved themselves, are worked out, precedent to a rest in the spiritual realms, or realms which we may call spiritual — spheres where aspirations are fulfilled, high and lofty hopes are realized, and where the expanding native faculties of the soul find full and adequate fields of self-expression.

XIII—The Visible Worlds

The visible world that we humans know somewhat of with the sense-apparatus that evolution has given us at the present time is merely one cross-section of the Boundless All. As the human host, or any other host indeed, passes on in its evolutionary course into what are now the invisible worlds, any one such invisible world which the human host then enters will be for the time being, its 'physical' cross-section of the Universe.

Our meaning should be very plain. What we call a physical world is merely that world in which we happen to be sojourning at the time and cognize through the sense-apparatus of the vehicles in which we then are. Consequently the adjective 'physical' applies *mutatis mutandis* with as much accuracy and right to the lowest of any such invisible worlds as it does to our present world.

When we pass out of this present physical sphere, it will become invisible to us; and the world into which we shall pass will be the visible world. This conception or rather fact of evolutionary experience lies behind the meaning of certain technical words used in the ancient world-religions and world-philosophies, such as are found in the Sanskrit, where the *rupa-* (or 'material') and the *arûpa-* (or 'immaterial') worlds or planes are mentioned; and these words are to be construed strictly in accordance with what has just been said.

It may be of assistance to delineate the hierarchical structure or constitution of the Universe, by the following diagram. We employ for purposes of illustration the names given to the respective planes or spheres that are used for that purpose in Brâhmanism.

Other religions have their own respective names and respective methods of dividing the hierarchical structure.

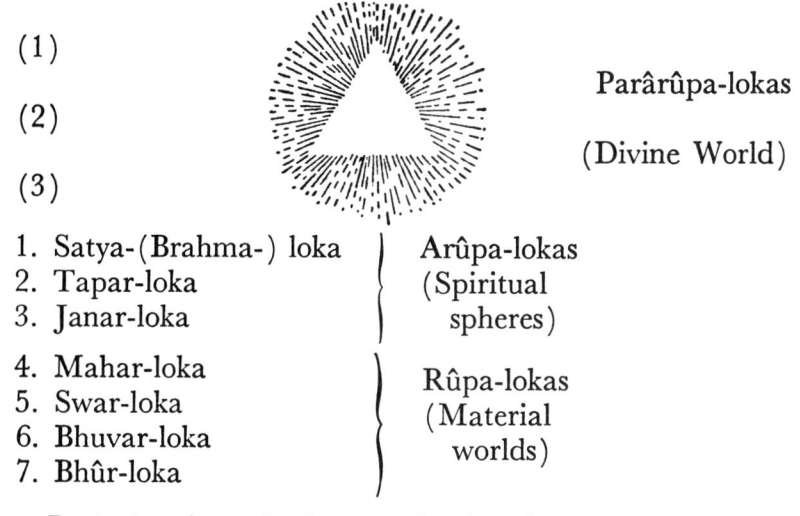

(1)

(2)   Parârûpa-lokas

(3)   (Divine World)

1. Satya-(Brahma-) loka   Arûpa-lokas
2. Tapar-loka   (Spiritual
3. Janar-loka   spheres)

4. Mahar-loka   Rûpa-lokas
5. Swar-loka   (Material
6. Bhuvar-loka   worlds)
7. Bhûr-loka

Beginning from the bottom, the four lowest are called the *rûpa-* or material worlds. These are the worlds of 'form' in ascending degrees of ethereality, that is to say, the higher they are the more ethereal they are. The Sanskrit word *loka* means 'place,' 'locality,' or 'world'; whilst *rûpa* means 'form.'

Now 'form' is here employed technically — not in the strict, popular sense in which it is used in English. It signifies rather an atomic or monadic aggregation about the central and indwelling consciousness, thus forming a vehicle or body thereof. *Arûpa* equivalently means 'formless,' but this word 'formless' is not to be taken so strictly as to mean that there is no form of any kind whatsoever; it merely means that the forms in the spiritual worlds as outlined in the above scheme are of a spiritual type or character, and of course far more ethereal than are the 'forms' of the *rûpa-lokas*.

We might express the technical meaning better by saying that *rûpa-lokas* are *lokas* or worlds where the body-form or vehicle is very definitely outlined in matter; whereas in the *arûpa-lokas*, or the spiritual worlds or spheres or planes, the vehicle or body is to be conceived of rather as an enclosing sheath of energic substance. If we were to speak of the entities of these *arûpa-lokas* as containing bodies of light, it would be close to the real idea, because even in modern physical science, light is substantial — as Theosophy, and therefore the Ancient Wisdom, likewise teach it to be, although not a substance exactly of our material world.

Nevertheless, these *arûpa-lokas* or the three worlds above the *rûpa-lokas,* are as seemingly solid and substantial to their respective inhabitants as is our own material sphere *Bhûr-loka* to us, and as are the other three *rûpa-lokas* to their respective inhabitants. All this matter of solidity or substantiality is obviously merely a relative question. The three highest *rûpa-lokas* to us inhabitants of the lowest or *Bhûr-loka* are of course relatively immaterial to us, and so indeed they are. Even more so are the three higher or *arûpa* or spiritual spheres much more immaterial or ethereal to us, though as substantial or seemingly solid to their inhabitants as is our physical sphere to us.

Note further that the seven lokas of this schematic diagram, which include the three of the *arûpa* and the four of the *rûpa,* include all the *manifested* universes — that is to say, the universes subject to manifested imbodiment, counting from the spiritual down to the spheres of most material density, and therefore actually including—though not sketched in this schematic diagram—even what we Theosophists allude to as the 'Mystery of the Eighth Sphere.' Concerning this last or Eighth Sphere nothing further can be said in a published work except that it is a sphere even more material than is our earth, and may perhaps be best and most briefly described as the sphere of 'absolute' matter, in other words it is the lowest possible stage or step of our own Home-Hierarchy, in which matter has reached its ultimate in density and physical accretion.

Beneath this last stage begins a new Hierarchy; just as on the higher stage, above our own present Home-Hierarchy (could we consciously ascend along the various stages or degrees or rungs of the Ladder of Life), we should pierce through the laya-center or 'singular point' there existing into the lowest possible stage of the next superior Hierarchy.

As regards the 'triangle in radiation' which the schematic

diagram also presents, which we have called the *Parârûpa-lokas*, this represents in symbolic form the aggregative summit or top of the Ladder of our own Home-Hierarchy, and is to us Children of this Hierarchy our Divine World.

This Divine World is not only to be considered as the divine Seed whence flow forth in the cosmic Periods of Manifestation the seven grades or steps below it which the diagram shows, but it is also the Goal into which all shall again be ultimately resolved when such a hierarchical or cosmic Period of Manifestation shall have concluded its course of evolution in self-expression.

We now propose to set forth with more definiteness the real characteristic and nature of our physical sphere, which, in a larger sense perhaps than the Brâhmanical system employs, Theosophy would place in the lowest or seventh degree or stage of the above scheme, the *Bhûr-loka*, and would include therein not only our earth and our solar system, but our entire physical Home-Universe, all within the physical encircling bounds of the Milky Way.

The first conception we should grasp, absolutely essential to a correct understanding of our theme, is the fact that the Universal Life-Consciousness-Substance which pervades everything and which is at the back of and 'above' all of our own Home-Universe, manifests in every minutest part or detail of that Home-Universe. Such manifestation naturally takes the form, speaking in a general way, of its source. In other words, it takes the form of Life manifesting as individual *Lives*. Therefore, every minutest point — for a 'point of consciousness' is even smaller than the infinitesimal figure which chemists call an atom — every minutest point of the Kosmic Being is a monadic Center or Life.

As H. P. Blavatsky sets the matter forth in her own inimitable style, in her *The Secret Doctrine* (I, 49):

Esoteric philosophy teaches that everything lives and is conscious, but not that all life and consciousness are similar to those of human or even animal beings. Life we look upon as "the one form of existence," manifesting in what is called matter; or, as in man, what, incorrectly separating them, we name Spirit, Soul, and Matter. Matter is the vehicle for the manifestation of soul on this plane of existence, and soul is the vehicle on a higher plane for the manifestation of spirit, and these three are a trinity synthesized by Life, which pervades them all. The idea of universal life is one of those ancient conceptions which are returning to the human mind in this century, as a consequence of its liberation from anthropomorphic theology. Science, it is true, contents itself with tracing or postulating the signs of universal life, and has not yet been bold enough even to whisper "Anima Mundi!"

This limitation of scientific thinking was expressed with the voice of authority by the wiseacres of science in H. P. Blavatsky's day, but as the great Florentine Galileo Galilei is reported to have said, "Nevertheless it moves." Science, too, is moving ahead rapidly; and today we have the brightest luminaries in their scientific writings not merely hesitatingly pointing with uncertain finger to their acceptance of a cosmic life-energy behind all phenomena, but in some cases these luminaries are courageous enough and intuitive enough absolutely and openly to proclaim it.

We have given in another chapter the statement of Professor Eddington to the effect that life and consciousness are at the back of matter and energy, and this is equivalent to saying that everything that is, is a Life. Hence all the visible worlds existing in our visible sphere are but huge agglomerates of living entities or lives in all-various degrees of evolutionary development. Not only are they all — suns, planets, comets, nebulae, meteors, and what not — each one of them based in even its physical being on such aggregates of Lives, infinitesimal and other, but on some of these celestial bodies at least there are also, as there are on our earth, hosts of living entities possessing self-conscious mind and will, such as we human beings on this earth have.

It is these Lives that, driven or rather urged by their self-evolved karmic potentiality behind them, follow the various pathways of karmic destiny, and eventuate in this or in that or in some other form or self-expression of the invisible host behind.

As H. P. Blavatsky again says so very truly in *The Secret Doctrine* (I, 260-61):

Science teaches us that the living as well as the dead organisms of both man and animal are swarming with bacteria of a hundred various kinds; that from without we are threatened with the invasion of microbes with every breath we draw, and from within by leucomaines, aerobes, anaerobes, and what not. But Science never yet went so far as to assert with the occult doctrine that our bodies, as well as those of animals, plants, and stones, are themselves altogether built up of such beings; which, except larger species, no microscope can detect. So far, as regards the purely animal and material portion of man, Science is on its way to discoveries that will go far towards corroborating this theory. Chemistry and physiology are the two great magicians of the future, who are destined to open the eyes of mankind to the great physical truths. With every day, the identity between the animal and physical man, between the plant and man, and even between the reptile and its nest, the rock, and man — is more and more clearly shown. The physical and chemical constituents of all being found to be identical, chemical science may well say that there is no difference between the matter which composes the ox and that which forms man. But the Occult doctrine is far more explicit. It says: Not only the chemical compounds are the same, but the same infinitesimal *invisible lives* compose the atoms of the bodies of the mountain and the daisy, of man and the ant, of the elephant, and of the tree which shelters him from the sun. Each particle — whether you call it organic or inorganic — *is a life*. Every atom and molecule in the Universe is both *life-giving* and *death-giving* to that form, inasmuch as it builds by aggregation universes and the ephemeral vehicles ready to receive the transmigrating soul, and as eternally destroys and changes the *forms* and expels those souls from their temporary abodes. It creates and kills; it is self-generating and self-destroying; it brings into being, and annihilates, that mystery of mysteries — the *living* body of man, animal, or plant, every second in time and space; and it generates equally life and death, beauty and ugliness, good and bad, and even the agreeable and disagreeable, the beneficent and maleficent sensations. It is that mysterious LIFE, represented collectively by countless myriads of lives . . .

Everything, no matter how small, no matter how great, is an evolving *Life*, and hence, as every one of these visible bodies in the Universe around us is but an aggregate of such lives, we have here a clue to the real meaning of many of the ancient philosophers who spoke of the suns and stars as being living entities, or what the ancient Greeks called 'ensouled entities' ζῶα, *Zôa*, from which comes the word 'Zodiac,' used even in our current astronomical books, and meaning the circle of the 'Living Ones'; and which the Latin philosophers called *Animals* — a word of course which they used with the original Latin meaning of *animate entities*, and not in the restricted meaning of modern European speech, signifying only the beasts.

Even some of the greatest of the early Christian Fathers taught exactly the same thing — that the suns and stars were 'living beings,' for such indeed is the explicit teaching of the great Greek theologian Origen, as well, doubtless, as of Clement, another one of the great Christian Fathers, and, like Origen, belonging to the Alexandrian School of Christian theology. Of course every student of Christian ecclesiastical history knows that many of the doctrines of Origen were officially condemned and anathematized, first at the Home-Synod convoked by the Patriarch Mennas, under authority of the Imperial Rescript issued by the Emperor Justinian I, a Synod held about the year 538; and Origen's opinions were again condemned at the Fifth General or Ecumenical Council held in 553, also by order of the Emperor Justinian. But this condemnation and anathematization was engineered very largely by the secular powers of the time in response to the urgings of a powerful body of the then existing priesthood, and was an act which, while it changed the theology of the Christian Church in succeeding centuries to a large degree, took place over the very vigorous protest and complaints of an almost equally powerful body of the then existing Christian priesthood and community.

For the sake of their intrinsic interest, a few passages from Origen are quoted here. In his work on *First Principles,* chapter vii, section 2, he speaks as follows:

Not only may the stars be subject to sin, but they are actually not free from the contagion of it;

and in section 3, he says:

And as we notice that the stars move with such order and regularity that these movements never at any time seem to be subject to derangement, would it not be the height of stupidity to say that so consistent and orderly an observing of method and plan could be carried out or accomplished by beings without reason . . . Yet as the stars are living and rational beings, unquestionably there will appear among them both advance and retrogression.

Again Origen observes in his tract *Against Celsus,* chapter xi:

As we are persuaded that the sun himself and the moon and the stars also pray to the supreme deity through his Only-begotten Son, we think it improper to pray to those beings who themselves offer up prayers.

And again in the same tract *Against Celsus,* chapter lxvii, Origen remarks once more, quite after the Christian manner of his time:

> For we sing hymns to the Most High only and to his Only-begotten who is the logos and also God; we praise God and his only-begotten, as also do the sun, the moon, the stars, and all the multitude of the heavenly host.

Furthermore, in order to show the early Christian view about the innate vitality working in and through the celestial bodies as vehicles of that vitality, we find in the *Letter to Avitus,* of the Latin Father Jerome, the following passage which repeats Origen's teachings:

> Respecting the heavenly bodies, we should notice that the soul of the sun, or whatever else it ought to be called, did not begin to exist when the world was created, but before that it entered into that shining and luminous body. We should hold similar views regarding the moon and the stars.

It is also interesting to note that despite the condemnation of the views of Origen and his School by the two Constantinopolitan Councils, those views prevailed more or less in secret throughout the Christian community, and lasted until a very late period of Christian history, indeed even into the Middle Ages. The ecclesiastical writers of the Dark and Medieval periods have many passages with reference to the sun and stars which, historically speaking, are understandable only on the supposition that they are more or less distorted reflections of the views of Origen and his School.

The exact meaning of this old doctrine of the celestial bodies being animate entities, each one having its past and its present and future as such an animate being, was very largely lost even at the time of the Councils of Constantinople. The idea was not that the stars and other shining celestial bodies were in their physical forms 'angels' or 'archangels,' but that each one was the 'dwelling' or vehicle or channel of expression of some 'angelic' entity behind it. Certainly this conception approaches far closer to the Wisdom-Religion of the archaic ages, today called Theosophy, than might appear on first thought, although our own views are founded on sound philosophical principles and scientific facts of invisible Nature.

But all such doctrines as those of Origen were already largely degenerated in the time when Origen and his School enunciated them to the Christian Community, and were, furthermore, more or less distorted from their original Pagan meaning by the theological mental bias of the men who taught them. It is to the Ancients themselves that we must turn, if we wish to gain a clearer and more definite outline of the original thought. And it may be said in passing that it is from Plato in especial, and from Pythagoras and his School, that are derived these doctrines which certain ones of the Christian Fathers took over and modified for their own special purposes.

The truth of the whole matter is this: each and every celestial body, whether it be nebula, comet, sun, or star, or hard rocky planet like our own earth-sphere, is a focus or psycho-electric lens, through which pour the energies and powers and substances passing into it from the invisible spheres, after the manner that we have before hinted at. It is through the laya-centers, or through Sir James Jeans' 'singular points,' that these Circulations of the Cosmos take place, and each such sphere, whether star or planet, comet or nebula, has at its heart such a laya-center or channel of communication, through which pass in both directions, upwards and downwards, the forces and powers and substances just spoken of.

Furthermore, these Circulations pass not merely to higher realms, that is to say upwards and downwards so far as any physical sphere in the superior worlds is concerned, but also pass upwards and downwards so far as the inferior but also invisible worlds or planes are concerned.

Turning for a few moments to our physical science, we have the most progressive of its luminaries setting forth a body of speculations regarding the atom and the characteristics of atomic physics which lends itself in a most admirable way in support of the Theosophical teachings regarding the same things.

When material substance existing in and of the atom, the ultimate material constituent — and we here allude of course to the electronic theory — is said to be naught but electric charges, respectively of positive and negative type, which by their interactions produce the physical universe surrounding us, we enter at once upon the invisible realms, for these invisible realms are causes of the energies working in and behind and through the atomic sphere or body or garment or veil — call it by what name you like — which forms the material world.

Nor is this all, for there are brilliant minds today which are beginning to speak of certain still more subtil and particular points of material substance, which they call photons, which apparently either exist in the core of the electron and thus compose the electronic activity itself, or are connected with the protonic or central nucleus of the atom.

The future will doubtless show more clearly what actually does lie behind and within the electron, and how and why the latter, in connection with the protonic nucleus of the atom, produces the phenomena of radiation. Other scientists also of a philosophical type are now beginning to talk of 'emergence,' at least in biology; that is to say that behind or within living entities in particular, and doubtless in the so-called inanimate sphere of matter, there are factors which 'emerge' through the rigidly governed physical activities of the material world. We may mention Professor Lloyd Morgan, a British scientist, in this connection, and other scientists who belong to his school.

All these ideas or speculations or theories or hypotheses are like the straws which show which way the wind is blowing: the new spirit which has entered into the minds of scientific men, driving old ideas like chaff before it; and all these theories of course are directly related to and depend upon the characteristics of the physical world which surrounds us.

These theories come to us from two directions: from a study of the atomic structure in the microcosmic sphere, and from a similarly advancing study, on a macrocosmic scale, of the worlds or spheres of physical space.

One of the most beautiful as well as profound and interesting teachings of the Ancient Wisdom regarding the visible worlds — an observation which applies with equal force to the invisible — is that each such visible world is not merely a focus of the subtil and ethereal essences and energies pouring through it, but exists as an entity within the life-sphere, or within the encompassing life, of an Entity still more vast; so that, as Paul of the Christians truly said with reference to Man, each such visible globe "lives, moves, and has its being" in some other Entity of still greater magnitude.

Who can say where and when limits should be placed to this view? In natural reality there are no limits in any direction. But there are indeed limits or frontiers in a secondary sense, in view of the hierarchical structure or constitution of the Universe. Each such Hierarchy of course has its beginning and has its end, its highest and its lowest points, and these are the frontiers of the limits *for itself*. But they are not real limits in the last analysis, because both the beginning and the end of any Hierarchy may be considered the point of junction or union with a superior or an inferior Hierarchy, respectively, thus continuing in both directions the endless Ladder of Life.

There is another and still more fascinating manner of looking at this endless chain or concatenation of entities and things: the continuation of the hierarchical structure through and into the invisible realms, or, in other words, continuation extending ever more inwards; and indeed this is the point of prime importance for anyone to understand who wishes to get some comprehensive view of what is meant by the words, "the hierarchical structure or constitution of the Universe."

Nature, in the sense of the Boundless All, is *per se* frontierless and limitless in all directions; and through the All extends the illimitable network or web of Cosmic Being. It is these Hierarchies which form the inner constitution of the Universe, and each such Hierarchy may be figured to the mind as an organic entity or organ of the Cosmic Organism. In a very similar manner man's inner constitution is builded — for it is indeed but a reflection or mirroring as the ancient Hermetists would have put it of the constitution of the Universe. Just as man in all the stages or degrees of his inner constitution (in other words, in all his principles) is builded up of vast hosts of Lives in which he is the monadic and inspiring entity and through which he works and in which he lives and moves and has his being, precisely so is the Universe constructed.

All these Hierarchies are builded up of incomputably numerous multitudes or hosts of Lives, and through them all and in them all lives and works and has its being what the ancient Pythagoreans called the Cosmic Monad. Remember, however, that these Cosmic Monads are as numerous in Boundless Infinitude as are the countless hosts of minor beings in which they live. Each one such minor entity, it matters not at all what its evolutionary stage may be, has its own monadic center, and therefore is a learning and evolving entity.

The general principle of cosmic cooperation, to use familiar words, which is so readily deductible from these observations, is one of the phases of the doctrine of Universal Brotherhood, for this interlocking and interblending scheme extends everywhere, in the invisible worlds as well as in the worlds which are visible. Another phase of this doctrine is that all things whatsoever, great or small, are rooted in the same Cosmic Source, whence they proceeded in the beginning of the primordial periods of World-Evolution, and towards which they are journeying back.

Every visible world is therefore the seat of a most marvelous complexity and activity of Life — or more accurately, of Lives. It is in these worlds, invisible or visible, that these hosts of evolving entities find their fields of self-expression. Our own earth is a very good example, with its various families of offspringing children, which we call the various kingdoms: Mineral, Vegetable, Animal, and Human, as well as the three Elemental Kingdoms which precede the Mineral. All these entities are evolving together, albeit in different evolutionary grades.

Here we see the wide basis that morals have in the hierarchical construction of Nature, for morals, however men may view them, or however they may be delineated in human philosophical outline, are based on this hierarchical structure of Nature itself. No man can live unto himself alone. He must, whether he will or whether he nill, live unto others as well. The single human being is but one individual droplet in the vast and onrushing River of Evolving Entities. It is when man realizes his essential oneness with spiritual Nature, and his inseparable links with the visible and the intermediate spheres, that he begins to understand his duties to all other beings, and begins truly to live, and to extend the range of his sympathies to all that is. Thereby he comes into harmonious relationship with all that is, and instead of opposing and battling with other entities and things, he becomes helpful, and obtains a growing understanding of them, because in proportion as he understands himself, he understands other entities also.

XIV—Evolution

Evolution as taught in the archaic philosophy, and therefore taught by the Theosophy of our own times, is based, as a process, on what we may briefly call the unfolding or unwrapping of what had previously been infolded and inwrapped. It is therefore, as a word, used in the exact etymological sense.

When, indeed, the Theosophist uses the word 'Evolution,' the picture immediately comes to mind of a very general process applying as well to worlds or spheres or planes, as to any one or to all of the innumerable hosts of entities inhabiting those worlds or spheres or planes which compose the entire universe. All are, considered both collectively and in particular, but passing phases or 'events,' stages in progressive development. Thus Man, originating in the beginning of past aeonic evolution as an unself-conscious god-spark, travels through the various phases of evolutionary progress or growth, and each one of such phases is to be considered an 'event'; and this process has continued to the present time, and will continue indefinitely into the future, till the very end of the present Cosmic Period of Manifestation.

The Monad began its long pilgrimage in the beginning of a past Cosmic Period as an unself-conscious god-spark. This 'event' was followed from phase to phase, each such phase being a new 'event,' until it found itself in that phase of its evolutionary journey on and through our earth called the Mineral Kingdom. It passed through this Kingdom in the course of long ages through the process of unfolding the innate energies and powers flowing forth from itself, gradually bringing the intermediate links, or intermediate nature, between the Monad and the Mineral Kingdom, into becoming fitter and more perfect vehicles to the Monad; so that ultimately the evolving Monad found itself in the Vegetable Kingdom.

Passing through this Kingdom during the course of long aeons, the constant perfecting of the intermediate vehicles between the Monad on the one hand, and the plant-bodies on the other, brought these intermediate links into a still more sensitive and quasi-conscious condition, so that they became fit for enshrining the Monad in the Beast Kingdom.

The Monad passing through all these various phases or events of the Beast Kingdom in its evolutionary progress, continued, as before, in a larger measure of progressive unwrapping of ever higher or more spiritual energies flowing forth from the inner Monad itself, till the sensitized beast-nature became more fit to express, in still larger degree, still higher and nobler energies and forces flowing forth from the Monad; and at this point, then, we find the journeying Monad manifesting in the Human Kingdom.

But here a very important point must be noticed, so important, indeed, that we dwell upon it somewhat strongly. The process as just described does not in any sense mean that the elemental became a stone; nor that the stone became a plant; nor that the plant became a beast; nor that the beast became a man; for if this were so, it would be preaching the old Darwinism over again in simply newer and somewhat different phraseology. That is not the idea at all, and it is one which the Theosophical teaching of Evolution repudiates. Here are the differences between the popular doctrine of Evolution, which is more accurately described as 'Transformism,' as the French properly call it, and the Theosophical teaching of Evolution:

First: The Ancient Wisdom postulates the deathless and ever-enduring spiritual Monad or Life-Consciousness-Center: a purely spiritual being, existing as a separate Individuality throughout the aeons of our present cosmic period of Evolutionary Manifestation.

Darwinism teaches nothing of the sort, but says that all beings arose out of inert and lifeless matter, how, no one knows. But such was the declaration, although, as we have earlier explained, scientists today are beginning to talk about a doctrine of 'emergence'; and this is a very hopeful sign of a more spiritual viewpoint working through the scientific imagination.

Second: the Theosophical teaching of Evolution, we reiterate, does not set forth that the Monad *becomes* an elemental, nor that it *becomes* a stone, nor that it *becomes* a plant, nor a beast, nor a man. It teaches that the Monad unrolls or unwraps or unfolds from itself — in other words, emanates various energies or powers which, as they aggregate around their monadic source, form a composite vehicle or body in which, and through which, the Monad works, and through which it manifests itself on the lower planes.

These intermediary vehicles or bodies grow or evolve progressively in a cyclical development; and thus become ever more fit vehicles for the manifestation of the transcendent powers flowing forth from the spiritual Monad. The Monad never leaves its own spiritual sphere. It sends, as it were, its rays through these intermediary vehicles or bodies, down into the material world; and of course these rays find an ever easier path of expression as these intermediate vehicles become more perfect, fitter to express the powers inherent in the monadic rays.

It is thus clear that the Monad, never leaving its own spiritual realms, simply 'overshadows' or illuminates all the relatively gross material vehicles through which it passes, and which form the various phases or 'events' of its growth.

To the contrary of this, all the scientific theories know nothing of this Monad behind or rather above the various physical bodies which that science alone knows anything about and studies. This science traces only a gradual increase in the material beings or entities which are the subject of its researches, and from this gradual increase of faculty and organ it deduces the unquestioned truth of an evolutionary progress. But it has mistaken that process. It sees an actual transforming of the lower physical entity into the higher physical entity; and this transforming of body into body is what the Theosophist repudiates. All the various physical vehicles or, in other words, the living beings and entities in and through which the monadic rays manifest, and which are the phases or events through which the Monad passes, are indeed nothing but that — 'events.' They come, they live, and they pass; but the Monad working through its evolving, intermediate and living vehicles continues forever.

It is the gradual increase in 'perfection,' to use a popular word, of these intermediate vehicles in which the monadic rays work, which constitutes Evolution; and the various Kingdoms thus also in the last analysis are built up and made more perfect by the inner urge or drive within.

Third: The Theosophical teaching of Evolution sets forth that the various Kingdoms of Nature are themselves plastic phases or 'events': transitory appearances of interior energies expressing themselves through these various Kingdoms, and indeed forming those Kingdoms, much as the interior forces of man's constitution form his body.

When such a body is worn out, it is dropped, and the intermediate entity, the 'reincarnating ego,' passes on to its rest, but only to return after a certain lapse of time and inform a new physical entity. In other words, it assumes a new human body in the next incarnation. European science knows nothing of Reincarnation, or of the process just sketched, except by hearsay, and of course in one sense it is not to be blamed for refusing to accept something which its physical studies have not yet enabled it to prove. Nevertheless such theories as that of 'emergence,' as enunciated by Dr. Lloyd Morgan and his school, are long steps in advance and show the direction in which modern scientific speculation is advancing.

Furthermore, Evolution in the Theosophical sense, means that such a progressive growth or development takes place coincidentally and co-ordinately on at least three planes: the monadic (for the Monad itself is evolving in its own high realms); the psycho-intellectual or the human; and the astral-physical. It is in this concurrent scheme of evolution that lie the secrets of the progressive development of even the physical beings of our own world; for these beings, after all is said, but reflect or mirror the general growth or forward advance of what takes place in the case of the inner intermediate entities which inspire and drive on these beings of the physical sphere.

What, then, is the Monad? The Monad is a spiritual entity, a life-consciousness-center. Each Monad is a spiritual being, which in long past aeons of development — in other words, in other Manvantaras or periods of Cosmic Manifestation — had passed through all the inferior or lower phases or 'events' of growth until it finally reached conscious quasi-divinity.

One of such previous 'events' was in all senses equivalent to what is called the human stage as manifest on our earth. In other words, a man is an entity in which spirit and matter are more or less equilibrated. It is the destiny of the human beings of the present period of cosmic evolution on this earth ultimately to attain the same high spiritual stature and status that these Monads have already reached. These Monads are, therefore, only our forerunners on the path of an ever-expanding evolutionary perfection — a perfection which never reaches an ultimate.

Similarly, the infinitesimal lives which compose man's body, and which are the life-atoms invigorating the atoms of physical chemistry in which they live and through which they work, are ultimately souls, so to speak, evolving towards the human stature and condition of progressive development.

Thus we see all through Universal Nature one common Rule of Action or Operation of Natural being: the drive or urge or tendency to betterment. This is Evolution in the Theosophical sense, and the student or reader can work out the details as widely and as largely as he may choose to do so.

Every stage of evolutionary advancement is an 'event.' This word is an excellent one, because it contains the meaning of a passing or transitory phase of growth; it destroys in the mind the tendency to crystallization of ideas, and to consider the various things and entities which surround us as unchanging in their essence, and changing, if at all, only in their outer appearances or bodies. The exact reverse of this is Nature's law. Everything changes, every thing advances; every entity changes, every entity advances; every entity, every thing grows, develops, and therefore every entity or thing is a phase or 'event'— in other words, a stage of growth of that indwelling and impelling entity in its progress to higher and greater and better stages or events.

The Monad itself, therefore, is a spiritual 'event'; man is a human event; the mineral is also an event; the worlds and spheres and planes in which these various beings live and move and have their being, are themselves but 'events.' For everything changes — in other words grows — passing from the less perfect to the more perfect, from the inferior to the superior; and all things and all entities: divine, spiritual, intellectual, psycho-astral, or physical, whatever they may be, and wherever they may be: are unwrapping, rolling out, bringing forth from within themselves, if we speak in a collective sense, the intrinsic, inherent, innate energies, powers, faculties, of the Causal Self residing in the core of each.

That causal Self is the source of all, and the whole course of Evolution is the raising up unto ever higher standards of self-expression, of the spiritual grandeur within, of all the entities and beings which form the hierarchical hosts of the Boundless Universe. Everything helps everything else; nothing and no entity lives unto itself alone; every entity and everything is but a part of another entity still more grand, still more sublime. This is the secret meaning of the saying of Paul of the Christians, that "In It we live and move and have our being."

It is at once apparent that the Theosophical view of Evolution is distinctly a spiritual one—necessarily so, because Evolution, as conceived by the Ancient Wisdom, is fundamentally the activity of spiritual powers manifesting throughout the spheres of Universal Being.

It is precisely in this that lies the great distinction between Darwinism, as taught under its various forms by its scientific exponents, and the teaching of Evolution as Theosophy sets it forth. So far as the mere details of the progressive development of the physical beings on earth go, the Theosophist is more than willing to leave to the researches of biologists, their elucidation and classification; but when it comes to questions of causes or to scientific questions having a wide philosophical import and basis, the matter is a very different one.

It seems to the Theosophist a matter of mere time until the

real nature of Evolution considered as a natural process shall have become more or less clear to scientific thinkers, and then doubtless the Theosophist will see the same close approach to our ancient teachings that scientific discovery and scientific deductions from these latest discoveries have alraedy been instrumental in producing in the present day.

To put it in simple language, the missing factor in scientific transformism is the idea that every animate evolving entity has a 'soul' and in a sense is a 'soul.' When the science of the future shall have realized that physical beings cannot exist without an inner focus of energy—call this inner focus 'soul' or by any other name that you may please to adopt—then the philosophical science of the future will with every year tend to become more Theosophical.

On precisely the same grounds do we feel that when the science of the future shall have come to understand, and understanding to realize, that the physical world is but the expression of the energies and ethereal substances flowing into it, and thereby composing it, from spheres which to our present sense-apparatus are invisible—and which we may call the 'soul' of the physical world—then too shall we in all probability, indeed of necessity, see the science of that future day becoming with the passage of each year more and more Theosophical.

When that future shall have arrived, science will have become distinctly religious, but religious in a cosmical sense and not in the restricted sense that this word 'religious' is ordinarily understood to have in Occidental countries. Then a new and very beautiful Religion of Nature will take the place of the present period of agnostic uncertainty — that is what it really is, let people say what they may. A system of thinking builded upon uncertainties and changing from day to day, *pari passu* with each fresh and epoch-making discovery, may be all right in a certain sense perhaps, but it most certainly offers no principles of structure which are either permanent or satisfying. The mind and heart of man instinctively call for some basis of reality which, if not unchanging, at least is self-consistent and enduring, and of course there can be no reality outside of natural fact and law.

Now, when we speak of a Religion of Nature it must be remembered that the word 'Nature' is employed strictly in the Theosophical sense, that is to say, in the sense of a Cosmic Organism, consisting of both visible and invisible worlds or spheres or planes, and ensouled by vast Hierarchies of living and fully self-conscious entities of a spiritual character and type. Whether these be called gods or spiritual beings or by some other name, matters not at all. It is the conception that is important. Scientific thinkers are becoming restive under the rapidly accumulating facts of discovery for which there has as yet been evolved or found no unifying and satisfying system, bringing them all into coherent and logical form. In other words, modern science is soulless, and this word is not used with any desire to be disrespectful, nor forgetful of the splendid work of our scientists in doing all they can to unveil Nature's secrets. This they most certainly are doing, using all their efforts, to penetrate behind the veils of the outward seeming. Truth is perhaps the holiest thing that man can aspire to, and unquestionably the best minds in science are seekers of Truth.

Of course in time such a Religion of Nature will be found or formulated, and it will be founded entirely on the facts of the spiritual Universe. But it is a great pity that work towards that end has not already begun with a larger degree of definite purpose. Opinions such as those of Professor Eddington, before alluded to, are of course a great step ahead. Once that men realize that the substratum of all natural being is Consciousness, a new light shall have dawned.

Now, Evolution is, in fact, not a thing in itself, but a procedure of Nature, and is wholly governed by the karmic causes originated in previous periods of the existence of any evolving entity whatsoever. And since Evolution is but the bringing forth into kinetic manifestation of seeds of activity sown in its own fabric of structure, it is of course evident that it is Karma, or Nature's fundamental law of cause and effect, which is the originating cause of all evolutionary activity.

Closely involved in the conception of Evolution is another operation of Nature which we may call the Law of Cycles, or

Nature's repetitive operations. This is an exceedingly interesting branch of study, one which is so obviously manifest in the worlds surrounding us that its existence can hardly be denied, except by the wilfully blind. Everywhere we find Nature repeating herself, although such repetition of course is not merely a running in the same old ruts on each recurrence of the cyclic activity, for each recurrence is the expression of a modification, more or less great, of what has preceded. Day succeeds night, winter succeeds summer, the planets circulate around the suns in regular and periodical courses; and these are but very familiar examples of cyclical activity.

Man himself in his course of repeated incarnations is another example of the same method of Nature's working, and, as just said, Evolution and cyclical activity are closely involved, the one with the other. Indeed, it may be said that these are not so much two distinct processes of Nature as they are two aspects of the general process of natural growth in progressive development. Cycles in Nature show the time-periods of periodic recurrence along and in which any evolving entity expresses the energies which are itself, so that cycles and evolution are like the two sides of a coin: the one shows the time-periods or cycles, and the other side manifests the energic or substantial qualities appearing in manifestation according to these cyclical time-periods, but back of this apparently double, but actually single, process lie karmic causes.

The thought may perhaps become more clear if we consider the evolutionary progress of any evolving entity (or any host of evolving entities) as a continuous or uninterrupted series of 'events,' in the sense already outlined. These 'events' are the self-expressions of the energies flowing forth from the evolving entity, its different phases of self-expression; and as each evolving entity is a bundle of forces, each such bundle having its own characteristic or type, its own individuality, it becomes obvious that this individuality can express only what is in itself, indeed, what *is* itself; and this continuous and uninterrupted expression of the powers of the indwelling Self proceeding along the lines of its characteristic individuality, furnishes not only the time-periods or cyclical aspect of the process, but also the changing qualities of the energic substances involved, which are the evolutionary aspect.

A tree, for instance, at the proper season of each year, will burgeon into leaf and blossom, finally producing fruit; and then at the proper time-periods these manifestations of the indwelling vitality will fade or pass away. Each such recurrence is an event in the life-cycle of the tree, and repeats itself from year to year. Just so in the case of an evolving Monad (or any other entity, or any expression of such an evolving Monad—a human being, for example), each incarnation is but the renewed coming forth into manifestation of the karmic results, of the Chain of Causation and of Consequences, originated in the past life and lives. These of course proceed according to the energies involved, which had their beginning, their period of maturity or culmination, and their decrease or decay. These last must proceed according to cyclical periods.

This manner of looking upon Evolution as a continuous series of 'events,' the one succeeding the other throughout time, and each one being the fruitage or consequence or resultant of the preceding event, is invariably considered by the Theosophist to contain a deeply ethical significance, using the word 'ethical' in a larger sense than is perhaps usual.

A man who considers himself as such an evolving entity, self-expressing himself in such a continuous and uninterrupted series of 'events,' realizes that the old-fashioned ideas of an immortal and changeless soul having one term of life-expression on earth, and thereafter entering upon an endless period of a more or less crystallized destiny, are as unnatural as they are impossible of acceptance by any thoughtful and logical mind. Instead he sees himself to be a growing entity, a learning thing, continually assuming garments builded of circumstance and time, and as continually casting them aside when their use and purpose have been respectively fulfilled.

Evolution therefore in the Theosophical view of things is a distinctly spiritual process, for in Spirit it has its roots and action and all its ultimate motivating qualities. When we say 'Spirit' here, we mean of course the spiritual Monad, as before described, and not some vague and intangible quantity or essence which is assumed to be separate from the matter existing throughout the spaces of Space. Such a universal essence is not denied, but it is merely the vital stuff or substance of the Cosmic Entity in which all the Monads inhere and of which these Monads are themselves, so to say, the life-atoms, and it is in no sense of the word separate and distinct in its roots from the remainder of the Universe.

The Spirit here spoken of in the particular sense which we are now studying, means those individualized centers of consciousness-life which the Theosophist calls 'Monads,' adopting for the purpose the old Pythagorean term. It is a good term because each such Monad is in its essence or in the core of itself an individualized and deathless entity, lasting throughout the entire term of manvantaric evolution, throughout a great Cosmic Period of Life-Manifestation. It is of course true that at the end of such a Cosmic Period of Manifestation, these Monads re-enter the bosom of what we may briefly call the Boundless All, for their term of monadic rest and recuperation; but they will again issue forth for a new Period of Cosmic Manifestation when the cosmic time-clock points to the karmic hour.

The destiny of a Monad is thus to be sketched precisely along the same lines that characterize the destiny of any individual reincarnating human ego, for indeed any such reincarnating ego or highest human self is but a copy in miniature of what its 'prototype in heaven,' the Monad, is. Analogy is the one greatest guiding rule in any attempt to explain the operations of the Universe and of the entities included within its immense bosom. One fundamental and universal system of laws operates throughout the ALL, and hence it is of course a simple matter of logic that the part shall obey, or rather follow, the general operation of these cosmic laws, for the inseparable parts of the Whole can do no otherwise.

But we repeat: this is in no sense fatalistic, for just as the cosmic spaces of Space themselves are the enshrouding garment or veil of some immensely superior Cosmic Entity possessing consciousness and will or freedom of choice in its own spheres or realms, so does likewise every one of the innumerable Hierarchies of the hosts of entities composing that Hierarchy as its life-atoms, have each one its own individual character or monadic center; and this is equivalent to saying that it has its own individual sphere of free will or moral and intellectual choice.

Envisaging Evolution as an entirely spiritual process in the last analysis, makes the study of it one of surpassing interest, for it is immediately seen to be the manner of working of the indwelling hosts of consciousnesses which not merely inform and infill the Universe, or any specific part of it, but are actually the fabric or framework or web of that Universe itself.

XV—Evolution
(Continued)

No Theosophist has ever denied that there is a certain modicum of truth in the views of Nature that were brought into modern physical science more or less through the writings of Charles Darwin; but by this we do not mean that the Theosophist is a Darwinist. We have already most emphatically denied this. The first edition of Darwin's book, *The Origin of Species*, was published on November 24, 1859; and his second work, epoch-making in its way, *The Descent of Man*, was published in 1871. In these two books, Darwin set forth his conception of the evolutionary process as a series of additions to, or in some cases subtractions from, the physical equipment of evolving entities, by means of what he called "natural selection," or the "preservation of favored races in the struggle for life."

The idea lying behind these two works is that Nature is a purely mechanical process, eventuating in the varied phenomena of the world which surrounds us; and that the energies inherent in Nature and producing these phenomena were in some mysterious manner endowed with the power of selecting out what Darwin called 'fit' entities, in other words, entities or beings which by chance had brought forth certain physical characteristics enabling them to survive and reproduce their kind in a manner superior to other contemporaneous physical beings.

Now, of course no one denies that as regards two entities, one of which is fit and the other unfit as regards a certain environment, the fit has the better chances to survive; but it is very evident that merely restating a natural problem in new words, is giving no explanation of the problem at all. It is not solved merely by stating the facts of the case in a new formulation. Furthermore, the fittest is by no means the best, and the most limited experience of life shows us that sometimes it is the best which goes to the wall. For instance, shark and a man in the water offer an example of a case where one, the shark, is well fitted to live in that particular environment, and the man is not. The shark will survive and the man will drown; but the man is unquestionably the better, the more evolved, of the two.

What was lacking in Mr. Darwin's work was the conception of an inner conscious or quasi-conscious urge or impelling drive which brought forth not merely the fit, but also the best, in any particular set of circumstances; and merely to say, as Mr. Darwin did, that the better of two in the long run survives, is merely saying what everybody knows, and is offering no explanation at all of the phenomena of life. The great value of Darwin's work, in the effect that it had on immediately succeeding generations, was its calling attention to the unexplained fact of progressive development, and also the destructive effect that it had on the crystallized theories and notions of the time.

In certain merely secondary matters we do not deny that there is some truth in Darwinism, but we cannot see that it really explains anything in Nature whatsoever; and indeed Mr. Darwin himself rather pointedly said that his literary work was descriptive rather than explanatory: at least this is the substance of a number of his remarks.

Again, the supposition of Darwin, and of his followers even today, that the human race is an evolution from beast-ancestors and more particularly from the anthropoid stock, is, in the Theosophical view, not only unproved but untrue, and later evolutionist-biologists have done splendid work in showing pretty much the same thing.

It is often said today that Darwin did not teach the descent of man from the apes; but this statement is unfortunately altogether untrue. In several places in his published works Mr. Darwin makes the very definite declaration to the contrary, deriving man in an unbroken line from that particular branch of the anthropoid stock which is commonly called the Catarrhine or Old-World division of the anthropoids. For instance, in his *Descent of Man,* chapter vi, 'On the Affinities and Genealogy of Man':

> Now man unquestionably belongs in his dentition, in the structure of his nostrils, and some other respects, to the Catarrhine or Old-World division.

And again on the next page, he remarks, in speaking of the Catarrhine group:

> We may infer that some ancient member of the anthropomorphous sub-group gave birth to man.

And again, over this page, he continues:

> And as man from a genealogical point of view belongs to the Catarrhine or Old-World stock, we must conclude, however much the conclusion may revolt our pride, that our early progenitors would have been properly thus designated. But we must not fall into the error of supposing that the early progenitor of the whole Simian stock, including man, was identical with, or even closely resembled any existing ape or monkey.

And again he says, in the same chapter, a paragraph or two farther on:

> We are far from knowing how long ago it was that man first diverged from the Catarrhine stock; but it may have occurred at an epoch as remote as the Eocene Period.

In view of these citations and a large number of others that could be made from Darwin's works, it is simply idle to deny that the great English naturalist derived man from the ape-stock, merely because he says that man could not have been derived from "any existing monkey or ape." Of course not. The trees of the present period are obviously not derived in direct lineal descent from the ferns and mosses of the present period! It is the alleged derivation of man from the anthropoid stock which we find to be utterly unsupported by any natural fact.

Unquestionably a large number of resemblances and even possible identities in some few cases exist in ape and man. These are natural facts, which certainly no Theosophist would ever deny; and, furthermore, with an insistence even stronger than that of the Darwinist, we point to these resemblances and few identities as certain proofs of the relationship of the apes to man. But we offer an explanation of these facts which is widely different from, in fact what we may call a polar antithesis to, that suggested by Mr. Darwin, and followed by his school.

It is perfectly true that the apes have some human blood in their veins, but there is not one drop of ape-blood in the veins of man. This entire matter is so well set forth by H. P. Blavatsky in her *The Secret Doctrine,* in various places, that it would be a mere waste of time to go into the details here; and to *The Secret Doctrine* the reader is referred for further information, if he cares to pursue the subject.

Man is the most advanced of the living entities on earth today, and being the most advanced, the immediate supposition is that he is so because the oldest of the animate stocks on earth. Being the oldest, he has had the most time in which to evolve forth from his indwelling monadic essence in greater degree than the inferior stocks have been able to do, the innate or inherent energic and substantial characteristics of that monadic essence, which thus expressing themselves through their ultimate vehicle, the physical body, have changed it correspondingly.

Evolution is a cyclical process, as already said, and this fact is so perfectly obvious that even the most recalcitrant Darwinist, or the most positive and determined materialist, is not blind to the fact. Even from Darwin's day, it was noted and commented upon that as the geological record is uncovered, one very interesting fact is observed with greater clearness and more fully as that geological record becomes better known, and it is this: there seem to have been in past ages on earth, evolutionary waves or cyclical periods during which one or another stock *apparently* suddenly appears in the geological record, advances steadily to its culmination or maturity of development of form and power and size, and then fades away and apparently in some cases, as suddenly disappears, while in other cases remnants are carried on over into the succeeding age.

Such cases of succeeding evolutionary waves are very noticeable in three instances: first, in the Age of the Fishes, which took place during what it is usual to call the Primary or Palaeozoic Era. This was the geological era when the sea swarmed with fishes of all-various kinds and sizes, which fishes then represented, *as far as the geological record shows*, at least the supposedly highest known forms. This last we do not admit, but we are here speaking of the geological record alone, and not of the Theosophical teachings.

The second of these waves, which occurred during the Secondary Era or Period of time, is what is called the Age of Reptiles, when reptilian monsters of many kinds and often of huge body, were, so far as the geological record shows, the masters of the earth.

The third instance occurred during the Tertiary—or perhaps it began in the last period of the Secondary, and continued into the Tertiary—and this third evolutionary wave or cyclical period we may call the Age of the Great Mammals, which then in their turn, succeeding the Reptiles, were the masters of the earth.

In each of these three cases, as the geological record is studied, we can see the beginnings: we can see the growth in size and power, the culmination or the maturity or full efflorescence of the particular stock. Then comes decay and a final passing of the bulk of the animate beings belonging to that particular evolutionary life-wave, making place for the new stock, which in its turn has its dawn, reaches its full margin in the expansion of its physical powers and size, and then in its turn passes away; and so forth.

These evolutionary waves comprise a subject of study which is fully explained in Theosophy, and they furnish interesting examples of the cyclical nature of Evolution as hereinbefore spoken of. Wave succeeds wave, each wave reaching a higher level of evolutionary activity than did the preceding wave; and is in its turn followed by another wave, bringing on the scene beings or entities and things of a new and different type.

It has been customary to say that the fishes gave birth to the reptiles, and that the reptiles gave birth to the mammals, to the great beasts, and these great beasts brought forth man through the highest of their own type, which, as supposed, was the ape. But the difficulties in the way of the acceptance of this theory are far greater—and no one knows this better than the modern transformists themselves—than are the arguments in favor of it. The Theosophical teaching runs directly to the contrary. It sets forth that while it is true that these evolutionary waves succeed each other, each such wave represents or manifests the coming on the scene of physical existence on our earth of a new Family or a new Host of evolving entities. It says, furthermore, that each one of these hosts has its dawn, its noonday, and its evening, and that the physical bodies in which these hosts of evolving entities dwell, die or pass away in due time, and that the hosts themselves pass on to inhabit vehicles or bodies of a higher evolutionary character which these hosts themselves bring forth.

It is not the bodies of these hosts which give birth to the superior bodies which follow them, as the Darwinist and other theories say; but it is the succeeding waves, each one of a stronger and fuller type of self-expression, of the Monads composing such an evolving host, which in their psycho-astral principles grow constantly more perfect and fitter vehicles for the manifestation of the monadic essence.

Evolution is essentially a process arising from within, and not existing wholly without; or, in other words, Evolution means the monadic essence constantly expressing itself in ever fuller measure, and constantly raising the visible and invisible vehicles through which it manifests itself to better and fitter vehicles for the expression of itself.

In one sense, therefore, in the Theosophical view, Evolution is not only cyclical but teleologic, purposive, working towards a destined end, which in fact is an ever fuller expression of the monadic essence. But this purposiveness in Evolution, this inherent urge or drive to betterment, is in the entity itself, and is not imposed upon it from without, either by a god or gods existing outside of and separate and different from the evolving entity, or, on the other hand, by physical nature alone.

Physical nature furnishes the environment or fields within which the monadic essence works, and it is in these physical fields that the various races of physical bodies which biological science calls the various Classes, Orders, Families, Genera, and Species, of physical living beings, exist, and are the means for the ultimate self-expression of the evolving host of Monads or consciousness-centers.

We return again to the key-thought of what Evolution is, as taught by the archaic Wisdom-Religion, Theosophy: it is a continuous and uninterrupted series of beings appearing one after the other, enchained by karmic effects or actions one to another—each one the fruitage of its predecessor, and eventuating in its successor; and this continuous and uninterrupted series of beings is an endless concatenation of 'events' of evolving Monads in the sense we have already set forth.

Evolution is cyclical, for it has a beginning, a culmination, and an end—which is but a new beginning along other lines; and the motivating or rather the energizing causes behind this majestic process of natural as well as intellectual and spiritual growth, flow forth from the consciousness-center or Monad within the evolving form, in strict accordance with the seeds of karmic action sown by previous acts, and thus working in and through the conditions and circumstances which then exist.

It is thus that the fabric of character is built; it is thus that the destiny of the future is founded; it is thus that consciousness expresses itself in continuous and uninterrupted action. What is called 'death' is no real interruption, but is a passing or transference of the invisible energies composing the evolving entities to the invisible worlds or planes or spheres, where the cyclical evolutionary activity pursues an uninterrupted course without break of continuity.

When we realize that man, as an example of such an evolving entity, is a composite being, consisting of a spiritual-divine Monad; of a reincarnating ego; of a temporary 'event' called a human ego; and of a vital-astral-physical body; it is at once seen what death is—the casting off of the least evolved or most imperfect of these living vehicles. In other words it is the dropping of the physical body, and the continuance of the evolutionary course as regards the remaining portions of man's constitution.

In due time, after the death of the physical body, the intermediate or soul-nature or human nature in its turn is dropped. All the best of it, all the finest energies or functions, are withdrawn or indrawn into the monadic essence, which then, as before, pursues in its own spiritual realms the sublime course of evolution characteristic of itself. Then, when the energies which we have called the 'finest energies' (formerly withdrawn into the monadic essence and forming the reincarnating ego) have passed a certain period of time in rest or repose—or in what may perhaps be properly termed an intellectual adjustment in spiritual equilibrium—the seeds of thought and action previously sown in the fabric of the reincarnating ego itself and thus forming part of its own being, awaken. They begin to manifest themselves anew, and by a species of psycho-magnetic attraction for its former spheres and planes of activity, the reincarnating ego is drawn back to the earth whereon it had formerly lived, and enters anew another human physical body. It starts a new life-cycle, the fruitage of its past life and lives, and which again will be the field whereon shall be sown the seeds ultimately producing the next succeeding reimbodiment. Thus this wonderful process continues, each step or stage of growth in the normal course being superior to the last.

We omit in the present study all questions of retrogression, for there are occasional instances of apparent degenerative return to a more imperfect but always human incarnation. These last cases are very rare, and do not concern us here, for they are what may be called exceptions to the general rule.

It is these seeds of thought, of emotion, and of energic impulses carried over from the tree, so to speak, of the former life, which are destined to blossom forth into the career of the individual next to be: in other words, to furnish the series of 'events' and the various vehicles for the reimbodiment of the Monad in its next cycle of evolutionary activity on earth.

. . . .

In order now to round out the scheme of Evolution we have set forth and to give the more complete Theosophical picture of the great Root-Races, as we Theosophists call them, through which the human race has passed, we present the following observations drawn from *The Secret Doctrine* by H. P. Blavatsky.

In the first place, then, and in the early portion of the evolution of this globe—our Earth, which is the most material of a chain of seven interblending and interlocking spheres, the other six of which are progressively more ethereal as they ascend towards the spiritual realms—when the human life-wave first entered into the 'physical' atmosphere of this earth in those far past aeons of time, it did so as Beings clothed with light — or at least we may so phrase the matter for easy understanding.

The earth then opened a new period of evolutionary activity. Previous to the descent of the human life-wave from those other and higher globes of the earth-chain of seven spheres, the earth had been in a course of evolutionary preparation. This means that it had become from an ethereal and nebulous sphere in its beginning, one now fairly well compacted or concreted in the material sense, although far more ethereal than it is at the present time.

The human host, when the time came for it to appear on this earth-globe, did so in bodies of concrete light, these bodies having a globular, or perhaps more accurately, an ovoid or egg-shaped form. These were the 'physical bodies' of this first period of human evolution, the First Root-Race.

These ovoid bodies had no physiological organs whatsoever, and the vital functions were carried on by a process very similar to what would now be called osmosis, including both endosmosis and exosmosis. The manner of propagation of this First Race was entirely sexless, and was carried on by what would today be called fission, or the separating off from the parent-body of a part or a half of itself, which thereupon grew and became another entity similar to its parent. This lasted many millions of years and it might be remarked in passing that this First Race appeared on earth some tens of millions of years ago, or possibly more.

It was succeeded by the Second Great Race of mankind, the Second Root-Race, which was more material in all senses of the word than the First, but still preponderantly ethereal. It likewise was asexual in character, and its method of propagation was by budding. A small 'bud' or swelling appeared on the body of the individuals of this race, and finally detached itself from the parent in order to grow into a being in all respects similar to the parent from which it came.

There followed it the Third Great Root-Race, much more physical or grossly material than its predecessor the Second Root-Race, but still far more ethereal than the human beings of the present time. Its method of propagation was in the beginning also asexual, by 'spores,' which method very soon, racially speaking, assumed the form of hermaphroditism. Its young were born from it in the shape of small ovoid bodies, which method of propagation is still extant on earth in egg-laying creatures such as the fowls and reptiles.

At about the middle of this third Root-Race there ensued one of the greatest events in the history of the human species, and this was the *Awakening of Mind,* or Intelligence, which had been entirely latent in the First and Second Root-Races, which were, mentally speaking, in much the same state that a man of the present day is in when in what is called a trance. They were but faintly, if at all, conscious of themselves, and the consciousness of the first two Races might perhaps be likened to that manifested by an infant or very young child of the present day.

The Third Great Race from about the middle point of its existence on earth—an existence which lasted for many millions of years—began to grow more and more towards becoming a race containing individuals such as we are today; and in its last portion, did indeed fully develop the separate sexes as now known. From this time began to appear the beginnings of real civilizations, and towards the end of this Third Great Race civilizations existed of a glory and splendor which we have not yet surpassed. This, of course was many million years ago.

This Third Great Race was followed by the Fourth Great Race, called technically the Atlantean for the reason that the *main* continental system on which it lived and flourished and built up its brilliantly material cycle of civilizations, lies under what are now the stormy waters of the Atlantic Ocean.

It may be remarked in passing that it is one of the geological teachings of the Ancient Wisdom that continental systems succeed each other in cyclic regularity in time. What is ocean becomes dry land, bears its races of men, and then disappears or is submerged to give place to succeeding and more evolved races existent on new lands, rising or emerging out of oceanic areas which were formerly part of the aquasphere of the earth.

This Fourth Root-Race was in every respect and in all senses the most material, grossly material, body of human stocks known in the history of the earth, and coincidentally with its middle point of evolutionary development the earth likewise reached its condition of greatest material concretion or solidity. Since then, both the earth and the men who live on it have rebecome more refined, more ethereal, for the evolutionary turning-point, alluded to before, then took place, and the beginning of the pathway towards a more ethereal condition of things occurred.

It is to this great Fourth Root-Race and its brilliantly material civilizations and great Initiates, that most of the religious and philosophical mythology of the ancient peoples refers when it speaks of the 'giants of antiquity,' of the great Sages and magicians of past time, and of the wickedness of former generations of men. All this is set forth with marvelous power in *The Secret Doctrine,* to which the reader is referred for fuller information.

When this great Fourth Race had about half-way run its course, there appeared the beginnings of the Fifth Root-Race, and this Fifth Root-Race is the present Race of mankind, to which we ourselves belong. We shall be succeeded by two other Great or Root-Races, each one, just as ours is doing, evolving constantly towards a more ethereal expression of energies and substances, on its return journey to Spirit from which all beings and things originally came. The earth likewise follows the same etherealizing process, but at a much slower rate of speed than do the humanities succeeding each other in cyclical periods.

In order to give a somewhat definite geological view, it may be said that the First Root-Race appeared, in all probability, in what it is customary to call the late Primary Age (or Palaeozoic Age) of Geology, and possibly in the Devonian, or Coal-Periods. Because of the fact that the geological periods, as taught today, are by no means certain as regards their duration or their points of beginning, it is extremely difficult to place our Races in them with any pretense of accuracy.

It is quite possible that the First Race had its beginnings in the Coal-Period. The Second Race also very probably had its origin in the later Carboniferous or possibly even in the early Permian. The Third Great Race was contemporaneous with the enormous reptiles of the Triassic and Jurassic Periods of the Secondary Era; whilst the Fourth Great Race certainly appeared before the Tertiary, and the great Sages and Seers specifically state that its primal beginnings may even be placed back in the very last period of the Secondary Era, probably therefore in the Cretaceous.

It was in the very beginning of the Eocene Period of the Tertiary Era that this Fourth Race made its first real appearance, and it reached its culmination of brilliant material splendor, and its catastrophic fall, in the Miocene. Our own Fifth Race, as a race *sui generis* (and racially descended from the Fourth Race which preceded it), is at least a million years old, but the primal beginnings of our Fifth Root-Race go back farther than that, and perhaps may be traced into the early Miocene, which witnessed the catastrophal downfall or destruction of the great Fourth Root-Race.

Finally, in response to the question that might be asked regarding the lack in the geological record of any evidences of the First, the Second, and the Third Root-Races, the answer is simple enough. The First Race was extremely ethereal in physical texture, much more so than even the earth then was. And so was the Second Root-Race, although more materialized than was the First. Obviously, races having bodies of so tenuous and vaporous a texture could leave no fossilized impress even on a more or less etherealized earth, as it then was. Nor could even the Third Race in its early portions do so, for it was still much more ethereal than the globe on which it lived.

However, it must be remembered that the geological record is extremely imperfect, so imperfect indeed that what we know of it is not a page here and there in a big volume, so to say, but not even all the paragraphs of that one page, nor even all the sentences of one paragraph. The geologic record furnishes us with only an occasional word or phrase, or sentence perhaps, here and there on such a page, and mostly towards the end of the page.

The fourth Race of course was quite sufficiently material easily to affect the earth on which it lived, for the men of that Race were not only mighty builders, but their bodies were intensely physical and gross, more so even than our own; fossilized remnants of these bodies it is quite possible will be found when further discoveries open up further paragraphs of the book of the geological record.

Thus then, in the preceding sketch of Evolution as taught by Theosophy, we see once more the power of thought that the Great Theosophist, H. P. Blavatsky, possessed, and the high grade of intellectual discernment which enabled her to gather, in her *The Secret Doctrine*, the large number of facts and instances which she there adduced in support of her re-statement of the teachings of the Ancient Wisdom in modern times.

What she there taught was practically unknown and unsuspected when she wrote. But since her passing, Theosophists have checked off, one after the other, as they have come to pass, ever closer approximations by the most brilliant minds in modern scientific speculation to the teachings which she there laid down.

We come back to the question we have asked before: Whence did she get these teachings? If she invented them, she was indeed a genius without peer in the history of the world, for these supposititious 'inventions' are being yearly shown to be facts of Nature, as modern scientific discovery and deduction bring them to our view.

But no Theosophist ever looks upon H. P. Blavatsky in this light. While recognizing her intrinsic greatness of spirit, of mind, and of heart, the Theosophist above everyone else realizes that the hand which wrote *The Secret Doctrine* and the brain which dictated to that hand, were inspired by intellects still loftier—the Great Teachers of the Ancient Wisdom from whom H. P. Blavatsky, from the beginning of her public work to the end, claimed to receive the doctrines which she gave to the world.

We conclude this chapter with the following thought: Evolution is a fact, growth is a fact, the great Seers and Sages of the ages are a fact and they are the individual products of cyclical evolutionary law. They are as much a necessity in Nature's scheme, so far as our earth is concerned, as is anything else, and to deny the existence of the Teachers of Wisdom who sent forth H. P. Blavatsky into the world is equivalent to denying the fact of cyclical evolution itself.

They are the Fine Flowers of the human race, the noblest human expression of the monadic essence. Between them and us there are all-various grades or degrees of intemediate grandeur, and between them and the gods there are other similar grades and degrees of still nobler beings who are the examples of a still more splendid evolutionary growth.

XVI—Man

It is customary in Western lands in speaking of the 'human race,' to think only of the *physical bodies* which the host of Monads inhabits. This extraspective method of viewing Man is entirely owing to centuries of miseducation along religious and philosophical lines, and to the great development during the last three hundred years of European science in its physical aspects. But to look upon the outstanding figure, Man, earth's noblest inhabitant, after this manner, is obviously taking a very restricted and imperfect view, for it leaves imperfectly and improperly considered the real faculties which make Man Man—his spiritual, intellectual, moral, and psychical characteristics.

It is of course perfectly proper to look upon man's physical body as an entity, for it is one; and for physical science to study that physical body is most excellent for it is indeed a very wonderful natural product—wonderful and mysterious indeed.

But man's physical body is something more than the mere product of physical nature, for it is due to the co-operation of the higher faculties with the forces of matter which have made that physical body even what it is, and it is these higher faculties which have thus, by their co-operation, distinguished it so markedly from the physical bodies of the lower entities such as the beasts and the various ranges of plant-life.

Man has a physical body in and through which he works, because he cannot avoid having one, for it is simply the outermost or physical expression of the very complex bundle of energies which in their aggregate make Man what he is. This bundle of energies self-express themselves through the physical body of Man exactly in proportion as that body has been raised through evolutional development to become a more or less fit and adequate transmitter of this bundle of energies existent in the invisible worlds. Strictly speaking, therefore, when a Theosophist refers to Man he speaks of necessity more particularly of this bundle of energies.

Thus we must come to view Man as a composite entity: a fact upon which we necessarily lay great emphasis. And it is the variations in the functioning of the composite factors of this bundle of energies which produce not merely the different varieties of physical man, but the far larger and greater differences which exist as between individual men in their spiritual, intellectual, psychic, and moral attributes.

Now, the essential root of man, as we have already made clear, is a monadic center, a consciousness-life-center, a center of permanent and enduring character; for the Monad lasts with undiminished consciousness and energy throughout the vastly long cycle of the cosmic Period of Manifestation in which the various worlds and planes and spheres of the solar system are at present evolving.

This period of cosmic manifestation, when calculated in human years, runs into a figure which may be represented by some fifteen digits. When such a period of cosmic manifestation comes to its necessary and karmic end, not only are all physical and intermediate planes of existence withdrawn into the vast spiritual fields of being — or into what the ancient Pythagoreans call the Cosmic Monad—but likewise all the individual Monads which are the roots of individually manifested entities and things are themselves of course withdrawn into the same greater or cosmic Monad, and therein pass their period of aeons-long rest. From this they reissue into manifestation again for a new cycle of activity, but on planes and in worlds and on spheres superior to those which presently exist, which future worlds and planes and spheres will be the necessary karmic or effectual product of the presently existing ones.

It is thus seen that the life-cycle of the solar system is in the Great what Man, in his series of reincarnations, is in the Small. This of course is only what is to be expected, because, the Cosmic Organism is ruled by one general system of 'laws' working in one general organization of substance existing in various degrees of ethereality or materiality; and it is therefore a logical necessity that any individual part or portion of this vast cosmic aggregate is subordinate to and subject to the cosmic bundle of energies which compose and rule the mighty Whole. Man, therefore, does not exist unto himself alone, but is merely one Atom, one Particle, of the almost incomprehensibly great aggregate of which we have just spoken.

Precisely as the Universe has its series of principles or substances from the very spiritual or super-spiritual (Divine) down to the physical, so has Man. It is customary in our Theosophical philosophy to divide these principles and substances of Man into seven conveniently distinct parts. When we say that any one of them is 'distinct', however, we do not mean that it is radically separate from the other six: we mean merely distinct for purposes of enumeration, much as the modern scientific physicists will speak of gravitation and of the phenomena of electro-magnetism as distinct, although these scientists now know that electro-magnetism and gravity are fundamentally or essentially one.

These seven substance-principles of which man is composed are usually enumerated as follows, beginning with the highest and ending with the lowest:

1. Âtman — Self: Pure Consciousness *per se*. The essential and radical power or faculty in us which gives to us, and indeed to every other entity or thing, its knowledge of or sentient consciousness of Selfhood. This is not the Ego.

2. Buddhi — The faculty in Man which manifests as understanding, judgment, discrimination, etc., and which is an inseparable veil or garment of the Âtman.

3. Manas   The center of the ego-consciousness in man and in any other quasi-self-conscious entity.

4. Kâma   The driving force, the seat of the living electric impulses, desires, aspirations, considered in their energic aspect.

5. Prâna   Usually translated 'Life,' but rather the electrical veil or 'electrical field' manifesting in the individual as vitality.

6. Linga-śarîra   The Model-Body, popularly called 'astral body,' because it is but slightly more ethereal than the physical body, and is in fact the model or framework around which the physical body is builded, and from which, in a sense, the physical body flows or from which the physical body develops as growth proceeds.

7. Sthûla-śarîra   The physical body.

One point about this classification is of extreme importance. These various principles, excepting Nos. 7 and 6, and also in a degree No. 5, are more truly what should be characterized as cosmical principles. In other words, they are the general substance-principles which are derivatives from the life-forces of the surrounding Universe. Man of course has them all, and they in their totality make Man all he is, and thus in their aggregate and interworkings and interlockings and interblendings, make him the bundle of energies which we have alluded to before.

But there is another method of dividing the human principles, which is perhaps somewhat easier of comprehension and which we give in the schematic diagram hereunder.

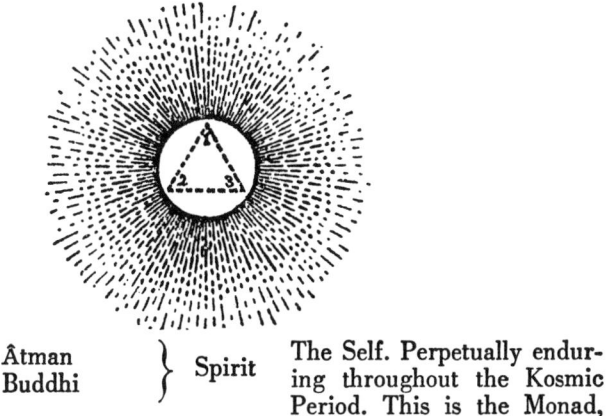

Upper Duad	Âtman Buddhi	} Spirit	The Self. Perpetually enduring throughout the Kosmic Period. This is the Monad, unconditionally immortal.
Intermediate Duad	Manas Kâma	} Soul	Seat of the Ego. Dual: part aspiring upwards, which is the Reincarnating Ego; and part attracted below, which is the ordinary Human Ego. Immortal in Reincarnating Ego; mortal in Human Ego.
Lower Triad	Prâna Linga-śarîra Sthûla-śarîra	} Body	Mortal throughout. The physical human frame and its invisible forces and substances.

Here we see that the seven principles of man are divisible into two Duads and one Triad. The uppermost Duad is the immortal and perpetually enduring Self, the seat of the selfhood in man and indeed in all beings and things: in other words, the seat of the characteristic individuality of the entity, called in Sanskrit Swabhâva. This is unconditionally immortal.

The second Duad, or the intermediate nature, is the ordinary seat of human consciousness, and is composed of two parts: an upper or aspiring part, which is commonly called the Reincarnating Ego, or the Higher Manas; and of a lower part attracted to material things, which is the focus of what expresses itself in the average man as the Human Ego, his everyday ordinary seat of consciousness.

The three principles forming the lower Triad are unconditionally mortal considered as an aggregate, although of course the respective seed-elements of them being drawn from Nature's cosmic reservoirs, are in themselves and considered as cosmic principles, immortal *per se*. This will be clearly perceptible when the reader recollects that the Sthûla-śarîra or physical hierarchy of the human body is builded up of cosmic elements, in their turn formed of atomic entities, which although subject individually to bewilderingly rapid changes and reimbodiments, nevertheless are more enduring in themselves as entities than is the physical body which they temporarily compose.

It is the interconnection and interblending and interlocking of all these substance-principles which make Man what he is. All these principles in the last analysis are cosmic principles; and what makes the Man is the particular gathering together of them in human form around the monadic individuality. It is the teaching of Theosophy that every entity and thing is septenary in constitution, even as Man is, for he is no exception at all in the Universe, as regards his inner constitution.

Evolution, then, consists in the constantly increasing degree in which the higher substance-principles, the two upper Duads in the diagram, are enabled to manifest themselves. When they do so through the lower Triad more easily than before, this denotes an advance in evolutionary progress; and when they manifest themselves but feebly, we see the effect in the lower races of mankind, or in the entities below the human, such as the Beasts and the Plants.

Even in the case of one human individual as he grows from infancy to maturity, we see exactly the same thing. The infant can manifest but very imperfectly the transcendent powers within him, or more accurately 'above' him, simply because the physical vehicle has not yet grown or evolved into becoming a capable and adequate channel for these powers; but as the child grows through youth to maturity, we see day by day these transcendent powers showing themselves with greater fullness, and reaching a limit in any one life which is set or determined by the karmic causes or seeds of development lying latent in the growing child, and unfolding as growth proceeds.

From all this the meaning of H. P. Blavatsky's words in *The Secret Doctrine* (I, 224) become clearer. "Collectively," she writes, "men are the handiwork of hosts of various spirits; distributively, the tabernacles of those hosts; and occasionally and singly, the vehicles of some of them."

Man is indeed, collectively speaking, the handiwork of the hosts of various cosmic spirits, of the multitudes of Monads existing in the hierarchical construction of the universe surrounding us, which give to man his respective various substance-principles. He is also, distributively, the tabernacle of these hosts of monadic entities or cosmic spirits, because he himself as a human host is but the manifestation on earth of one such corporate aggregate. And, most interesting perhaps of all, most wonderful perhaps of all, is the fact that occasionally individual men are the chosen vehicles of some transcendent intelligence, of some highly evolved superhuman being which (or who) manifests through him.

Now such a superhuman being — and the word superhuman should not be stressed too strongly — is one of the great World-Teachers; for each one of the great Sages and Seers is in very truth the more or less perfect or complete representation on earth *in human shape* of the spiritual and transcendent Being which each such great Sage and Seer is in his own higher parts.

We see therefore the meaning of the statement that man is a god manifesting through a temple or tabernacle of flesh — in other words, an incarnate god. The meaning here is obviously not the superficial one, that such a god has no intermediate links of connection with the physical body through which its splendor streams. On the contrary, it is precisely these intermediate links, the intermediate nature of the individual — his various garments or veils enshrouding the monadic splendor — which have been evolved up to a point of being able to 'step down' the glorious energies of the spiritual and super-spiritual parts of man's being.

In connection with the two diagrams above set forth, it should also be stated that man is rooted in the cosmos surrounding him by three principles. These can hardly be said to be *above* the first or Âtman, but are, so to say, that same Âtman's highest and most glorious parts. They could be represented above the second schematic diagram by the symbol of a sun or a globe radiating light, and containing a dotted triangle. Thus it can be seen that man is a child of the Universe in all senses of the word, and that his innermost or highest principles are universal in scope, because radically a part of the Spiritual Universe.

Let us now ask ourselves what is 'death'? In the second of our schematic diagrams the human constitution is divided into seven principles, sub-divided again into a superior Duad, an intermediate Duad, and a lower Triad. Death occurs when a general break-up of this constitution takes place. Nor is this break-up a matter of sudden occurrence, with the exceptions of course of such unusual cases as mortal accidents or suicides, which form a subject beside the present discussion. Death is always preceded, varying in each individual case, by a certain time spent in the withdrawal of the monadic individuality from an incarnation, and this withdrawal takes place coincidentally with a decay of the seven-principled being which man in physical incarnation is. This withdrawal process precedes physical dissolution, and is a preparation of and by the consciousness-center for the forthcoming existence in the invisible realms.

This withdrawal actually is a preparation for the life to come in invisible realms, and as the septenary entity on this earth so decays, it may truly be said to be approaching rebirth in the next sphere. Death occurs, physically speaking, with the cessation of activity of the pulsating heart. There is the last beat, and this is followed by immediate, instantaneous unconsciousness, for Nature is very merciful in these things.

But death is not yet complete, for the brain is the last organ of the physical body really to die, and for some time after the heart has ceased beating, the brain still remains active and the memory, although unconsciously so to the Human Ego, for this short length of time, passes in review, every event of the preceding life. This great or small panoramic picture of the past, is purely automatic, yet the soul-consciousness of the Reincarnating ego watches this wonderful review incident by incident, a review which includes the entire course of thought and action of the life just closed. The entity is, for the time being, entirely unconscious of everything else except this. Temporarily it lives in the past, and memory dislodges from the âkâśic record, event after event, to the smallest detail, passes them all in review, and in regular order from the beginning to the end, and thus sees all its past life as an all-inclusive panorama of picture succeeding picture.

There are very definite ethical and psychological reasons inhering in this process, for it forms all together a reconstruction of both the good and the evil done in the past life, and imprints this strongly on the fabric of the spiritual memory of the passing being. Then the mortal and material portions sink into oblivion; whilst the Reincarnating Ego carries the best and noblest parts of these memories into the Devachan or heaven-world of post-mortem rest and recuperation.

Meanwhile the end called death has come, and unconsciousness, complete, and undisturbed, succeeds until there occurs what the Ancients called the 'second death'.

The lower Triad is now definitely cast off and the remaining quaternary is free. The physical body of the lower Triad follows the course of natural decay, and its various hosts of life-atoms proceed whither their natural attractions call them. The Linga-śarîra or Model-Body remains in the astral realms, and finally fades out. It should be remembered that these astral realms are not one single plane, but a series of planes growing gradually more ethereal or spiritual as they approach the inward spheres of Nature's constitution or structure. The life-atoms of the prâna, or 'electrical field,' fly instantly back at the moment of physical dissolution, to the natural prânic reservoirs of the planet.

This leaves man, therefore, no longer a heptad or septenary entity, but a Quaternary consisting of the two Duads already spoken of.

The 'second death' now takes place when the lower or intermediate Duad in its turn separates from, or rather is cast off by, the upper Duad or monadic essence. But preceding this event the monadic essence gathers unto itself from this lower Duad what is called the Reincarnating Ego, which is all the best of the entity that was, all its purest and most spiritual and noblest aspirations and hopes and dreams for betterment and for beauty and harmony. It is this that the monadic essence gathers into itself, where it remains as the egoic center in the state called Devachan. In this devachanic condition the Reincarnating Ego remains in the bosom of the Monad (or of the monadic essence) in the state of the most perfect and utter bliss and peace, reviewing and constantly reviewing and improving upon its own blissful imagination, all the unfulfilled possibilities of the life just closed that its naturally creative faculties automatically suggest to this devachanic entity.

Man at this point is no longer a Quaternary of substance-principles, but is now reduced to the Monad with the Reincarnating Ego sleeping in its bosom, and is therefore a spiritual Triad.

When the 'second death,' or dissolution of this second or intermediate Duad, has finally taken place, the lower portions of this second or intermediate Duad remain in the etheric or higher astral spheres which are intermediate between the devachanic and the earthly, as the Kâma-rûpa. In time this Kâma-rûpa gradually fades out in its turn, its life-atoms at such dissolution passing to their respective reservoirs. It is this Kâma-rûpa which legend in the various ancient world-religions speaks of as the 'Shade,' and which it has been customary in the Occident to call the 'spook.' It is, in short, all the mortal elements of the Human Ego that was, which Human Ego is now disintegrated.

This, then, is the process of death so far as the individual ego is concerned, but it should not be supposed for a moment that the perpetually spiritual Monad itself is in a state of passive negativity. Very much to the contrary; it is always active, always sending forth from itself a new ray or stream of spiritual activity, which, in these invisible realms or worlds, makes its various veils or garments or bodies. And these various bodies form the living entities in which it manifests in the invisible spheres and which are in a very true sense living beings.

The Monad therefore passes from sphere to sphere on its upward journey from earth, carrying with it the Reincarnating Ego, or what we may for simplicity of expression call the Earth-Child, in its bosom. (Plutarch in his very esoteric essay 'On the Apparent Face in the Orb of the Moon,' speaks in rather veiled but yet to the Theosophist plainly understandable language of this 'second death'.)

The intermediate worlds or spheres or planes are very many, ranging from the lowest or the merely etheric or astral worlds, up to the highest or the spiritual worlds, and it is in these invisible realms that the monadic individuality lives for a time in each, during the course of its gradual ascent.

The time comes when, having passed through all these invisible realms connected by chains of causation with our own planet, it—this monadic essence or individuality—passes on to higher planetary spheres, and in each such planetary sphere continues manifesting or evolving its various sheaths or garments or vehicles or bodies of shape and character appropriate to and fit for each sphere. This continues until the ascending cycle of the interplanetary pilgrimage is concluded, and then its return journey on the descending cycle earthwards begins.

As it slowly 'descends' again through these higher intermediate spheres earthwards, coincidentally does the Reincarnating Ego, hitherto sleeping in devachanic bliss in the bosom of the monadic individuality, slowly begin to reawaken to activity. Just as a man will lay himself down on his bed, tired, and enjoy a blissful sleep of repose and recuperation, and awake in the morning ready for the duties of the new day, so does the Reincarnating Ego act. Gradually it feels, at first unconsciously to itself, the attraction earthwards, arising out of the karmic seeds of thought and emotion and impulse sown in the preceding life on earth, and as these attractions grow stronger, it finds itself under the domination of a strong psychomagnetic attraction driving it to the earth-sphere.

The time finally comes when it is drawn to the family on earth whose karmic attractions are the nearest to its own characteristics, and it then enters, or attaches itself to, by reason of the psycho-magnetic attraction previously spoken of, the human seed which will grow into the body of the human being to be. Thus reincarnation takes place, and the Reincarnating Ego reawakens to life on earth in the body of a little child.

All these processes are governed strictly by natural law, and to a large extent, so far as the entity implicated in the process is concerned, are automatic, as all natural laws are more or less. This automatism, however, is in no sense the unguided or unmotivated workings of inert or dead matter, but is the fruitage of seeds of activity sown by the reincarnating entity itself in the former life, which thus provides for itself the fabric of the body in which it will next manifest itself on earth, as well as the circumstances and environment in which it will find itself involved. Justice rules it all, a justice arising out of the nature and actions of the reincarnating entity itself and in no sense depending upon the activity of any god or gods outside of the human being, or on any merely mechanistic principles of brute matter.

As regards the destiny followed by that portion of man's constitution which pursues its wonderful pilgrimage through the spheres, the ideas involved are for the average man so abstruse and intricate that it would be practically impossible to give a clear outline in a few paragraphs; but the following may be said. Closely connected with the earth and its six invisible but companion-spheres, which with the earth form its Planetary Chain, there are seven other planets of our solar system with which all Monads at any time manifesting on earth have relations as close and as intimate as they do with our own Planetary Chain. Each one of these seven other planetary spheres is itself a Planetary Chain consisting of the visible planet and six companion-spheres, and in each one of these seven Planetary Chains the monadic entity pursues a karmic evolutionary course of Rounds, similar on all general grounds to the evolutionary course which it pursues in and through our own Planetary Chain.

These seven other spheres therefore are what the ancients called the Seven Sacred Planets, called 'sacred' on account of their intimate evolutionary relation with our own earth. The earth and they are inseparably bound together with bonds of destiny originating in the very origin of the solar system, and coming over from the preceding solar system of which our present one is the karmic consequence.

H. P. Blavatsky in her *The Secret Doctrine* speaks of "the adventures of an atom," referring not solely to the physical atom of chemistry, but also to the Spiritual Atom which the Monad in a sense is, and says that no romance ever written or imagined could be more wonderful than are in fact such Adventures of an Atom, were one able to trace them in full. This is very true indeed, and such Adventures are the journeys and pilgrimages of any Monad whatsoever belonging to our solar system.

From what we have outlined it must be perfectly clear that Man when moving on earth is a heptad or septenary entity, and that within a very short while after the death of the physical body, after the dissolution of the lowest Triad, he no longer is in any strict sense of the word a 'man' at all, but a psycho-spiritual quaternary entity. But when the second death occurs, he then no longer is a quaternary entity or an entity formed of four substance-principles, but strictly speaking is withdrawn into the highest Duad in the shape of the Reincarnating Ego.

All this may seem like a gradual process of deprivation of faculty and power, to those who are not accustomed to philosophical thinking or who imagine that Man as a complete heptad or septenary entity as he is on earth is the standard or representative type. The exact contrary, however, is the real truth. Every increase in number of the substance-principles composing an entity means a corresponding decrease in freedom of spiritual faculty and power, and therefore of life, because each such substance-principle added as a veil or sheath, by so much the more beclouds and dims the transcendent Light always streaming forth from the heart of the Monad.

Death means freedom, it means release, it means the rupturing of the veils and sheaths or garments which becloud or enshroud this inner Transcendent Spiritual Sun. Man's destiny in the far distant future is to become ever more and more alike unto his monadic essence, more akin in faculty and power to his Transcendent Self, until the time shall come when he shall have become a god on earth. And although even in those times, so long as an earth-incarnation lasts, he will be a septenary entity, nevertheless all the lower veils and garments or sheaths will have become so etherealized and spiritualized that the dimming of the splendor of the Inner God will be vastly less than it is at present.

It has been said that man is a composite entity, like everything else, and this is strictly true. It has been said also that every entity whatsoever, and wheresoever it may exist, is but one of the smaller entities composing the being of an Entity still more vast. This means, therefore, following the ancient law of analogical reasoning, that Man himself in all his vehicles or bodies is composed of such entities smaller than he, and each one of these, whether we call it a life-atom of his lowest Triad, or the Human Soul of the intermediate Duad, or the Reincarnating Ego of the upper part of the intermediate Duad, is a learning thing, an evolving being. Each one such has an individuality of its own rooted in a monadic life-consciousness-center; and all these are bound together as a host of evolving entities, and in their turn are rooted in the over-ruling or supreme Monad of any such host or multitude.

From this we may deduce that the self-conscious entity whom we popularly call man, is, strictly speaking, not his monadic essence, which is his Inner God, but the Reincarnating Ego, or the higher part of the intermediate Duad, as man's constitution exists during life in incarnation on earth.

There is also the Human Ego, which is the more human expression of this Reincarnating Ego, and this Human Ego, strange as it may sound, is only a part of man's consciousness which is himself, for his Reincarnating Ego partakes of the Monadic essence in which it lives and moves and has its spiritual being; and yet is different from it. We may liken the idea to a tree formed of a trunk producing many branches, these developing into minor branches, these again into branchlets, these into twigs, and each twig into a leaf. The combined multitude of parts thus form a host indeed in themselves, and yet each member of this host has an individual personality of its own.

This rough illustration of the tree is a very old one, but it is suggestive, and the application of the rule of this interlocking and interblending series of consciousnesses is as strictly followed in Nature in the higher realms as it is in the lower realms.

The idea, therefore, is that the Human Ego is a developing and learning thing, growing out of something nobler, tending to become a Reincarnating Ego; and the Reincarnating Ego is constantly evolving or tending to become something nobler than what it was before, to become what the core of its own particular individuality is—a monadic essence. And the monadic essence, including these others, and which is our higher or spiritual Self, is in its turn evolving onwards to become something still greater than itself—a Divine Thing.

Thus also the very atoms of which man's lower Triad is composed, are each one of them a learning and growing entity, each with its own particular individual monadic essence, yet rooted in the general monadic essence of the septenary structure which man in earth-life is.

How true, therefore, the old Theosophical saying is, that no one can live unto himself alone, because every entity everywhere is merely a part of a larger entity, and is itself composed of a host of minor entities. This is the philosophical rationale of the doctrine of "Universal Brotherhood as a fact in Nature."

We see, then, that so far as life consciousness is concerned, Man is composed of a Self, of which the instinctual feeling in the septenary entity is 'I *am*.' Furthermore, he is composed of an individual Ego, his reincarnating aspect, of which the instinctual recognition in the men living on earth is not only 'I *am*'—which is the stream of consciousness from the essential Self—but also '*I* am *I*.' This latter is the egoic consciousness, as contrasted with the spiritual consciousness of abstract selfhood expressing itself in the two words 'I *am*.'

Very wonderful indeed are the Theosophical teachings, and very wonderful indeed are the ideas and reflections which flow forth from these teachings, when the earnest and truth-loving and truth-searching student ponders over them. How consoling it is, this sheer consciousness of selfhood! It assures one of the deathlessness of his own inmost being, and of the utter impossibility of termination of the consciousness of this essential selfhood, although the egoic selfhood or egoic consciousness of the growing and evolving reincarnating entity, or of its child the Human Ego, is interrupted by the process called reincarnation, a process arising out of the necessities of natural law.

When man thus feels his utter oneness with the Universe, which these thoughts lead him to feel and to understand; when he realizes that he is not alone in infinitude, but is one of numberless hosts of other similar beings, all interblending from a life-consciousness standpoint, there comes into his heart such a sense of rest and peace that this alone is a treasury of blessing beyond all appraisement.

Occidental folk are so unused to thoughts of this kind, and so miseducated to think that a distinct individuality utterly separate in life and consciousness from all other individualities is the *summum bonum* of being, that it requires some effort of the imagination to throw off this fantasy of falsity.

XVII—Karma

Karma is a Sanskrit word, and as a word means Action. But when used in a philosophical sense, it has a technical meaning best translated into English by the word 'consequence.' The idea is that every movement of a living entity, be that movement spiritual, mental, psychological, physical, or other, is immediately or at a later date succeeded by a consequence or an effect closely akin to that movement, of which the movement is the cause; and that this consequence or effectual action is an *inevitable* result of the causative action which preceded it and gave it birth. Also that this linking together of action to action, and of cause to effect, or of consequence to its precedent movement, is a universal rule, and applies not only to man or to any other animate entity on earth, but to the Universe both in general and in particular.

It is not, by any means, what is known in the Occident as Fatalism, for the karmic results or consequences flow forth only as effects from some one entity which originated them or gave them birth; and upon that entity these causal movements recoil sooner or later, as effects or consequences. Fatalism, on the other hand, means the doctrine or belief of a rather restricted class of minds, that the Universe is governed by some transcendent personal or individualized power which impresses upon such Universe all precedent causes, and therefore all consequent effects, and that it is hopeless for the entities or beings or things composing such a supposititious Universe to try to escape from the over-ruling and over-powering energy or energies thus manifested.

Karma, therefore, is essentially, in the last analysis, a doctrine of Free Will, for naturally the entity which initiates a movement or action: spiritual, mental, psychological, or physical or other: is responsible thereafter in the shape of consequences and effects, that flow therefrom, and sooner or later recoil upon the actor or mover.

Of course it is true to a certain extent — since everything is interlocked and interlinked and interblended with everything else, and that nothing and no being can live unto itself alone— that other entities are of necessity, in smaller or larger degree, affected by the causes or motions initiated by any individual entity. But such effects or consequences on entities other than the prime mover, are only indirectly a morally compelling power, in the true sense of the word 'moral.'

An example of how one entity can affect another in the manner just spoken of, is given in what is meant by 'family karma' as contrasted with one's own individual karma: that is to say, the network or web of circumstances and events which belong to the family of which he is a part. Or, again, national karma, the series of consequences pertaining to the nation of which he is an individual; or again, the racial karma pertaining to the race of which the individual is an integral member.

The reason for this secondary series of consequences is not different, however, when we go to the roots of things, from action initiated by the individual entity himself, because the doctrine of Karma also sets forth that the family or the nation or the race to which such individual entity belongs, is so on account of the karmic consequences or effects originally initiated by that individual which brought him into that *milieu* or set of circumstances. He himself builded for himself, in some past time, incarnation in that family or in that nation or race. So, in a very real sense, the family or national or racial karma in which he finds himself involved, he is in his own particular minor degree himself responsible for. So really it all comes back to the same thing.

Rooted as man's monadic essence is in the Boundless All, and furthermore in the highest and most spiritual aspects of the Boundless All, it is also seen at once that the *universal* karma of cosmic being is therefore the ultimate background of the karma of the individual, because the individual is inseparable from that universe. Indeed things are what they are because they compose a vast aggregate, indeed incomprehensible in its universal reaches, of co-operating energies and powers, of which every one is but an expression of karmic consequences. And this is but another manner of saying that everything that is, collectively and distributively, in general and in particular, is but the consequence or consequences of actions or movements which have preceded the present state of things; and, furthermore, that the present state of things will be succeeded by another web or network of incoming and interlocking energies and forces and beings which will be the resultants or consequences in every sense of the word, of what exists at present, both in the universal and in the particular.

We may speak of Karma as the 'fundamental law of the universe,' if we so choose, and there is no particular objection to this phrase, except perhaps in the one word 'law.' Karma is not a 'law' in the ordinary human sense of an enactment or rule of action laid down by some supreme law-giver. Not at all. It is, as the Ancients would have said, existent in the very 'nature of things.' Beings and things act or move, and by the very nature of things produce consequences, and so on indefinitely; for the original movement or act is but the consequence or result of some other consequence or result which preceded it, and so on in both directions endlessly: endlessly back into the past, and extending endlessly forward into what we call the future. This is the Chain of Causation we have referred to earlier.

Just as the root of universal nature, or of any individual entity or being or thing, is pure consciousness, pure abstract substance, so likewise is Karma in the last analysis but the fundamental activity of such consciousness itself, whether manifesting in the universal or in the particular, whether in a universe or in and through an individual entity. To say just what Karma is in other words, would be extremely difficult. It IS because it is the profound mystery of the operation of the essential being of consciousness itself.

Nature proceeds in cycles, because Nature is founded in and on consciousness. And it is the characteristic of consciousness to know, and it is the characteristic operation of knowledge to repeat what it knows, and this repetitive action of indwelling consciousness produces through the boundless ranges of the Universe the cyclical action or the cyclical movements which are apparent all around us. It is these cyclical movements again which bring forth the various evolutionary activities, for indeed cyclical movement and evolution are so much the same thing that it would require a good deal of imagination to see any profound distinction between them once that the doctrine of Karma is clearly understood.

As we look around us and observe the operation of the wonderful spheres in the dark violet dome over our heads, and notice the vast fields of differentiation in the smaller and minor things which compose the entities living and dwelling in and on our earth, we are compelled to admit that it is just this vast number of interworking and co-operating agents of some deeply indwelling and over-ruling energy which perhaps attracts the thought and imagination of man more than anything else.

All men at some time must have asked themselves the question: Why is it that the universe is builded as it is, with such vast hosts of beings of all kinds and classes and in all degrees of advancement, and all apparently working towards some end, which, on the surface of things, seems beyond human understanding? We have already given the key for solving this apparent riddle, for it is only an apparent one. That key is what has just been pointed out: that all these hosts of differentiated entities and things are the consequences or results—visible or invisible as the case may be—of the operations or actions of evolving consciousnesses impelled to follow their various paths of action by the karmic heritage inherent in each one of them.

Size or lack of size has nothing to do with the matter. The Universe being nothing really but hierarchies of imbodied consciousnesses, each one with its own karmic load upon it — or heritage, if the word be preferred—of necessity that Universe is differentiated into all-various and bewildering multitudes of beings and things. And yet each one of these in its inmost of the inmost, is, as we have emphasized before, a Monad working in the surrounding *milieu* made by itself and by other similar Monads interlocking and interblending and interworking, and all evolving on their upward way.

Some are very far along the path, and we humans call these highly progressed ones, gods or cosmic spirits, or Dhyân-Chohans. Others are far in the rear of the vast hosts of evolving multitudes. And others, like us human beings, stand more or less at the middle point of this aggregate of developing consciousnesses.

If one were to say that Karma, whether in the large or in the small, whether universal or particular, is but the operation of the essential entities themselves — in other words, of the Monads—he would say truly. Really, that is just what Karma is. Whatever else it may be called, one thing is absolutely certain, and that is that Karma is nothing at all outside of, or superior to, or over-ruling the entity which manifests the Karma belonging to it, because native to it: flowing forth from its own heart of hearts, from the core of the core of the inmost of the inmost of itself. In other words, an entity's Karma is the self-expression of its individuality flowing forth in the form of evolutionary activity.

Universes, worlds, solar systems, nebulae, comets, planets, cosmic spirits, men, elementals, life-atoms, matter, and all the various planes and spheres of being, are not merely the resultants or consequences of each one's preceding and individual aggregate of karmic causes, but are each one for itself originating new karmic causes constantly and from itself alone.

The question has been asked: "If I understand your Theosophical teaching aright, Karma is but another name for your God. Is Karma therefore the supreme God?" It took some little time to explain to this inquirer the real nature of Karma, and it was not uninteresting to watch the effect that this explanation had upon his mind. An unbeliever himself in any kind of supreme divine power, he nevertheless, paradoxically enough, seemed disappointed that Karma was not an over-ruling god; and after the explanation, with some difficulty and labor of exegesis, had been laid before him, he said: "Why then, you don't believe in any god, you Theosophists; you are just sheer materialists!" Another explanation was needed, in order to show that, on the contrary, the Theosophist teaches that the Universe is full of gods in the higher ranges and reaches of the cosmos, but that each such god is what it is on account of the evolutionary path tending towards a constantly increasing perfection, which it had itself trodden in the past.

Furthermore, it required some time and pains to enable him to see that there was no end of the evolutionary process, and likewise no beginning; and that he was leaping from one absurd extreme to another, in saying that because Theosophists do not believe in the teachings of Theism, therefore they of necessity belong to the school of the materialists. It was necessary also to explain to him that the Theosophist most positively is not, in any sense of the word, a materialist; for matter, in the Theosophical conception, is but the aggregate of the multitudes of spiritual essences or Monads which are passing through a particular and definite phase of their evolutionary journey *on this our own plane*, which Monads, in this phase, are in a dormant or sleeping state, so to speak, and that this aggregate of dormant Monads produces what our senses perceive as, and what our mind calls, 'matter.'

Everything ultimately and fundamentally is consciousness, or to speak more accurately, is numberless multitudes of consciousnesses or life-consciousness-centers, called Monads. Spirit and substance, or equivalently consciousness and vehicle, are fundamentally one.

Theosophy, therefore, may be called an Objective Idealism, idealistic in principle, but not denying withal the relative objective reality of the so-called physical and other manifested worlds, which form what men popularly call matter or substance. And as this rule of things prevails over the entire Universe, and lasts throughout eternity: because as one or another Universe leaves the ranges of matter and rebecomes spirit, other Universes equivalently pass downwards in their evolutionary journey through what is called matter: it is therefore seen that both matter and spirit, in the last analysis, are only two phases or 'events' in the modern philosophical or Einsteinian sense.

All such 'events' or stages of growth are transitory and relatively unreal, and therefore are explained by that other branch of the Theosophical philosophy which deals with what is called *mâyâ*, a Sanskrit word meaning 'illusion,' or the magical delusion worked by our imperfect human mentalities upon our understanding of Nature. In other words, things are not what they seem, for there is a Reality behind the seeming.

Mâyâ or 'illusion' does not mean that things and entities, the Universe and all other cosmic aggregates, are unreal in the sense of non-existent *per se;* but it does mean that the perceiving and understanding entity, through its own innate imperfections, because its understanding is not yet sufficiently evolved readily and correctly to grasp the reality behind, misunderstands the essences of things, and through this functioning of the mind clothes those essences with illusory garments. This is the real meaning of mâyâ.

Karma, therefore, is in no sense of the word Fatalism on the one hand, nor what is popularly known as 'Chance' on the other hand. It is essentially a course of action which the entity himself lays down for himself, and which his feet follow as a path of conduct. No one is responsible but himself for what he prepares for himself, and this, as said above, is Nature's fundamental law. There is great hope and comfort in this thought, for it means that "there is always another chance."

We are the makers and carvers of our own destiny, and are at the present time traversing the destiny, or undergoing it, which we in past times in other lives have carved out for ourselves. Both in character and body we reap what we sow, as the New Testament of the Christians puts it, and this expresses very graphically and briefly the essential meaning of the doctrine of Karma.

H. P. Blavatsky alludes to the matter in *The Secret Doctrine* (I, 642-44):

> KARMA-NEMESIS is the creator of nations and mortals, but once created, it is they who make of her either a fury or a rewarding Angel. . . . . There is no return from the paths she cycles over; yet those paths are of our own making, for it is we, collectively or individually, who prepare them. Karma-Nemesis is the synonym of PROVIDENCE, minus *design*, goodness, and every other *finite* attribute and qualification, so unphilosophically attributed to the latter. An Oc-

cultist or a philosopher will not speak of the goodness or cruelty of Providence; but, identifying it with Karma-Nemesis, he will teach that nevertheless it guards the good and watches over them in this, as in future lives; and that it punishes the evil-doer—aye, even to his seventh rebirth. So long, in short, as the effect of his having thrown into perturbation even the smallest atom in the Infinite World of harmony, has not been finally readjusted. For the only decree of Karma—an eternal and immutable decree—is absolute Harmony in the world of matter as it is in the world of Spirit. It is not, therefore, Karma that rewards or punishes, but it is we, who reward or punish ourselves according to whether we work with, through and along with nature, abiding by the laws on which that Harmony depends, or—break them.

Nor would the ways of Karma be inscrutable were men to work in union and harmony, instead of disunion and strife. For our ignorance of those ways—which one portion of mankind calls the ways of Providence, dark and intricate; while another sees in them the action of blind Fatalism; and a third, simple chance, with neither gods nor devils to guide them—would surely disappear, if we would but attribute all these to their correct cause. With right knowledge, or at any rate with a confident conviction that our neighbors will no more work to hurt us than we would think of harming them, the two-thirds of the World's evil would vanish into thin air. Were no man to hurt his brother, Karma-Nemesis would have neither cause to work for, nor weapons to act through. It is the constant presence in our midst of every element of strife and opposition, and the division of races, nations, tribes, societies and individuals into Cains and Abels, wolves and lambs, that is the chief cause of the 'ways of Providence.' We cut these numerous windings in our destinies daily with our own hands, while we imagine that we are pursuing a track on the royal high road of respectability and duty, and then complain of those ways being so intricate and so dark. We stand bewildered before the mystery of our own making, and the riddles of life that *we will not* solve, and then accuse the great Sphinx of devouring us. But verily there is not an accident in our lives, not a misshapen day, or a misfortune, that could not be traced back to our own doings in this or in another life. If one breaks the laws of Harmony, or, as a theosophical writer expresses it, "the laws of life," one must be prepared to fall into the chaos one has oneself produced. . . . .

. . . Karma-Nemesis is no more than the (spiritual) dynamical effect of causes produced and forces awakened into activity by our own actions.

There is no religion, no philosophy worthy of the name, which does not contain this doctrine of Karma under one or another formulation, for the doctrine arises out of the very essence of any man's sense of justice, of retributive justice; and such action of retributive natural justice is but Nature's way of bringing about the rearrangement of natural harmony disturbed by the thoughts and acts, emotions and feelings, aspirations and desires of some or of all living entities.

In our chapters on Evolution we have spoken of the various entities and things which infill or compose Universal Being, as 'events'. And so indeed they are. They are all 'events,' because they are all transitory, temporary. Not one of them, no matter how great in evolutionary advancement, no matter what its magnitude in size, and no matter where we may class it in the frontierless range of Universal Being, is absolute—all are transitory, and each one of them, therefore, is also a passing phase or event of the cosmic life.

There is nothing which is not transitory, nothing which is utterly permanent, changeless and living forever. How could that be? How can anything reach an ultimate beyond which there is no further possibility of growth and progress? For growth and progress mean change. How can such a thing as the 'changeless' exist? Such a conception would mean that the changeless, did it exist, could have had no past, and can have no future, for there would be no growth and progress in it, nothing but changeless immobility; and such a conception is as repulsive to our intuitions as it is repugnant to our reflective minds.

Some things are relatively more changing than others, but this is only to be expected. Things which live their life in wide and long cycles of time, appear to us men who live in a smaller and more restricted period of existence, to be more or less changeless, but this view arises out of the imperfection of our knowledge of things. Everything is changing because growing; there is nothing changeless, says our majestic philosophy, in the Boundless All, for that would be equivalent to utter, eternal immobility. Life, movement, progress, evolution, are everywhere, and the most thoughtless of men must see in this conception how wide are the fields of hope which Theosophy presents to our mind's eye. Always advance, always progress, always upwards during illimitable duration.

So far as men are concerned, or entities who occupy in other spheres of the celestial spaces a status of being equivalent to that of humanity on this earth, what we Theosophists speak of as Reincarnation is the method by which karma works in and through us humans, because it is we ourselves who produce karma eventuating in reimbodiment in bodies of flesh or their equivalent.

We act, and Nature reacts, and this reaction against our initiating movement, takes the form, in the present period of human evolution, of reincarnation. Reincarnation itself is a special instance of a more general natural process, which we call Reimbodiment.

Indeed, from one point of view it would be quite proper to say that the doctrine of Karma is but another way of expressing the multiform and all-various activities of existence — of the Universal Life: for the action of Karma is universal. Nor can we call Karma either conscious or unconscious. It is neither good nor bad, never had a beginning, never will have an end. Its action in a sense is purely automatic, for, reduced to final principles, it is but the indirect functioning of the consciousness in the core of the core of every being.

The Secret Doctrine (II, 304-6) refers to Karma-Nemesis again in the following very graphic words.

... Karma-Nemesis, or the Law of Retribution. This Law—whether Conscious or Unconscious—predestines nothing and no one. It exists from and in Eternity, truly, for it is ETERNITY itself; and as such, since no act can be co-equal with eternity, it cannot be said to act, for it is ACTION itself. It is not the Wave which drowns a man, but the *personal* action of the wretch, who goes deliberately and places himself under the *impersonal* action of the laws that govern the Ocean's motion. Karma creates nothing, nor does it design. It is man who plans and creates causes, and Karmic law adjusts the effects; which adjustment is not an act, but universal harmony, tending ever to resume its original position, like a bough, which, bent down too forcibly, rebounds with corresponding vigor. If it happen to dislocate the arm that tried to bend it out of its natural position, shall we say that it is the bough which broke our arm, or that our own folly has brought us to grief? Karma ... has not involved its decrees in darkness purposely to perplex man; nor shall it punish him who dares to scrutinize its mysteries. On the contrary, he who unveils through study and meditation its intricate paths, and throws light on those dark ways, in the windings of which so many men perish owing to their ignorance of the labyrinth of life, is working for the good of his fellow-men. KARMA is an Absolute and Eternal law in the World of manifestation; and ...

believers in Karma cannot be regarded as Atheists or materialists—still less as fatalists: for Karma is one with the Unknowable, of which it is an aspect in its effects in the phenomenal world.

Intimately, or rather indissolubly, connected with Karma, then, is the law of rebirth, or of the re-incarnation of the same spiritual individuality in a long, almost interminable, series of personalities. The latter are like the various costumes and characters played by the same actor, with each of which that actor identifies himself and is identified by the public, for the space of a few hours. The *inner*, or real man, who personates those characters, knows the whole time that he is Hamlet for the brief space of a few acts, which represent, however, on the plane of human illusion the whole life of Hamlet. And he knows that he was, the night before, King Lear, the transformation in his turn of the Othello of a still earlier preceding night; but the outer, visible character is supposed to be ignorant of the fact. In actual life that ignorance is, unfortunately, but too real. Nevertheless, the *permanent* individuality is fully aware of the fact, though, through the atrophy of the 'spiritual' eye in the physical body, that knowledge is unable to impress itself on the consciousness of the false personality.

Karma has sometimes been called the 'law of ethical causation,' and in one aspect it can indeed be so called. But such a phrase deals with only one part of the operations of Nature and omits mention of the universal sway or sweep of karmic activity. Karma 'rules' the so-called 'inanimate' world fully as much as it does the hearts and minds of men, and of course when we say 'rules' we employ popular phraseology. Strictly, Karma no more 'rules' or 'governs' or 'directs' than does the automatic action of the ocean the ebb and flow of the tides, for Karma is not an originating power exterior to the acting entity or thing. So far as individuals are concerned, it is the indwelling consciousness of the acting entity which originates and sets in motion the operation of Karma.

It is most important, however, not to conclude that karmic action is a mere automatic resultant of inner and lifeless matter, for in the Theosophical pilosophy nothing is lifeless, but everything has a life of its own type and kind. The 'automatic action' of Karma here spoken of has a different meaning from what the words might seem to imply to one whose mentality is still more or less under the cloud of the old-fashioned materialism.

Nature is harmonious throughout. Its heart is harmony itself;

and an action by an entity in the hosts of animate beings which make Nature, is subject to the reaction of the surrounding weight of the Universe upon it, moving to restore the equilibrium disturbed by such action. And this combination of the action of an originating consciousness and a reaction upon it is Karma.

Karma, therefore, in another sense is Readjustment, the re-establishing of the natural harmony of Nature, which the action done, or left undone when it should have been done, has thrown into local and temporary disturbance. Thus, therefore, we repeat, there is nothing fatalistic about the doctrine of Karma. It is action originating in the free will and consciousness of some entity which induces the reaction of Nature. This combination we call Karma.

There is one very important point about this subject which perhaps is clear enough in the outline of the Theosophical philosophy already made, but which it may be advantageous to speak of again here. It is this: the heart of Nature or the essence of Nature, because it is Harmony, is what the ancient Greek philosophers would have called Love. As H. P. Blavatsky so beautifully puts it in her *The Voice of the Silence*, Compassion is Nature's fundamental law. The importance of this observation rests in the following: it is the bounden duty of every human being to help Nature and to work with her. As H. P. Blavatsky also says in the same treatise:

> Help Nature and work on with her; and Nature will regard thee as one of her creators and make obeisance.

Gentleness, kindness, pity, compassion, love, mercy, in fact all the fine and ennobling attributes of the fully developed human being, belong distinctly in their action to this line of co-operation with Nature's fundamental essence and being. The man who would stand idly by when another is in trouble, listening with stony-hearted indifference to the cries of misery or of pain without stirring to relieve the distress, is acting directly contrary to Nature's fundamental law. He is taking upon himself a heavy burden of karmic responsibility, which Nature in its re-establishment of harmony will visit upon him to the uttermost.

It is futile and an entire distortion of the sense of the doctrine of Karma, to think that because some human being is undergoing disaster or is in a situation of distress and suffering, therefore he should be left unhelped and uncomforted on the sole supposition that he is 'merely working out his karmic deserts.' This idea is monstrous and runs directly counter to all the teachings of all the great Seers and Sages of all the ages. *The Voice of the Silence,* one of the most beautiful devotional works of any time, puts it clearly:

Inaction in a deed of mercy becomes an action in a deadly sin.

The Buddha, the Christ, and such other Great Ones have left behind them in no uncertain words the doctrine of our ethical responsibility to others, calling upon us to be up and doing in our duty towards others. Outside of other considerations, one must be exceedingly dense of understanding not to realize that there is no developing power in life which is so certain and so quick as self-forgetful action in compassionate service to others. Such service teaches us how speedily to find the resources of our own hearts and to see the wondrous mysteries lying therein. It also teaches us how most quickly and surely to develop the finer parts of our intellectual faculty. Benevolence combined with beneficent action in service to others, may truly be described as the royal road of discipleship, and indeed only a strong-hearted man or woman can follow this path consistently, and with tact.

It is easy enough to go through life involved in one's own personal and purely selfish affairs; but the effects or consequences of such a course of living are bitter in the extreme, and turn to the ashes of death in the mouth. Such a course of life shrivels the character and bemeans it, simply because the sphere of action is so restricted and localized, whereas benevolence eventuating in beneficent action, is the quickest cure for all the pettiness of mind and heart to which we are so sensitively alive when we see them in the characters of those who surround us.

There is one more point regarding the doctrine of Karma: the student of ancient literatures, particularly those of the Orient, has doubtless met with observations to the effect that when a man has reached the status or condition of Mastership of life —in other words, has become one of the great Sages and Seers, or indeed, perhaps has reached a still more lofty stature in spirituality—he is then 'above Karma,' above karmic action, and has passed beyond its sway. But we should always remember that Karma is not only universal but has neither beginning nor end, and that the highest god in highest heaven is as much subject to Karma as is the humblest ant climbing up a sand-hill, only to go tumbling down again.

Is there a contradiction in these two statements? There is not, although there may be a paradox. The following is the explanation of the apparent contradiction. A man or an entity, whatever its high state of evolutionary development may be, passes beyond the sway or sweep of the karmic action of the hierarchy to which he belongs when he has become at-one with the loftiest part or portion of such a hierarchy. For the time being, he has reached quasi-divinity, and as all the movements of his nature are then entirely harmonious with the hierarchy in which he now stands at the summit thereof, it is obvious that being one with the nature of that hierarchy and 'working with Nature' in this respect, he is beyond the sway or 'rule' or 'control' of the general field of karmic action in that hierarchy. That hierarchical karma has no further sway over him, for he is therein a Master of Life.

But in the universal sense, and because hierarchies in the Boundless All are numberless, the hierarchy in which he now finds himself a Master of Life is but one of hosts of other hierarchies, some of them far lower, and others far higher. As compared with the Boundless All, his own hierarchy shrinks to the dimensions of a mere mathematical point, so to say, and becomes simply an aggregate hierarchical Atom in the fields of universal life. This means that as the evolution of such an entity progresses, he enters into still larger and sublimer spheres of action, wherein, at his entrance, he finds himself on the lowest rung of that new Ladder of Life, and immediately falls under the sway or 'rule' or 'governance' of the Karma of this sublimer hierarchical sphere.

We must never forget that man is a composite entity. He has both heart and mind, and a due and proper understanding of Nature and of Nature's laws and operations can be obtained only by an employment of all man's faculties, omitting none. An over-accentuation of the human mentality is bound to lead the student astray, just as much as an over-accentuation in thought or action of his emotional parts is bound likewise to lead him astray.

But when heart and mind work together, and man realizes that they are but two aspects of the one indwelling consciousness, the Inner God, then ensues a harmonious development of all man's parts, and the true realization of what life means. One of H. P. Blavatsky's greatest achievements, we believe, in this connection, was that she pointed out so clearly and proved so forcibly the natural truth that man's spiritual development depends first upon a harmonious adjustment of both mind and heart, and their final unification in the consciousness of the real existence of the continuous inspiration of the essential Divinity within.

XVIII—Reincarnation and the General Doctrine of Reimbodiment

The General Doctrine of Reimbodiment applies not solely to man, but to all centers of consciousness—to all Monads whatsoever, wheresoever they may be on the evolutionary Ladder of Life, and whatsoever may be their particular developmental grade thereon. Every life-consciousness-center, every Monad or monadic essence, reincorporates itself repeatedly in various vehicles or 'bodies.' These bodies may be spiritual, or they may be physical, or they may be of a nature intermediate between these two: in other words, ethereal. This rule of Nature, which applies to all Monads without exception, takes place in all the different realms of the visible and invisible Universe, and on all its different planes, and in all its different worlds.

When a Monad is undergoing such a course of reimbodiment on our earth, in the present stage of human evolution, it takes place in human bodies, in bodies of flesh; and this is Reincarnation. But before this special phase of reimbodiment began, in far past ages of the earth's history, the reimbodiment of the human Monad was indeed the evolutionary course then followed, as it now is followed, but it did not then take place in bodies of human flesh. It is the Theosophical teaching that when the present passing phase—for that is what it is—of Reincarnation has reached its end, then Reimbodiment as an evolutionary method will continue, but in bodies then not of human flesh, but composed of ethereal substance; and at a still later time the Monad will clothe itself in veils or garments or sheaths of matter still more ethereal, which we may actually speak of as being spiritual.

The process of Reincarnation is not difficult to understand, and the student or reader who cares to pursue the subject no farther, may gain all the knowledge that he desires from an attentive perusal of our Theosophical works; but for those who desire to go more deeply into the rationale of the General Doctrine of Reimbodiment, the facts and observations which this and the following chapter will contain, may be of assistance.

There are seven words used in the Theosophical philosophy in connection with Reimbodiment, which are not all synonymous, although some have almost the same meaning:

1. Pre-existence
2. Rebirth
3. Reimbodiment
4. Metensomatosis
5. Metempsychosis
6. Transmigration
7. Reincarnation

Four only of these may be said to contain the four different basic ideas of the general Doctrine of Reimbodiment. These are Pre-existence, Reimbodiment, Metempsychosis, and Transmigration.

Pre-existence is the most easily explained. It simply means that the human soul-entity existed before birth. This is a doctrine by no means typically Theosophical, but belonged likewise to the early teachings of Christianity, as is evidenced in the writings that remain to us of Origen, the great Alexandrian Church-Father, and his School.

Reimbodiment in meaning goes much farther. It states not only that the soul-entity exists before birth, but also undergoes a series of reimbodiments before birth on earth, and during all its course of evolutionary progress through the invisible spheres.

Metempsychosis imbodies ideas still more profound and fundamental, and signifies that the monadic essence or the life-consciousness-center, or Monad, not merely is pre-existent to physical birth—not merely that the soul-entity reimbodies itself—but also that the Monad, during the course of its aeonic pilgrimage through the spheres, clothes itself with, or makes unto itself for its own self-expression, various ego-souls, which flow forth from it: that they have each one its characteristic and individual life, which, when its life-period is completed, is gathered back again into the bosom of the Monad for its period of rest, at the completion of it to reissue therefrom upon a new cyclical pilgrimage. This last series of ideas has already been briefly spoken of in preceding chapters, in connection with the Reincarnating Ego, one of these soul-egos, ego-souls.

Transmigration, the fourth of these words, is a much abused term. In European and American countries it is commonly supposed to be synonymous with Reincarnation, but with the added idea that the human soul-entity, if its karma after physical life be a heavy or evil one, then at death passes into the body of a beast. Let us say at once that this is not the Theosophical teaching. "Once a man always a man," is a very definite statement of the Ancient Wisdom, or Theosophy; and the references in Oriental and Greek and Latin literature to what is mistakenly called Transmigration and Metempsychosis, as signifying rebirth in bodies of beasts, contain an esoteric teaching concerning the life-atoms of the deceased entity. As construed by Europeans, these references are distorted into an entire misunderstanding of what the original significance and meaning of the Oriental and Greek and Latin doctrines were. Theosophy positively repudiates the idea that the human soul-entity ever, at any time, reincarnates in the body of a beast. This is against Nature's rigid laws, and never happens.

Transmigration technically means that the life-consciousness-center passes from one form of life to another form of life: migrates as it were, from one realm to another realm, but always pursuing its own upward course in evolution. Transmigration contains, in fact, the combined meanings of Evolution and Karma, in other words, karmic evolution, as signifying the path followed by the Monad in migrating from sphere to sphere, from spirit to matter, and back again to spirit, and in the course of this pilgrimage entering into vehicle or body after vehicle or body.

Here then briefly explained are the four main words of the seven above mentioned. Of these four the most important is Metempsychosis, perhaps, although the ideas contained in all four must be kept clearly in the mind, if the student wishes to have a definite outline of the nature of the pilgrimage followed by the monadic essence.

As regards the other three words of the list of seven given: Rebirth and Reimbodiment are very much the same, with the difference that Reimbodiment definitely sets forth the series or succession of bodies, and their nature, which the evolving entity takes unto itself, and in which it lives, and through which it works on this and other planes and in other worlds. Metensomatosis is practically the same as Reimbodiment. It is of course a Greek word, and its signification is perhaps somewhat more limited than is Reimbodiment and really means merely the taking up of successive physical bodies on earth. It is, therefore, practically identical with rebirth.

In no case is the word Reincarnation identical with any of the other six words, though of course it has grounds of strong similarity with Pre-existence, because obviously the entity pre-exists before it reincarnates; and on the same grounds it is similar to Rebirth, Reimbodiment, and Metensomatosis. Such differences of meaning as exist are in a closely reasoned exposition of the General Doctrine; but the shades of meaning are of no particular value to the average reader.

Undertaking now a brief sketch of the meaning of the General Doctrine of Reimbodiment: as before said, the evolving entity, or more accurately the monadic essence (except during its intervals of cosmic rest called pralayas), passes its entire existence in manifestation in a series of corporealizations succeeding one another regularly throughout any such cosmic period of manifestation. Each one of such corporealizations or imbodiments is a veil or garment or sheath partly evolved by the monadic essence from its own inner energies and substances, and partly built up of life-atoms drawn from the reservoir of the sphere in which it is, or from the world in which it is, during such particular corporealization or imbodiment.

These imbodiments range from the spiritual to the material within the confines or frontiers of any one Hierarchy. This is really but another way of saying that the general course of reimbodiment is the general course of Evolution, for each one such imbodiment is the evolutionary child or successor of the one which preceded it, and is of course therefore likewise the karmic parent of the one which follows it.

The doctrine is that in the beginning of any cosmic Period of Manifestation, the Monad or monadic essence reissues forth from the bosom of the Cosmic Hierarch or Cosmic Monad, and immediately clothes itself with garments of spiritual substance, which, for the sake of easy understanding, we may perhaps call garments of spiritual light—light, in Theosophy, being ethereal or spiritual substance.

It passes a certain period of existence in these garments, beginning to weave the web of destiny according to the Karmic roots or seeds brought over by it from the preceding period of Cosmic Manifestation, and now beginning to become active.

The course of any such cosmic Period of Manifestation for the Universe involved, and for all the hosts of entities that it contains, passes from the divine or superspiritual through the spiritual into the ethereal, thence through the ethereal into the material, wherein the greatest degree of condensation of substance is reached.

Passing through these material phases of its evolutionary progression, the Universe as an entity begins the reascent towards the superspiritual origin from which it in the beginning had set forth, and just as it had passed through various and increasing degrees of materiality on the downward arc, so now does it reascend towards that spiritual source through various and differing degrees of gradually etherealizing substances.

In each and every one of the various worlds, planes, and spheres contained in these different degrees or stages of the Ladder of Life which the evolving Universe is, every Monadic essence of the countless hosts of Monads infilling that Universe evolves forth from itself bodies corresponding and appropriate to such various worlds and planes and spheres. These bodies which the monadic essence corporealizes itself in, are partly drawn from its own essence and partly made up from the lifeatoms of the corresponding sphere or spheres. These life-atoms, however, are in no sense of the word foreign to the individual Monad or monadic essence, for they are in their turn living entities or evolving atoms, which the Monad in the previous period of Cosmic Manifestation had thrown forth from its own essence, and which, on the return of the Monad, rejoin it through what we may call psycho-magnetic attraction.

The reader will remember what we have set forth in preceding chapters, to the effect that every entity everywhere forms a part—integral, inseparable in essence—of some entity still greater and still more evolved from which it originally came. Just so do these life-atoms, which the Monad reincorporates into its various imbodiments or veils or bodies, return to it when its spiritual-psycho-magnetic influence is felt by these life-atoms upon the entrance into their respective spheres of such monadic essence during the course of its pilgrimage.

This really wonderful series of Cosmic Adventures, both of Monad and of life-atom, furnishes a subject of study of the most fascinating character for our hours of quiet thought. The general principles of the Doctrine of Reimbodiment thus briefly sketched lie in the background of all the great world-religions and world-philosophies of the past, and indeed actually furnish in those religions and philosophies the esoteric or secret side of their doctrines. These esoteric or secret sides of course were always taught "at low breath" and "with mouth to ear," as the sayings go. The Mysteries of Antiquity comprised an elucidation of these secret teachings given to the Epoptae or fully initiated ones; and we may say in passing that the main reason for the great secrecy which surrounded the Ancient Mysteries was originally and very largely based on the impossibility of making them understood by the odinary run of men without due and adequate preparation, or, in other words, a course of intellectual and moral training lasting through many years. Not all men were found fit to be the depositaries of this sacred knowledge; and the penalties following unauthorized divulgation of these mystic secrets were very heavy indeed.

We have now set forth *in parvo* the main outline of the general Doctrine of Reimbodiment. However, in order to bring the matter more definitely to the mind's eye of the reader, let us turn for a while to the subject of Death, which is a dissolution, on one side, of bodies, and the preparation for a new state in the invisible realms, and trace the Adventures of a Spiritual Atom, in other words of a Monad, as it leaves human incarnation preparatory to embarking on one of its journeys through the spheres.

As we have already pointed out, Death is preceded by a period of preparatory phases initiated by the principles of man's inner constitution, which culminate in the dissolution of the Lower Triad, as outlined in the second of the schematic diagrams in Chapter XVI. What men call old age, senility, and physical decay, are the physical resultants of this preparatory withdrawal of the monadic essence from conscious participation in the affairs of earth-life, and may be with a great deal of truth compared to the period preceding the birth of a child.

The inner constitution — which here means the Reincarnating Ego and to a certain extent the Human Ego and of course the uppermost Duad — prepares itself for a new birth. At least the monadic essence does. And a portion of this preparation consists, as said, in the gradual withdrawal of the Reincarnating Ego and an accompanying dulling of the faculties of the mortal Human Ego, its Child.

The Lower Triad composed of the physical body, of its vital essence or electrical field (Prâna), and of the model-body, compose an aggregate which is, as an aggregate, unconditionally mortal, and therefore falls to pieces with the rupture of the 'golden thread of connection'—in other words when the stream of consciousness from the monadic essence is broken, or rather withdrawn. The life-atoms composing this prânic or 'electrical field' of vitality, as soon as the rupture of consciousness takes place, fly with the rapidity of lightning to their appropriate reservoirs of the planet. But these life-atoms, just like the life-atoms of all the principles of man's constitution, are living entities, evolving and learning things. They do not remain in a state of dormancy or in sleep until their parent monadic essence, after many ages, returns again to physical incarnation. Each one of them almost immediately begins a series of transmigrations into other bodies coming into physical existence, each such life-atom of this Lower Triad existing on these three planes: that is to say, the physical plane, the astral plane, and the prânic plane. They enter into such bodies either at birth or indeed before birth, or after birth, in the shape of food or drink, or with the air we breathe, or in other manners, such as occurs in endosmosis. They are attracted to the bodies of those entities which are most akin to their own state of psycho-magnetic evolution, and these life-atoms themselves act according to the strongest impression left upon the fabric of their being by the man, just deceased, whose body they composed.

This is the real meaning of the ancient and Oriental doctrines which pass under the much misunderstood term 'transmigration'.

The two Duads which remain of the constitution of the man who was, follow the course already briefly described, to wit: the intermediate Duad breaks up into two parts: the upper part or Reincarnating Ego is withdrawn into the bosom of its parent Monad, its inner God, where it remains in Devachanic bliss and peace until its next incarnation on earth.

The other or lower part of the intermediate Duad, which is the dregs of the Human Ego that was, remains in the astral spheres as the kâma-rûpa or spook, which gradually, if left alone and not attracted by earthly magnetisms, fades out, as did the physical body which it had previously informed. Its life-atoms follow precisely the same course, in a general way, as did the three classes of life-atoms of the Lower Triad. They transmigrate continuously from living entity to living entity, but remain on their own psycho-mental plane.

The Upper Duad has now become a Triad by the inclusion within its bosom of the Reincarnating Ego, and this, strictly speaking, is what is called in Theosophical terminology, the 'human Monad.' Really, however, the Monad is the Upper Duad alone, but the attributive adjective 'human' is now given to it on account of the Reincarnating Ego which it now contains within itself.

This portion of the doctrine we have no need to consider further—that is to say, as concerns the human Monad—for it will be sufficient to remember that the Reincarnating Ego sleeps in ineffable bliss and peace in its Devachanic state until the call to Reincarnation on earth comes again after a lapse of time which varies according to the spiritual or material characteristics of the man that was. If his nature had been highly evolved and spiritual, reincarnation does not take place before many centuries have passed. If his nature had been material, reincarnation takes place much sooner.

The Monad, which we may now look upon again as a Duad, follows its own path or pilgrimage; for, on its own lofty plane or in its own lofty state or condition, it is an evolving entity as much as is the humblest of the life-atoms previously existent in the lower substance-principles of the man that was.

It passes from sphere to sphere, from world to world, from plane to plane, passing a certain time in each; in each evolving forth new sheaths and garments appropriate to such world or plane or sphere. These sheaths and garments become the new intermediate portion or intermediate Duad of the child-entity now coming into conscious existence in such world or sphere; and these sheaths or garments are fit for these other worlds. This is the meaning of Metempsychosis.

The Monad ascends first through the three ascending spheres of our earth's Planetary Chain, in each of which it follows the same general course of action that it did on this our earth (the lowest sphere of our Planetary Chain), evolving forth therein imbodiments in which it manifests for a time. Reaching the highest or the last of these three ascending globes of our Earth-Chain, it goes next to one of the Seven Sacred Planets of the ancients, and therein passes through an evolutionary course similar to what it did on our Earth-Chain. Finishing with this Chain, it goes to the next of the Seven Sacred Planets, and on the Planetary Chain of this second, it follows the same general course. And thus, through all the seven planets, the seventh bringing it back nearest to earth where it again 'imbodies' itself in—or rather overshadows—the frame of a human child to be; and this is done through the attraction towards such imbodiment felt by the Reincarnating Ego within its bosom, which thus, so to say, attracts the Monadic pilgrim to such reincarnation.

The Seven Sacred Planets of the ancients are the following,

given here not in the order of the monadic pilgrimage, but in the order in which they are usually set forth in the ancient writings: Saturn, Jupiter, Mars, Sun, Venus, Mercury, Moon. And it should be said in passing that the sun and the moon are here substitutes for two secret planets.

A very important point of this entire subject is the following: Every one of the various and many imbodiments or vehicles in which the monadic essence manifests itself during the highly varied and picturesque course of its pilgrimage through the spheres, is composed of life-atoms of degrees and kind and ethereality or materiality appropriate to the respective planes or worlds or spheres in which the monadic essence at any period of time may find itself.

The question then perhaps arises: Is there then no abiding center in man? Is he nothing, reduced to the last analysis, but an agglomerate or aggregate of life-atoms on each one of the planes of his inner constitution? Are his seven substance-principles then built up of nothing but life-atoms? If so, where is the life-consciousness-center spoken of? Where is the center of individuality?

These questions are extremely pertinent, but the answer to them is a very simple one indeed. Through all these various imbodiments there runs the stream of consciousness flowing forth from the monadic essence. Furthermore, in any one imbodiment, such as that of man on earth in any incarnation, this stream is colored by the child-stream of consciousness flowing forth from the Reincarnating Ego. Now this stream of consciousness, this golden thread of individuality, on which all the substance-principles of man's constitution are threaded like beads on a golden chain, is called the Sûtrâtman, a Sanskrit word meaning 'Thread-Self,' which is the stream of consciousness-life running through all the various substance-principles of the human entity—or indeed of any other entity.

It is this Sûtrâtman, this Thread-Self, this stream of consciousness-life, which IS the fundamental Selfhood in all beings. It is that which, reflected in and through the several intermediate vehicles or veils or sheaths or garments of the invisible constitution of man, produces the egoic centers of self-conscious existence.

The Sûtrâtman, therefore, is rooted in the Monad, the monadic essence, but its stream is colored by the individuality of the Reincarnating Ego hitherto sleeping in the bosom of the Monad, which now after Reincarnation is awakened into self-conscious activity. And this 'colored stream' working through the appropriate vehicles of man's inner constitution, in other words, through his mind and through his emotions, his aspirations, his intellect and so forth, produces the individual consciousness which man recognizes in himself.

One of the profoundest teachings of the great Greek philosopher Plato, outlined for instance in his *Meno*, his *Phaedo*, his *Phaedrus*, his *Laws*, and others of his remarkable Socratic dialogs, is that regarding the origin of human consciousness when reflected in its instinctive and intuitive operations. Plato taught, following the Pythagoreans, that this was due to previous reimbodiments of the egoic center which man is, and that, therefore, all consciousness in its various degrees of development, and consequently all knowledge and wisdom and faculty, are but reminiscences of former existences, which reminiscences each new life develops and increases and improves. The great Greek philosopher called this body of reminiscences by the one word *Anamnesis*, or re-collection, meaning the gathering together again into a coherent unity of all the energic consciousness-activities that the being in the preceding incarnation was. This in a sense is truly Recollection or rememorization of the past: not indeed of details, but of the psychological resultants.

Any human being who cares to analyze his own consciousness must have some realization of the truth of Plato's statement, that the faculties and powers of consciousness which man shows forth could hardly have been developed in any one life-time, for they are a quite complete body of conscious energies which in their aggregate form a man's personalized individuality. The old materialistic doctrine of our fathers and grandfathers, that man's consciousness is but the psychologically recognized reflection of chemical changes taking place in the body, and particularly in the brain, is as inept and foolish as it is entirely inadequate to explain what the 'explanation' so called attempted.

Quite outside of the fact that every molecule of the human body is completely changed some half-dozen or more times during an averagely long life; and quite outside of the fact that this constant flowing of the molecular constitution of man should, according to the molecular theory, make man's individuality change completely from day to day, there is the other still more conclusive argument, which every normal human being knows perfectly well, that his consciousness is the same from the first moments in childhood when the individual first is cognizant of it, to the day of his death. The egoic stream is not merely unchanged, but increases in volume, as the body develops into its mature age. How the older school of materialists worked their mental gymnastics in reconciling these irreconcilable contradictions, furnishes one of the most puzzling, if amusing, episodes in modern European philosophical thought.

The argument of course is childish. Plato was distinctly right. Not merely is consciousness reminiscence in the Platonic sense—that is, the coming anew into self-conscious recognition of the energies precedently working—but the recognition of his individuality by man grows stronger as the years pass, and as the innate faculties and powers of that individuality come more fully into actual manifestation. It is obvious that in any one life-time no such individuality could possibly have been built up, with its wide fields of cognition and recognition and the functioning of consciousness varying so widely as they do in different human beings. How unconscious lifeless matter could give birth to self-conscious cognition of matter, offers a truly unsolvable problem.

All this shows that the stream of consciousness which man calls his egoic individuality, is something which preceded his birth. So strongly has this obvious fact appealed to the greatest minds and loftiest spiritual intellects of the East, that all of them, without exception, have recognized the truth of, and taught the doctrine of, the repeated reimbodiments of the human egoic center.

It should be therefore very clear indeed that man, considered as an entity, is but an aggregate of life-atoms existing in various vehicles, from the physical, through the intermediate or ethereal, up to the spiritual; and any individual human entity, therefore, is in himself a copy of the Macrocosm or Great World. As the latter is a cosmic Hierarchy, so is man the Microcosm, its copy. He is therefore a Little World, and includes in himself, that is to say in his entire constitution, both visible and invisible, hierarchies of the hosts of these life-atoms in all-various degrees of evolutionary development. Through it all, however, runs the stream of consciousness, which, adopting a word of the archaic Hindû philosophy, we have called the 'Thread-Self,' or Sûtrâtman.

We have traced the pilgrimage of the monadic essence from the beginning of the cosmic Period of Manifestation down into the most material portions of its evolutionary journey in any one Universe, such as our own, and we have briefly sketched its peregrinations through this most material portion, and have pointed to its rising along the ascending arc towards the completion of its evolutionary journey back to the Divinity from which it sprang in the beginnings of the aeons of any such cosmic Period of Manifestation.

As Nature is repetitive in action throughout, as she works wholly after a cyclical manner or pattern; thus also is reincarnation, one of Nature's operations, in the small but a repetition of the general rule of the pilgrimage of the monadic essence in the Large or Great. Reincarnation takes place according to the same general scheme of action, in the case of man, that the imbodiments and reimbodiments of the Universe with its included Hierarchies of entities, take place in the Great. When, of course, the monadic essence, towards the close of such a cosmic Period of Manifestation, finally re-enters the Divinity from which it originally sprang, it does so as a fully self-conscious god or divinity, and it rests in what we may call its Paranirvâna for long aeons of what human beings would call time (during the pralaya or dissolution of such a Universe) before it reissues forth for a new cosmic pilgrimage, but on planes and in worlds and in spheres superior to those in which such a monadic essence is now journeying.

As regards the matter of Reincarnation or the repeated reimbodiments in flesh of the Reincarnating Ego, it should again be emphasized that the Reincarnating Ego on any such return into earth-existence does not enter into fleshly vehicles which are wholly alien or foreign to it, or with which it had previously had no connection whatsoever. That notion is entirely contrary to the real meaning of the doctrine and suggests a process altogether different from what actually takes place. It would be impossible for the Reincarnating Ego to take unto itself new bodies, whether visible or invisible, formed of life-atoms with which it had previously had no possible connection, for there would be no psycho-magnetic links between the Reincarnating Ego on the one hand, and these life-atoms on the other hand. The truth is altogether contrary to this. All the life-atoms building up, composing, making, the various bodies of flesh, and the various interior substance-principles which the Reincarnating Ego reassumes in any return to rebirth on earth, are, as has already been plainly said, life-atoms which originally issued forth from the bosom of the Monadic Essence in which such Reincarnating Ego itself is a child—one of such former life-atoms evolved into the stature of self-conscious humanhood.

As the Reincarnating Ego returns through the spheres earthwards, it takes up on each plane, on each world, or in each sphere, precisely those life-atoms which had builded the various vehicles both visible and invisible, inner and outer, which it had previously dropped as it ascended out of material existence, following the decease of its last physical body. It takes them up again, we say, and it can do no otherwise, for both these life-atoms are attracted to it as it passes through the respective spheres; and it, the Reincarnating Ego, is equivalently attracted to these spheres by the psycho-magnetic pull of these, its own former life-atoms awaiting it in such respective spheres.

These life-atoms, as we have already said, had, during the post-mortem rest of the Reincarnating Ego in the bosom of its Monad, undergone or followed their own respective transmigrations into the bodies of other beings, wherein they passed times proportionate to the strength of their karmic attractions thither. The moment that the psycho-magnetic pull of the returning Reincarnating Ego is felt by them, these hosts of life-atoms which formerly composed the various substance-principles of the former human entity's constitution in the former life and lives, are drawn to the returning Reincarnating Ego. Thus they build up for the returning Ego a series of six substance-principles, and therefore a physical body also, and this combination is in all *essential* respects, the personality of the man that was in his last life.

The meaning of all this is that the returning Reincarnating Ego gathers again unto itself the identical life-atoms which it had formerly used in its last incarnation or incarnations. It may be truly said, therefore, that the new physical body, indeed, the entire constitution of the new human being, is exactly the man that formerly was at the moment of death, but rejuvenated and renewed, although of course the various adventures of the life-atoms of the different substance-principles have modified and changed them more or less.

But the Reincarnating Ego itself has grown stronger in a psycho-spiritual sense, the resultant of its long rest and recuperation in the bosom of its parent Monadic Essence. Just so is a man refreshed and recuperated after a long night's sleep, and awakens to find his consciousness alert, active, in the body that he had when he laid himself down to rest.

Yet we must be careful here. The new man is essentially the old man rejuvenated and renewed, because the life-atoms are the same that he formerly had, which life-atoms compose his entire constitution, but in another sense, and a very true one, a very profound one, these life-atoms, and therefore the new man, are the Karmic resultant or fruitage or consequence of the man that was.

We cannot say that he is exactly the same man that he was before, because things have moved and changed for the better. Not only does the stream of consciousness run more strongly and more clear, but the life-atoms themselves have undergone all-various modifications which are the resultants of their peregrinations through the realms of matter. It is somewhat like a tree which in its perennial life dies down in the autumn for a while and remains a skeleton of the bare trunk and branches; and yet when the warm rains come in the spring, under the sunshine it burgeons and shoots forth a new garment of leaf-life. Shall we say that the new verdure, the new leaves, covering the branches with the new glory of their appearance, are exactly the same old leaves that were? Hardly. And yet they are all derived from the same life-stock, and as our Theosophical philosophy tells us, even the life-atoms that compose the former leaves are reimbodied in the new leaves; and just so it is with man.

We dwell with some emphasis upon this matter because it is important. We cannot say, if we speak with precision and necessary exactness, that the new man is the identical man who was, because that statement is not quite true. On the other hand, we cannot say that the new man is a different man from the old man that was, for that statement is not quite true.

It is in this very wonderful thought that lies the esoteric meaning of the old Buddhist doctrine that the human soul is mortal and dies even as the physical body dies, and that the fruitage or karma or karmic consequence of the man that was is the new man that now is. The Buddhists are right in saying that the man is the same and yet not the same, because it is in all senses of the word the karmic consequence of the man that was, the life-atoms being the same, and as we Theosophists say, the stream of consciousness being the same; yet as all have changed from what they were before, we cannot say that the new man is *exactly* the man who was. And thank the immortal gods that this is so!

As we have pointed out in other chapters, were there a changeless consciousness remaining in crystallized immobility, which passes, according to the popular theory of the Occident, from earth to heaven, there would be no possibility whatsoever of the continuous and ever-enlarging evolutionary march towards a constantly expanding perfection, which is actually what takes place. There would be, at the best, nothing more following the post-mortem state, than a wearisome repetition of the old memories and the old thoughts with a possible series of psychological modifications brought about by the exercise of will-power.

XIX—Reincarnation and the General Doctrine of Reimbodiment
(Continued)

It may be interesting to the generality of Occidental readers brought up under the influence of Christian religious thought to show that in the earliest historic periods of Christianity, a certain form of reincarnational metempsychosis, or metempsychosal reincarnation, was believed in and taught by a very important and in places powerful faction of the Christian community.

The greatest of the Christian spokesmen of this early Christian school, whose works in this line, in translation or in original, still remain to us, was Origen of Alexandria, born about 185 of the Christian era and supposed to have died in 253. Most of the references to early Christian metempsychosal belief in Origen's writings are to be found in his work *On First Principles*. It is very unfortunate for the student of early Christian beliefs that we do not possess a full text of Origen's original Greek work, and our knowledge of what that great Church-Father wrote is mainly derived from a translation into Latin of Origen's *First Principles,* made in later times by Tyrannius Rufinus, of Aquileia, who was born about 345 of the Christian era and who died 410, and was therefore a contemporary of the Latin Father Jerome.

Rufinus took great liberties indeed with Origen's original Greek text, so much so that it is impossible to exculpate him from the charge of mutilation of Origen's text, and even possibly of forgery in the sense of including in his Latin translation, and ascribing to Origen, ideas which very probably came from Rufinus' own mind. This literary dishonesty of Rufinus, however, he was not alone in possessing, even in the case of Origen's work, because he himself tells us in his Prolog to the

First Principles, that he merely acted as others did before him. His words are interesting, and therefore we quote them here:

> In translation I tried to follow as far as I could the rule observed by my predecessors, and especially by the distinguished man whom I have already spoken of, who, after translating into Latin more than seventy of the writings of Origen, which are called Homilies, as well as a large number of his writings on the Apostles, in which a good many 'stumbling-blocks' are found in the original Greek, so smoothed and corrected them in his translations that a Latin reader would come upon nothing discordant with our Christian belief. His example therefore I follow to the best of my ability. If I have not an equal power of eloquence, yet at least I pursue the same strictness of rule in my work, taking great care not to translate those expressions occurring in the works of Origen, which are inconsistent with and opposed to each other.

One is inclined to think that Rufinus was somewhat of a humorist in excusing his mutilations of Origen's text as being of matters "inconsistent with and opposed to each other." Why Rufinus and these others he speaks of should have set themselves up as judges of Origen's Christianity, the reader may himself easily understand. There is little doubt therefore that had we the full and original Greek text of Origen's *First Principles,* we should probably find that the great Alexandrian Church-Father was far more open in his teachings of his particular kind of metempsychosal Reincarnation than appears in the texts that have reached us. This conclusion is immensely strengthened by the condemnation of Origen's writings at the two Constantinopolitan Councils held in the sixth century, the first under the Patriarch Mennas, and the second, the Fifth General or Oecumenical Council, both convened under imperial rescripts of the Emperor Justinian I.

So thoroughly, in times preceding the sixth century, had Origen's ideas penetrated into the fabric of Christian theological thought—indeed of the entire Christian community—that it is small wonder that the growing religious materialism of the times took alarm at the differences in doctrine which Origen's teachings then showed as compared with the then established dogmata of faith.

Even although this double condemnation of the Origenistic doctrines succeeded in finally killing the spirit of the great

Alexandrian's teachings, it succeeded in doing so only after a great deal of quarreling and very bitter differences of opinion. As a matter of fact, a certain amount of the Origenistic thought survived until late ages in the Christian Church, as was evidenced by the opinions prevalent in eastern, central, and western European countries as late as the fourteenth century.

The various bodies forming the Cathari (a word meaning 'the Pure,' or as they were sometimes called, the Albigenses, and by other names in western lands) and the Bogomils in eastern Europe, as in Bulgaria and in Russia, sufficiently show, from what is at present imperfectly known of their doctrines, that they kept alive and taught ideas which were unquestionably widely prevalent in the Christian communities in the first centuries of the Christian era. It is popular among ecclesiastical writers to call these Cathari by the name of 'Manichaeans'; and doubtless there is some truth in this. But it is also equally true that even if certain doctrines of the Manichaeans can be shown to have existed in the beliefs of the Cathari between the tenth and the fourteenth centuries, some of the ideas of Origen were equally powerful among them.

Origen in his *First Principles,* Book III, chapter i — and here we can quote from a remnant of the Greek text — Section 21, speaks as follows:

> So the one nature of every soul being in the hands of God, and, so to speak, there being but one collection of reasoning entities, certain *causes of more ancient date* led to some of these being made vessels unto honor, and others vessels unto dishonor.

We have underscored the phrase 'certain causes of more ancient date,' because this is a clear and distinct reference to the pre-existent life or lives of the soul-entities who later, following inherent karmic causes, became some 'vessels unto honor,' and others 'vessels (or human beings) unto dishonor.'

We quote again from the original Greek a little farther on in the text:

> As, on the other hand, it is possible that he who, *owing to causes more ancient than the present life,* was here a vessel of dishonor, may after reformation become . . . etc.

Still more clearly does Origen speak in his *First Principles*, Book III, chapter iii, Section 5, as follows:

> Those who maintain that everything in the world is under the rule of the divine foresight, as is also our own belief, can give no other reply, it seems to me, in order to show that no shadow of injustice can rest upon the divine government of the world than by holding that there were certain exact causes of prior existence by consequence of which all souls before their birth in the present body contracted a certain amount of guilt in their reasoning nature, or perhaps by the actions, on account of which they have been condemned by the divine providence to be placed in their present life.

And a little farther on he continues:

> ... Even in such a case we must admit that there sometimes existed certain causes preceding the present bodily birth.

These last two citations from Origen are taken from Rufinus' Latin translation, and the immortal gods only know how guilty Rufinus may have been here of mutilating or changing or softening the text of his great Alexandrian predecessor.

Again quoting from Rufinus' translation of Origen's *First Principles*, Book III, chapter v, Section 4, speaking of the preexistence of souls, Origen, as Rufinus renders him, wrote as follows:

> ... Rational creatures had also a similar beginning. Indeed, if they had a beginning such as the end for which they hope, they must have unquestionably existed from the very beginning of the ages which are not seen. ... If this be so, then of course there has been a descent from a higher to a lower condition not only by those souls who have deserved this change by the variety of their inner movements of consciousness, but also by those who in order to serve the world, came down from the higher and invisible spheres to these lower and visible ones.

The reader must obviously see in this last quotation much of the very same archaic doctrine which we have been attempting to set forth, however the phraseology used by Origen (or by Rufinus) obscures the underlying ideas.

Furthermore, it is interesting to state that Origen likewise taught the pre-existence and reimbodiment of worlds, which of course is another old doctrine of the archaic Wisdom-Religion. In Rufinus' Latin translation of the *First Principles,* Book III, Section 3, we find Origen saying this point:

> We see that not then for the first time did Divinity begin its work when it made this visible world: but just as after the destruction of this visible world there will be another world, its product, so also we believe that other worlds existed before the present came into being.

It is plain enough from the quotations already made from Origen that not only did he teach a mere pre-existence in the spiritual worlds of souls or rational creatures, before their imbodiment on earth, but that he also taught an actual reincarnation or reimbodiment on earth of these soul-entities.

This is made very clear by what we find in Rufinus' Latin translation of the *First Principles,* Book IV, chapter i, Section 23:

> Every one, therefore, of the souls descending to the earth, is strictly following his merits, or according to the position which he formerly occupied, is destined to be returned to this world in a different country or among a different nation, or in a different sphere of existence on earth, or afflicted with infirmities of another kind, or mayhap to be the children of religious parents or of parents who are not religious: so that of course it may sometimes happen that a Hebrew will be born among the Syrians, or an unfortunate Egyptian may be born in Judaea.

Here there is obviously a distinct teaching of the doctrine of Reincarnation, and it is quite futile to argue, should such an argument ever be attempted, that Origen's teaching embraces a bare and sheer pre-existence in the spiritual realms without any repetitive incarnations on earth in human bodies. His last words run directly in line with the doctrine of Reincarnation.

Origen, of course, like most of the philosophers of ancient times, and even of his own period (for he himself had obviously been initiated in the Eleusinian Mysteries) does not teach transmigration of the souls of human beings into the bodies of beasts, and his opinion on this matter is clearly set forth in his *First Principles,* Book I, chapter viii, Section 3:

We think that those views are by no means to be accepted which some people most unnecessarily advance and support, to the effect that rational souls can reach such a pitch of abasement that they forget their rational nature and high dignity and sink into the bodies of irrational beasts, either large or small.

Origen again in his *Treatise against Celsus,* the Pagan philosopher, Book I, chapter xx, argues strongly against the misunderstood transmigration theory. He wrote as follows:

A view which is much worse than the mythical teaching of transmigration, according to which the rational soul tumbles down from the heavenly spheres and enters into the body of brute beasts, whether tame or savage.

And again in his *Treatise against Celsus,* Book III, chapter lxxv, Origen repeats his condemnation of transmigration as thus popularly misunderstood. In the same work, Book VII, chapter xxxii, he speaks as follows:

Our teaching as regards the resurrection is not derived from anything that we have heard about the doctrine of Metempsychosis, as Celsus thinks; but we believe that the rational soul, which is naturally immaterial, and therefore invisible in its nature, exists in no physical material place without having a body suited to the nature of that place. Accordingly at one time it puts off a body which it had found necessary but which is no longer adequate for its improved state, and exchanges it for another body; and at another time it takes up still another body in addition to the former, which other body is needed as a better clothing suited to the purer ethereal regions of heaven.

Here Origen of course voices again, in his vaguely Christian phraseology, other thoughts of the archaic Wisdom-Religion of the Ancients, which thoughts we have briefly outlined and spoken of as the peregrination of the Monadic Entity through the spheres.

In the same work, *Against Celsus,* Book VIII, chapter xxx, he speaks very cautiously, but yet from his standpoint quite correctly, during the course of an argument on whether it be right or wrong to eat flesh-food, as follows:

We do not believe that rational souls pass merely from one physical body to another physical body, nor that such rational souls may descend so low as to enter the bodies of beasts.

This teaching on the surface seems contrary to what Origen formerly said, and therefore opposed to Reincarnation or any form of reincarnational Metempsychosis, but such a conclusion is diametrically opposite to his meaning. He means exactly what the Ancient Wisdom meant as the ancient initiate philosophers taught it, and what Theosophy teaches: that Reincarnation is not the transference of the rational entity, or what we call the Reincarnating Ego, directly from one physical body to another physical body, with no intermediate stages of purgation or purification, and no intermediate principles between the physical body and the Reincarnating Ego. The Theosophist would deny such a distorted teaching as earnestly and as emphatically as does Origen—the former Eleusinian initiate and later Christian doctrinaire.

From the extracts which precede, and also from our knowledge of the wide-spread and deeply-rooted reach which the Origenistic dectrines had in the Christian community even as late as the sixth century, we can see how large a part his teachings had in the beliefs of the Christian community of his time in the third century of the Christian era. When we recollect also that the Latin Father Jerome, already spoken of, tells us in his *Letter to Marcella* that there were in his (Jerome's) time in the fifth century, a number of Christian sects which taught some form of Metempsychosal Reincarnation, we can readily understand how strong was the appeal which this doctrine, even in its distorted Christian form, must have made to the Christian community, and how long it lasted in time.

It is a practical certainty, however, that from a time even before the second century, or Origen's period, the peculiar form which the general doctrine of Reimbodiment took among the Christians was distinctly esoteric and secret. This is not a supposition based merely upon the intrinsic evidence to be found in early Christian patristic literature, a supposition more or less depending upon the mental bias of interpretation of the modern scholar, but is actually vouched for by one of the most orthodox of the early Church-Fathers themselves. We mean the Latin Father Jerome, who makes a specific statement in his *Letter to Marcella,* that this doctrine was, so far as the early

Christian sects of Egypt and of the Oriental parts of Hither Asia were concerned, an esoteric one; and from his words we can only judge that it was propagated more or less 'at low breath' and 'with mouth to ear.'

Jerome's words themselves are so interesting that no apology is needed for repeating them here, and we give the Latin in the footnote below, from which we make the following translation. He says:

> This impious and filthy doctrine spread itself in former times in Egypt and in the eastern parts; and, at the present time, is secretly, as it were, in the holes of vipers, spreading among many, polluting the purity of those parts; and, like an hereditary disease, insinuates itself into the few in order that it may reach the majority.*

It is of course also well known that in the early centuries of Christianity some of the different schools of Gnostics likewise taught a doctrine of metempsychosal Reincarnation, formulated after their own peculiar style; and for this statement of course the various encyclopaedias or historical works may be consulted. It is quite customary to ally some of these Gnostic sects with the early Christian bodies, as being 'heretical' divisions of the Christian community, although this opinion seems, in many cases, to be entirely arbitrary. However, if people insist upon it, the argument tells strongly for the position that we here take, because if they accepted some form of Reincarnation or reincarnational Metempsychosis, as indeed they actually did, and yet are and were claimed as Christians, the case needs no further argument, so far as they are concerned.

In the New Testament itself, there are a number of passages which, read as they stand, are more than merely 'dark sayings,' and make sheer nonsense unless the idea in the mind of the writers of these passages in the Christian New Testament was based upon some form of early Christian metempsychosal Reincarnation. The interview of Nicodemus with Jesus, and the

---

*"Haec impia et scelerata doctrina olim in Aegypto et Orientis partibus versabatur; et nunc abscondite, quasi in foveis viperarum, apud pleros versatur, illarumque partium polluit puritatem; et quasi haereditario malo serpit in paucis ut perveniat ad plurimos."

questions of the former, and the replies thereto, are a sufficient case in point, and show the general belief of the time, whether we accept the actual existence of Nicodemus or not. The point is proved by the fact that whether Nicodemus did or did not exist, the belief was so common in Palestine that it was taken for granted that all would understand the allusions, and the question therefore came very naturally from Nicodemus' mouth.

It is also well known that the Essenes, a Jewish sect, were believers in some form of metempsychosal Reincarnation, and we have the authority of the eminent Jewish historian Josephus, himself a Pharisee, that the great Jewish sect of the Pharisees held also to a form of metempsychosal Reimbodiment, and openly taught it.

The reader who is interested in pursuing the matter further may find the following references useful: Josephus in his *Antiquity of the Jews,* Book XVIII, chapter i, section 3, speaks of the Pharisees as believers in Reincarnation (as they understood it); and also in his *Jewish War,* Book II, chapter vii, section 14, has several long passages dealing with the metempsychosal Reincarnation beliefs of both the Essenes and the Pharisees; and he refers to the same matter again in Book II, chapter viii. Again in his *Jewish War,* Book III, chapter viii, section 5, Josephus reproduces his own address to the body of men under his command during their fighting against the Roman troops under Vespasian; and remembering that Josephus himself was a Pharisee, the remarkably clear declarations in these passages of a belief in Reincarnation show that the men to whom he spoke must have been perfectly well acquainted with it and that it was a commonly accepted belief of the day.

The Jews furthermore, certainly from the time of Josephus and doubtless from an indefinite period preceding his time, in their secret or esoteric doctrines called the Qabbâlâh — for the Qabbâlâh is the Theosophy of the Jews — taught Reincarnation openly, as also, by the way, they taught two others of the doctrines of the Ancient Wisdom, to which we have before alluded. One is the pre-existence of worlds as well as of human souls, and reimbodiment; and they also taught, as did Plato, that the consciousness and knowledge of man in any one life are but reminiscences of the consciousness and the knowledge of former lives.

Philo Judaeus, the great Platonizing Jewish philosopher, on a number of occasions speaks very strongly in favor of that particular form of metempsychosal Reincarnation which most appealed to him, and which actually had close links with the similar ideas held by Plato, his great Greek predecessor. For instance, in his tract, *On Dreams Being Sent from God*, Book I, section 22, he sets forth his belief in very clear words, and they are interesting outside of their corroborative value to our argument, in that they show the wide extent in which the General Doctrine of Reimbodiment, in one or another form, was held in his period.

It was during the first century of the Christian era, so called. Philo was an Alexandrian by birth, and of course was very largely affected by the syncretistic spirit of Alexandrian philosophy, which was so noticeable during his time. The entire purpose of his writings was to show the common grounds of mystical and theological thinking that, according to him, existed between the Platonic doctrines and the sacred books of the Jews. His argument of course is, more or less, that the Logos or Divine Spirit in humanity infused common ideas into human minds irrespective of race or time-period; and also he seems to argue in places that such great men as Plato, and, generally speaking, "the wisdom of the Greeks," derived what natural truth they possessed from inspiration having its origin in the Jewish scriptures. This idea is of course preposterous, but he argued it with undoubted sincerity, and actually succeeded in proving to any impartial and thoughtful mind that in all probability the Jews derived their wisdom from the other nations surrounding them, probably from the great philosophers of different periods, and from the Egyptians, and the peoples of the basin of the Euphrates and Tigris rivers.

In his tract before spoken of: *On Dreams Being Sent from God*, section 22, he speaks of the various kinds of souls, and of the celestial bodies as being animated entities, quite in common with the general teaching of antiquity, and remarks:

Now all these souls seem to descend upon the earth with a view to being bound up in mortal bodies, those namely which are most nearly connected with the earth, and which are lovers of bodily habitations. Others, however, soar upwards, and are distinguished from others of their class according to the times and characteristics which Nature has appointed unto them. All these souls, those which are influenced by desires for mortal existence and which have been previously familiarized with it, return to mortal life. But others, refusing bodily life as a great folly, and as a mere trifling, pronounce it a prison or a grave, and fleeing from it by the impulses of their nature as from a house of correction or a tomb, raise themselves on the light wings of their nature towards the aether where they devote all their life to speculations of a divine type, etc., etc.

It is really an amazing thing that so many people, some of them otherwise profound scholars in their respective lines, should be so blind to the evidences throughout the ancient literatures, coming from all parts of the world, proving that there did exist in ancient times a common and universally diffused Wisdom or body of doctrine concerning the nature and origin and destiny of the Universe, and therefore of man also, and that this body of doctrine was in all essential particulars — in other words, in all fundamentals — the same everywhere, whatever might have been the variations of form or of formulation which the body of doctrine referred to may have taken in different epochs of time and among different races of men.

Some form of metempsychosal belief or reincarnational Metempsychosis, is known by everybody to have existed in times preceding the Christian era all over the world, and such a belief also exists today over most of the world; and even in Occidental countries, although due to the long centuries of Christian belief it has been forgotten there, with the exception of sporadic instances of learned men who accepted it. It is today rapidly gaining many adherents through the efforts and teaching of the Theosophical Movement.

The time apparently is not far off when Reincarnation as a fact of Nature, and as taught by modern Theosophy, the true echo of the archaic Wisdom-Religion, will again be accepted by the majority of men. Already today it is a household word in every civilized country, and in European and American lands is a favorite subject of romance-writers, or dramatists, and of the movie producers.

We have spoken of the different formulations or methods of presenting the General Doctrine of Reimbodiment as taught by Theosophy, as formerly used or as now used in different parts of the world. The reason for these differences in form is one very easily understood. It is that the deeper or more esoteric teachings connected with this General Doctrine of Reimbodiment are by no means so easily understandable as are the general principles of it, and for that reason, these more recondite teachings were held as an esoteric collection of doctrines, which were given to men who had proved themselves worthy and fit to receive them, and who were sworn to the strictest silence regarding the knowledge imparted to them.

There were various grades of this knowledge existent in the ancient Mystery-Schools, and the manner of imparting, as well as the formulation of, the doctrines themselves, necessarily varied according to the time and the people in which or among whom such or another formulation of these more recondite teachings was given forth. But the clothes or garments in which a teaching is delivered are, after all, a very secondary matter. Nevertheless, and admitting this, the Theosophist feels that any truth of Nature, and therefore among them this General Doctrine of Reimbodiment, can be presented in a best way, and that this best way of presenting it is always to be preferred to any inferior method of setting any body of teachings forth.

The best way is that which most nearly represents to human minds the exact cyclical operations of Nature which fundamentally motivate the activities of those portions of man's constitution which undergo reimbodiment. The more photographically exact, so to speak, such a formulation is, the better it is. Therefore do we say that the Theosophical formulation is not only by far the most complete — even those parts of it which are presented to the general public — but is also the most skillfully prepared, and the most easily understood.

The reasons for this are that coming directly from the great Sages and Seers, who have been from immemorial time the

Guardians and Custodians of the Archaic Wisdom, our teachings have not been subjected to the deforming or distorting influences of social or political circumstances, such as most of the Mystery-Schools of ancient times were involved in. For in ancient times often the formulation of the truths concerning the General Doctrine of Reimbodiment was so intermingled with the general and popular mythology of the various countries, that distortion of form was an inescapable consequence of the resultant teaching. No such distortion of outline has occurred in H. P. Blavatsky's presentation to the modern world. This, however, does not mean that the Great Theosophist gave out all the details of the Ancient Wisdom to the modern world, and that she withheld nothing of its more important parts or aspects.

The contrary of this is true. A great deal was of necessity withheld, but what was presented was presented with absolute fidelity to the natural truth of the thing, and with strict loyalty to the instructions that she had received in this connection from the Great Teachers who sent her forth.

The observation that we make upon this matter of her reticence with regard to this one teaching of the General Doctrine of Reimbodiment apply with equal force to others of the grand body of Theosophical doctrines, of which she gave to the world so masterly and wonderful an outline in her *The Secret Doctrine*. That book is filled with natural verities which do not appear on the surface of the words, and for which the earnest student must dig and delve in the words themselves, as it were, as well as behind the words, in order to arrive at the deeper meanings which lie enshrined therein. It is a veritable mine of ancient wisdom regarding Nature and its structure and powers and faculties and energies. The Great Theosophist said very truly that while this her noblest work would not be understood, except in small degree, in the century in which she wrote it yet the coming century, the twentieth, would, before it had run its course, see that her *The Secret Doctrine* contains many if not all of the most abstruse mysteries of the nature of the Universe and of man.

That the General Doctrine of Reimbodiment in one form or other was at one time universal over the earth, is an undeniable fact, which none but those ignorant of the case would think of denying, although of course in all ages and among all races of men, individuals and minor bodies have held beliefs more or less resembling modern materialism.

The Druids for instance, in ancient Gaul and the British Isles and elsewhere, as well as the ancient Germans and doubtless the Scandinavians, all held one or another form of Metempsychosal Reincarnation, or of Reincarnational Metempsychosis, while in the countries surrounding the Inland Sea of Europe, every scholar or student of the classics knows how widely one or another form of the General Doctrine existed.

In Greece, the Orphics and the Pythagoreans and the Platonists all held the doctrine, and of course the Latins, who followed their lead, held it likewise, as is well instanced in the case of Ennius, the Calabrian Poet. Vergil also makes especial point of it in his wonderful work, the *Aeneid*, in the sixth book thereof, verses 724 and following, and it persisted down to the latest times of the last philosophers, such as Plotinus, and indeed prevailed in the entire Neo-Platonic School. Gnostics throughout Asia Minor and the Greek and Latin countries, also generally held it. We have spoken of its existence among the Jews, especially among the Essenes and the Pharisees, who openly taught it; and as the Pharisees composed the most numerous and influential of all the Jewish sects, we can readily understand how widely diffused it was among them. It is also found from the earliest times in the teachings of the Qabbâlâh, the Theosophy of the Jews. The Manichaeans of the Hither East also held it, and the Cathari continued even into the Middle Ages the Manichaean and Origenistic teachings.

About the time of the Renaissance in Europe, we find the doctrine still alive in the teachings of such men as Giordano Bruno, and in the seventeenth century it was written of and promulgated by the 'Theosophist' Jan Baptista van Helmont. Swedenborg also adopted it in an extremely modified form; while in the classical period of German literature, the doctrine of Metempsychosal Reincarnation furnished a very prolific field of thought for a number of the most prominent German philosophers and thinkers, such as Goethe, and Lessing who had probably taken the idea from Charles Bonnet. It was also spoken of and commented upon by Herder. The Scot, Hume, and the Austrian, Schopenhauer, mention it with profound respect.

Returning to times of antiquity, we may point out that, as is perfectly well known, the immense continent of Asia has always been practically unanimous in acceptance of the doctrine, not only in China, as among the followers of Lao-Tse and the various schools of Buddhism there prevalent, but also in Japan and Tibet; and it has flourished exceedingly in both ancient and modern India, as is instanced among the Brâhmans, and the early Buddhists there. Although the references to a belief in some sort of metempsychosal Reincarnation are much less easily found as concerns the opinions of the peoples dwelling in Mesopotamia, there nevertheless remain sufficient proofs of its prevalence there, to say that there likewise the doctrine, under one or another of its formulations, was as widespread and commonly believed in as elsewhere.

It is customary among modern scholars to say that the ancient Egyptians did not believe in any form of Reincarnation, this opinion being based solely upon the fact that the studies of Egyptologists have been so largely devoted to monumental studies and manuscript documents found in the tombs, that, as the saying goes, they do not see the wood on account of the trees. In other words, the details of the splendid researches in Egyptology begun by Young and Champollion have so blinded the vision of Egyptologists to the more general view, that they do not see that it is necessary to presume its existence in order to account for what they do study. In this the Egyptologists are entirely wrong. We believe that time will prove this fully, to the confusion of some of the more dogmatic modern scholars among them. It had always been accepted among European scholars prior to Young and Champollion that the ancient Egyptians did hold a belief in the General Doctrine of Reimbodiment, under one of its forms of metempsychosal Reincarnation and this belief was very largely based upon the statement of the great Greek philosopher and historian Herodotus — a man who at one time was called 'The Father of lies,' but who is now called 'The Father of History,' because modern research has shown how keen was his observation, and how accurate his descriptions.

We Theosophists prefer to believe in Herodotus, who spent a long time in Egypt, who knew the Egyptians well, and who had talked not only with the priests, but with the people, whether through interpreters or not is a matter of no consequence whatsoever. In a general way it may be said that the more we discover of ancient history the more does that knowledge prove the general, and often the particular, truth, of the statements in Herodotus' remarkable work.

The writers in *The Encyclopaedia Britannica*, on Herodotus, say of him on page 382 of the 11th Edition:

At all the more interesting sites he took up his abode for a time; he examined, he inquired, he made measurements, he accumulated materials. Having in his mind the scheme of his great work, he gave ample time to the elaboration of all its parts, and took care to obtain by personal observation a full knowledge of the various countries.

The italics of this citation are ours. Other writers, as for instance in the *Dictionary of Greek and Roman Biography and Mythology*, edited by the late Sir William Smith, D. C. L., LL. D., say only the truth of Herodotus when they write: "the accuracy of his observations and his descriptions still excites the astonishment of travelers in that country."

When we remember that this great Greek spent a long time in Egypt, and mixed not only familiarly with the people, but was given free entry, as his own work tells us, into the temples, and conversed upon esoteric and recondite matters with the learned priests themselves, we have reason to believe that when he tells us that the Egyptians accepted a form of metempsychosal Reincarnation, he knew better what he was talking about than do scholars of some twenty-four hundred years later, whose only argument against Herodotus' assertion is that they have not yet found what Herodotus said existed.

It would be an amazing thing if the Egyptians, so great and marvelous a people in scientific and literary and ethical and historic and religious and philosophical lines of thought and work, should have been ignorant of a doctrine which was not only universal, but as common sense and reflection show must have lain at the very basis of the psychological part of their own extremely mystical body of various religious dogmata.

The truth of the matter is that modern scholars do not understand the meaning of the ancient philosophies and religions, in most cases, unless that meaning be superficial and easily understood—that is, unless it lie so clearly upon the surface and be so openly expressed, that only a dolt could misunderstand it.

As it may interest the reader to have Herodotus' words before him, we give them here, as translated from the original Greek, in his Book II, *Euterpe*, Section 123:

> It was the Egyptians who first gave utterance to the following doctrine, to wit: that the soul [Herodotus here uses the word *psyche*] is immortal and that when the physical body decays, the soul enters into another living being which at the moment is ready for and appropriate to it. After it has passed through all the terrestrial and aqueous and aerial forms of life, it clothes itself anew with the body of a man then becoming ready for it. This wandering [or transmigration] it passes through in some three thousand years. There are a number of Hellenes also who follow this same doctrine, some of olden time and some of later days, giving it forth as their own. Although I know the names of these I do not here write them down.

And Herodotus was wise in not doing so, because, as an initiate of the Mysteries, he knew that after what he had just said concerning this belief of the Egyptians he could not designate who the Greek philosophers were, and what their particular forms of teaching were, without immediately giving the key to esoteric aspects which he had no right to give. That he was an initiate we know from his own words, and from several places where he speaks of the necessity of holding his tongue.

The belief which Herodotus here ascribes to the Egyptians, is not the teaching of Reincarnation, as is obvious from what has already been said in this book, nor is it the true teaching of Metempsychosis as the latter was taught in the Mysteries, although unquestionably the Egyptians knew both these true teachings as well as other ancient nations did. The particular and peculiar doctrine to which Herodotus here alludes, is the cyclical destiny of the psycho-vital parts of the human soul, in other words, of the lower half of the Intermediate Duad as this

Duad is outlined in the second of the schematic diagrams given in a former chapter.

This is but another way of saying that this particular Egyptian belief refers solely to the transmigration of the life-atoms forming the psycho-vital part of man's intermediate nature, and which reassemble or re-collect or come together again in a succeeding Reincarnation of the evolving soul-entity.

This particular Egyptian doctrine lay at the back of the custom which the Egyptians had, in common with some other peoples both of the ancient and modern world, of mummifying their dead. The entire object of mummification, as the Egyptians practised it, was a rather pathetic attempt to restrain, as far as it was possible, the transmigration of the life-atoms of the human Intermediate Duad and the Lower Triad through the lower spheres of life, by preserving as long as was possible the physical body from decay.

H. P. Blavatsky alludes to this matter in her magazine, *The Theosophist*, in the course of a short article which she entitled: 'The Transmigration of the Life-atoms.' How such a belief could have taken such firm hold of the imagination and religious emotions of the Egyptian people is in itself an interesting and rather pathetic psychological study. Unquestionably the priests knew that the custom of mummification was but an imperfect preventive of what it was originally intended to do, but due to some reasons at present unknown, the custom became so firmly established as to be one of the marked characteristics of Egyptian civilization.

Another writer in *The Encyclopaedia Britannica*, 11th Edition, under the title *Metempsychosis*, shows the usual modern, most lamentable ignorance of the real meaning of this teaching, for he confuses sadly Metempsychosis with Transmigration, and these with Reincarnation. He opens his article by saying:

> Metempsychosis, or Transmigration of the Soul, the doctrine that at death the soul passes into another living creature, man, animal, or even plant.

This is really amusing, and is a proof of the ignorance to which we have just pointed. In the first place, as we have already explained, Metempsychosis is not the same as Transmigration, although of course a Theosophist knows as well as anyone else that these words are wrongly considered by modern scholars to be interchangeable and synonymous in meaning. Secondly, Metempsychosis does not mean that the human soul passes into an animal or a plant, and we have set forth the reason why, as well as the true meaning of Metempsychosis, in preceding paragraphs; likewise that of Transmigration.

This writer further continues:

> Till full investigation of Egyptian records put us in possession of the facts, it was supposed that the Egyptians believed in Metempsychosis, and Herodotus explicitly credits them with it. We now know that he was wrong.

We now know nothing of the sort. All that we do know is that modern scholars have not found references to this doctrine sculptured on the monuments or painted on the papyri, and therefore say that it did not prevail in ancient Egypt, although they have the testimony of Herodotus, one of the greatest of the ancient Greeks, who tells us explicitly and precisely to the contrary. Herodotus lived in the fifth century before the accepted Christian era.

The General Doctrine of Reimbodiment, as Theosophy teaches it, is in no sense of the word Predestination or Necessarianism, as these words have been understood by the fatalistic theologians of certain phases of Christianity, wherein indeed may rightly be laid the charge of Fatalism. If Fatalism means, as it does, that all things in Nature, men therefore included, are but the creatures of an over-ruling Power which creates souls only to predestine them either to eternal weal or to eternal woe, then the charge of Fatalism certainly does not lie in the case of the Theosophists, who positively and emphatically repudiate this horrible idea.

Lest our words be thought to be unfair, we quote here Article XVII of the Thirty-nine Articles of the Episcopal Church of England, as they were laid down in Convention assembled in 1562-3, to wit:

> Predestination to Life is the everlasting purpose of God, whereby (before the foundations of the world were laid) he hath constantly

decreed by his counsel, secret to us, to deliver from curse and damnation those whom He hath chosen in Christ out of mankind, and to bring them by Christ to everlasting salvation, as vessels made to honor.

This seventeenth Article is mild in its tone and doctrine as compared with the Doctrine of Reprobation of the Westminster Confession of Faith, which also was formulated at Westminster by a Convocation of English Divines during the period 1643-1649. It should be remembered that Reprobation is a technical term in Christian theology, and means the doctrine that "God has predestined some to everlasting death." This Westminster Confession of Faith was largely drawn up by clergymen of the Anglican Communion having strong Calvinistic leanings, and in its Article III, 3, 4, we find the following:

By the decree of God, for the manifestation of his glory, some men and angels are predestinated unto everlasting life, and others foreordained to everlasting death. These angels and men, thus predestinated and foreordained, are particularly and unchangeably designed; and their number is so certain and definite that it cannot be either increased or diminished.

If this be not Fatalism according to every meaning that the word holds in common and theological and philosophical language, it would be interesting to know just what it does mean. Nothing of this sort was ever taught in ancient times when the great Mysteries of antiquity prevailed, which taught men not merely how to live but also taught them the secrets of universal Nature, and therefore of man's interior constitution and being. Nor is Fatalism, in any sense of the word, or on any grounds whatsoever, or in any possible construction, taught in Theosophy or endorsed by Theosophists.

We do not use the language we have here employed with any desire to cast unkind slurs upon the beliefs of other men. We venture to point out only the truth, that while our teaching of Karma, as expressed for instance in the workings of the general operation of Reimbodiment, means indeed an endless chain of causation, this chain of causation is one which lies in the nature of the evolving entity himself or itself, and for which that entity is solely responsible.

This is merely common sense, and it is sufficient to turn to the emphatic teaching of free will or of the free and unimpeded will in the flow of the stream of consciousness arising from the fountain-head in man's Inner God, to show how vastly different and more merciful, as well as how truly religious and philosophical, the Theosophical teaching is.

Such then is the real meaning of the General Doctrine of Reimbodiment; and it remains with the reader or student of our mystical Theosophical philosophy to draw the necessary conclusions, which doubtless he is quite capable of doing, for the principles upon which our teachings rest are in all cases easily understood.

How it could ever be argued, as has in a certain case been argued by superficial critics of an atrabilious turn of mind, that H. P. Blavatsky either invented her teachings, or plagiarized them from the books treating of ancient religions and philosophies, is another notion which passes comprehension. Any competent student should readily see that while all our Theosophical doctrines may be found here and there in the various ancient literatures, not one of these literatures contains a completely systematic formulation of Theosophy as H. P. Blavatsky gave it to the world, and it is precisely in this systematic formulation that we see the marvelous strength of her intellect and the penetrating power of her spiritual intuition. Indeed, we see far more than these movements of her soul: we see the effect of the teachings received from others greater than she, of whom she was the Mouthpiece and Messenger to the modern world.

And so we come to an end of this true story of a great psychological mystery, the biography of a soul rather than the outline of the life of a mere human personality. And in doing so, inevitably we have also presented a sketch of the essential teachings H. P. Blavatsky brought. In the greatest of her works, *The Secret Doctrine*, all that has been heretofore outlined in this present book is there contained, either in brief or in much fuller form than the compass of this volume permits. The true Theosophist loves his great first Teacher, with a love that is based on sound reasons and in no wise is dependent upon a merely personal predilection for one whose mental capacities and whose instincts of the heart provoked admiration. Not only did H. P. Blavatsky teach men how to know themselves, whence they came, what they are, and whither they are going, but she gave them new hopes in life, for she taught them a new meaning of Life, in elucidating the marvelous Wisdom-Religion of the archaic ages.

What work can be more sublime than giving back to man man's soul? And this in brief is precisely what the Great Theosophist, H. P. Blavatsky, did.

ADDENDUM
Biographical Sketch

As regards the very remarkable personality itself of Helena Petrovna Blavatsky there is little to add here to what has already been set forth in Theosophical literature. We give, therefore, only a hasty sketch.

She was born on July 31, 1831, old style (August 11 of the present calendar), in the town of Ekaterinoslav [now Dniepropetrovsk], Southern Russia, and in a family of historic distinction. Her father was Colonel Peter A. von Hahn, and her mother was Helena A. de Fadeyev. She was the granddaughter of General Alexis G. Hahn von Rottenstern-Hahn, a descendant of a noble German stock, originally of Mecklenburg, Germany, but then settled in the Russian Empire. On her mother's side she was the granddaughter of Privy Councillor Andrew M. de Fadeyev, and of Princess Helena P. Dolgorukov.

Her child-life was one of surpassing interest to any student of the beginnings of human greatness, for even then she gave promise of the spiritual and intellectual energies which later were to blossom forth in splendor in her mature age. She was a born Mystic in the ancient sense of the word; that is to say, one whose inner life was controlled by a dominating influence of spiritual type, surging through the mere personality as a stream of intimations and intuitions that could neither be stayed nor turned aside, and which ruled the destiny of the mere personality through which its spiritual stream passed.

On July 7, 1849, when she was seventeen years old, she entered into a formal marriage with Nikifor V. Blavatsky, Vice-Governor of the Province of Yerivan' in the Caucasus, who was 23 years her senior. But this marriage was a mere formality and within a few months at most it eventuated in a permanent separation. Thereupon began the series of travels at her father's expense in Egypt, Greece, and other parts of eastern Europe. Some time was also passed in London and in Paris, and in 1851 she visited Canada, Mexico, and the United States, in which country she is known to have been in Texas and in New Orleans.

It was in 1851 that she first met her Teacher personally in London, as she herself says. At the end of 1852 she was known to have been in Ceylon and shortly afterwards in Bombay; she was also in Java for a time and in other parts of the far Orient. In 1853 she was again for a short time in England, and in the same year, after crossing the Atlantic again, passed through New York and Chicago, and continued her travels westwards to the Pacific Coast.

In 1855 she was in India again, especially in Kashmir, and in 1856 she is known to have been at Leh in Ladak. About this time it is known that she entered Tibet under the protection of her great spiritual Teacher. In 1857 she left India and in the following year was for a while in France and Germany. She returned to Russia in late 1858, where she remained with relatives of her own family till about 1865. Leaving Russia again, she went to Hungary and possibly to Egypt where she met a very unusual character commonly spoken of as 'the Old Copt' with whom she studied ancient Egyptian lore. More than once in later years she met this mysterious figure again.

In 1867 she returned to the Orient, and some years afterwards revisited Cairo; she spent some time also during this period in Palestine and Greece. She reached Russia again in 1872. In 1873 she went to Paris, and in the summer of that year took passage for New York, in which city she arrived on July 7th.

In the following year she met Colonel Henry Steel Olcott and William Quan Judge, both of whom were to play important parts as collaborators with her in her great work and as co-founders of The Theosophical Society.

In 1874 H. P. Blavatsky began writing for various American publications. On September 7, 1875, at a meeting in her own rooms in New York, there was proposed the formation of a society for the study of various mystical and quasi-mystical subjects. On the following day, the Theosophical Society was formed there at her home. There were then present H. P. Blavatsky, Henry S. Olcott, William Quan Judge, and thirteen others. On September 13, the name 'The Theosophical Society' was adopted.

In 1877 H. P. Blavatsky's first great book, *Isis Unveiled*, was published. In 1878 she became a naturalized American citizen. On December 18, 1879, accompanied by Colonel Olcott, she left the New World for India in order to enlarge the work of the Society, leaving General Abner Doubleday as Acting President *ad interim* of the mother-society in New York, and William Q. Judge as Joint Recording Secretary. In 1879 *The Theosophist* was founded and edited in India by H. P. Blavatsky. In 1882 H. P. Blavatsky with her headquarters-staff took up residence at Madras, where a small property had been purchased for the purpose.

On April 7, 1884, H.P.B. left India for Europe, but in a later month of the same year returned to India. In 1885 she returned definitely to stay in Europe, living for various short periods in Würzburg, Germany; in Ostend, Belgium; and in Paris. In this year she began the writing of *The Secret Doctrine*, her greatest and most powerful work, in which she outlined the scheme of cosmic and human evolution and the nature of the Universe, which remarkable literary work ever since has furnished the foundation of the studies in Theosophy for her devoted followers.

In 1887 H. P. Blavatsky moved from Ostend to London, where she took up her permanent residence, first at 17 Lansdowne Road, and finally at 19 Avenue Road. In this year she founded and edited the magazine *Lucifer* in London. In 1888 her *magnum opus*, *The Secret Doctrine*, was published. The few remaining years between 1888 and May 8, 1891, the day of her passing from this physical sphere, was a very busy time for her. She not only wrote a large number of articles for her own magazine, *Lucifer*, and for *The Theosophist* in India, and for *The Path* of New York, but also for various Theosophical periodicals in European countries, and in addition to this she published *The Key to Theosophy* and *The Voice of the Silence*.

Under her inspiration and directing genius the various branches and centers of the Theosophical Society in European countries grew apace, while the literary and propaganda-work which she had inaugurated in India some years before pursued its own course, a course which can hardly be characterized otherwise than as rather slow and painful, because her departure from India had removed from the Indian sphere the immediate influence and inspiration of her pen, her tireless energy, and her wonderful mind. The work in America, meanwhile, even from a time as far back as 1882, had been growing steadily, and at the time of H. P. Blavatsky's passing the 'American Section,' as it was then called, was the most active, widely spread, and strong in membership of any of the various Sections of the Theosophical Society.

The Great Teacher, the Mover of men's hearts, and the inaugurator in very truth of a new civilization among men, a civilization founded upon spiritual ideals and cosmic verities, passed away quietly in her armchair, surrounded by a few of her attendants and friends, on the morning of May 8, 1891.

Legend has begun but has not yet succeeded in weaving around her memory and her personality those outlines of figure and type, based on reverential but imperfect knowledge, which at the present time portray to us Occidentals the distorted figures of other great World-Teachers of the past. True reverence should need no such fictitious embellishments of truth. A World-Teacher stands firm through the ages upon the basis of fact which is the work that he wrought; and let us hope that this grand and imposing figure, H. P. Blavatsky, may forever remain clear in our memories and sharp in the outlines of truthful delineation, untouched by the blurrings and embellishments of fancy and story, however reverential in origin such later fancy may be. We must see her as she was, not as fancy would portray her to have been; we must see her as she passed across the pages of history: grand, truthful, powerful, clear-cut, splendid, a martyr to her world-work, and a much misunderstood benefactor of her fellow-men.

* * * * *

This brief chapter gives only an outline-sketch of the life of H. P. Blavatsky, considered as a personality. Some of the dates given are uncertain, as available information is often contradictory. One of these days someone with full leisure at his disposal and with a mind stocked with wide reading on the fascinating events in the life of the Great Theosophist, will give to the world a full, truthful, and fascinating study of the great Russian woman who, without any reservation whatsoever, is to be called the most remarkable and interesting figure of her age—indeed, of any age known to history.

[For a much more complete outline of H. P. Blavatsky's life and work prior to her public career, the student is referred to *Blavatsky: Collected Writings*, Vol. 1, 1874-75, with bibliography and index, compiled by Boris de Zirkoff, as well as to subsequent volumes, through Volume XI, which include much additional biographical material and chronological surveys of the years from 1874 until her death on May 8, 1891.]

Lovely Life Progress

Divine Loving Light
Our Solar Self

Happy Life-Wealth

Education Humanity Foundation

© 2010

Many thanks to Geoffrey Hodson for his sensitive hearing of Archangel Bethelda's fabulous wisdom from above. Thank you master teacher O.Mikhael Aivanhov too for channeling lovely life-treasure through our universal Tree of Life.

Richard Shargel

Contents

The Quality of Our Feelings	4
Realizing Happy Loving Wholeness	10
Utmost Aspirations	18
Superb Wonderful Wealth – Archangel Wisdom, Male-Female Polarity, Avian Verse	22
Collectivity, Divine Loving Togetherness	33
Solar Harmony - Happy Wise Working with Light	37
Our Luminous World Family, Solar Living – Story of Our Solar Future, Life Centuries Ahead	43
Sublime Mountain	45
Breakfast in Sophia	54
The Market	59
Choir of Angels	65
Science of the Sun – Solar Respiration	75
Word from the Archangel	82
Solar Schooling - Initiate Education	88
World University	96

Lovely Life Progress
Divine Loving Light – Our Solar Being

The Quality of Our Feelings

I had a dream about divine love. I was in a room with a stereo I installed, playing excellent classical music to two men. I told the men, "What makes the huge quality of life's superb beauty and expansion happen perfectly is the stereo *speakers'* high quality." Thus utmost best music is heard, is felt and *lived.*

This superb symbolic meaning of a music speaker is, "The high quality of our *feelings* makes life's beauty and expansion happen perfectly."

We know from archangel Bethelda and the visionary sensitive master Geoffrey Hodson that feelings make sound; therefore we sing happy divine love above and around.

Prior to hearing music in my room I was outside. I told a person that I was going to have a few children in the room. The person answered that they would take too much space; that it would be better to have two ladies in the room. That meaning is obvious too.

Rather than your and my youth we need our inspired *maturity*, with its intuitive female-male wealth. Thus our mind and heart, with divine loving light, is nicely creative.

Thus too our life is wholly, ever *solar*. To me this is symbolized by flying birds: my creativity and loving life is 100 percent and best when it is 'forward-flying'. Another high symbolic image of happy progress is our constant riding of a horse with wings.

Yesterday morning these truths and realities had a wonderfully lovely aid from above. This was one of my most enrichingly beautiful experiences.

I was out watering my garden around the house. A quarter mile ahead above the trees I heard our best flying, singing birds. I wondered if the lovely vultures would fly toward me.

Here they come. Right over the trees, fifty ease-flying singing big birds fly straight forty feet over your head!

They say, "You're going for it nicely well, a hundred percent forward." A lovely affirmation from above. Yes, I'm flying forward, being servicefully creative toward a perfected future of divine loving solar well-being in the world. For you, all, and the lovely divinities above. And as well, earth and the solar system's divine loving solar future ahead is begun now in our present Aquarian Age.

The quality of our feelings also makes an enormous difference to earth upheaval.

It's known. For tens of thousands of years man's negative feelings like anger and war have been absorbed by the earth, making upheaval like earthquake, firestorm and hurricane. And therein is the solution. Make feelings clear and perfect. Radiate divine loving light to nature. Hundreds of millions of us doing this, for example, "Oh beautiful forest, nature, earth – divine loving light to You." - then upheavals *reduce*.

Psychologists Karl Jung, Sigmund Freud and many others tell us that we are birthed on models from above. Yes, it's true. Archetypes – models – in nature are ever present, birthing and developing beings. Absolutely, certainly, human and earth archetypes are solar, in the spiritual sun.

Solar Archetypes

Also above, we are told by earth's angels that happy loving fellowship is very important. Angels live in a perfected togetherness of happy love. Humanity too is gradually ascending to collective happy loving unity. One beautiful 'music' of this divine love is in Geoffrey Hodson's vision of our magnificent archangel Bethelda.

Archangel Bethelda receives brilliance from above in the white above her, and beams pure thought above in the white too.

Archangel Bethelda

The red below is Bethelda's music to us. Look at the size of the archangel's aura! It could be a half mile wide.

Bethelda tells us, "Your thoughts make form, your feelings make sound. Therefore beam music above."

Really. Doesn't clarity, a balanced pure heart with good feelings, feel nice? We are taught recently what path gives us a freedom from anger and negative feelings.

The cabbalistic Tree of Life has the way and means for us in nice detail. Our divine pure heart is archetyped in the Sun. Our transforming of anger to positive goodness is aided through sephira Geburah, its regent Kamael and planet Mars. When admiring and relating to a Tree of Life regent, when admiring and relating to a master initiate, like Buddha, Jesus or Aivanhov, then we directly receive from that regent.

Here is a huge benefit of feelings: relating to regents and masters with brilliant love, and receiving empowered great growth. Nature is so fabulous.

What a goodness we experience by singing in a church choir. One of man's greatest wealth's is experienced with choral music. Well, as a violinist orchestra player and singer I've sensed what our best music on the planet is.

I had a friend who was chairman of a University of California, Berkeley, department. He lived next door and invited me over to hear his favorite piece of music, Hector Berlioz's 'Requiem'. It is super classic.

Later I found that Berlioz's symphonic chorale titled 'Te Deum' (To God) was absolutely utmost. Other top chorales are 'Giuseppe Verdi's 'Quattro Messa Da Requiem' and Berlioz's L'Enfance du Christ'.

The latter chorale has an interlude for two flutes and harp that is played outside to hundreds at our world's wonderful life-conference center, l'Bonfin, in France. The people benefit magnificently, angels coming down tremendously. The seven minute interlude is played three times. And you likely have heard the saying, "A child's smile radiates to the most distant star." Well, here's another key truth in nature.

Singing, loving feelings and inspired creativity radiate around and above. I had a nice experience for you, in a choir.

In Ashland, Oregon's Methodist Church, a lady planted the church's front garden. Years later she passed away and the church did a Sunday service for her. I sang in the 35 member choir, led by likely the top choir leader in the nation, a music teacher at the local college.

While singing, I wondered if I would see the lady. And I did! I saw her up to my right, her head to mid-body, happily smiling from our kind loving-feelings to her. Thus I experienced with 200 people at once man's high happy goodness to all here and above.

So even a smile to your child radiates to all. And with these truths, events and realities you're reading, you and all are aided.

How humanity's future of loving divine light in perfected harmony shall be experienced is portrayed in our chapters ahead: 'Solar Living, Our Luminous World Family – Story of Our Solar Future, Life Centuries Ahead'.

Realizing Happy Loving Wholeness

With everyone working to realize happy loving wholeness, it then comes. Others' growth too subtly helps you; your advances helping them also.

A Paris, France author and journalist gave us a unique nice chapter on joy, 'Evolution Toward Perfection – The Way to Joy'. Here is the first paragraph.

'Joy is a sudden flowering of the heart, a dilatation, a feeling of expansion. The word itself is gay and relaxed, it writes joyfully: one is full of joy, one bursts with joy, one yells for joy! It's a shining word. Joy rises: we leap for joy! We give ourselves joyfully, we hear the joyous sound of bugles and joyful news. We are someone's joy, we are overjoyed at the sight of the one we love, we enjoy our holidays! In short, joy is good. Synonyms: cheerfulness, gladness, liveliness, delight, rejoicing, jollity, gaiety, jubilation and exteriorization. It's a merry word! To such an extent that the Master tells us, "You are better prepared to bear suffering than you are to bear the joy that lies ahead: the high vibrations of an intense joy such as you have never experienced."'

Yes, developing now and wholly coming ahead is wonderful happy harmony, our 'song' of perfected life. Steps are lovely and interesting.

We are given a lovely synopsis of superb developmental growth in the life-symbolism of a *tree*. Roots, trunk, leaves, flowers, fruit. Imagine the creative progress in these five. We learn this and much more in **The Seed** lecture.

A flower and fruit; archangel Bethelda tells us – "Be love, your angel self, that through your *beauty* God's splendor is revealed."

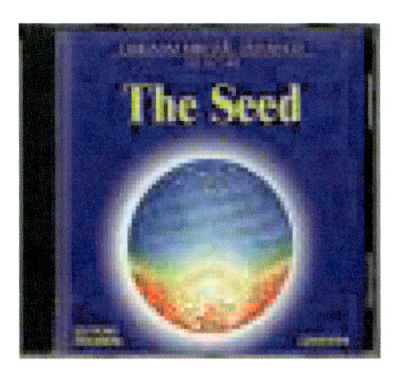

The fruit, as you know – our fruit of loving kind service to others – is beautifully utmost. A whole story of lovely realization is in your CD, 'The Seed'. Millions have learned beautifully from this lecture.

One's flowering of inner beauty and fruit of joyful service add nicely, ever.

A principle means for realizing perfected wholeness is in *hearing*. Our sixth sense is sensing what a person is thinking or going to say. Our developing seventh sense is straight intuitively sensitive hearing.

As ever, the world's top sensitive masters have intuitively heard straight from above, like we see in archangel Bethelda's white above her.

For realizing superb wholeness, the Bulgarian master teacher Peter Deunov gave us this reality about love.

"Human love changes and varies,
Spiritual love varies but doesn't change,
Divine love neither changes nor varies. It grows."

Well, one of our nice jobs is to amplify higher our love, through spiritual to *divine*.

Again, admiring and relating to divinities above helps a lot. Also, it's true that *we* are both human and divine. One of the big ways to realize our divinity is here in this quote from the book, 'Man's Two Nature's, Human and Divine'.

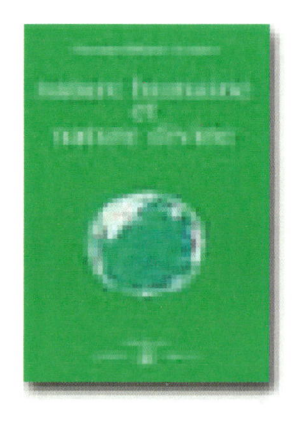

"Once a being has succeeded in creating a divine image of himself, this image will have a beneficial effect on all living creatures, on animals, plants and stones, on all Nature, because he will be emitting rays of light, forces and vibrations that will bring order, balance and harmony wherever he goes."

A lovely divine image is illustrated in archangel Bethelda's Presence. This divinity is also illustrated in symphonic chorales. A core of our realized loving wholeness is in realizing God's image within - not His likeness, but rather his image. A God seed and image is within every person.

God's image within us is illustrated in nature's divine portrait here for you.

Our Universe Within and Above

Inner pentagram, oneself.
Outer pentagram, the living universe.

Our Initiate Virtues

Philosopher's Stone Malkuth, **earth** *kindness legs*
Our legs carry us to where we can help others do good.

Fount of eternal life   Yesod, **moon** *justice* corresponding to the pure life   ***Hands*** are used to make a just distribution.

Universal panacea   Tiphareth, **sun** *love* the light that cures all ills   The ***mouth*** appeases anger, uttering words of consolation and healing.

Magic mirror   Daath *wisdom* showing the depths of eternal wisdom, enabling us to see and know all things   Our ***ears*** are used to understand and penetrate divine wisdom.

Magic wand Kether *truth* the caduseus of Hermes
the power to work miracles   With *eyes* we gaze on truth.

God's kindness, justice, love, wisdom and truth, **realized, applied,** both with one's motivated development and one's kind loving service.

How we're directly helped from Above is magnificent.

Here is how doctors, nurses and patients, plus nearby city residents at the lower right, are beautifully inspired.

New York City's Cornwall Park archangel *inspires* doctors, nurses and patients in Cornwall Hospital below, and the people in the lower left city.

Cornwall Archangel

Archangels are close, wonderfully inspiring us.

Blue archangel Bethelda gave sensitive intuitive master Geoffrey Hodson sixty seven pages for us, now in the book, "The Brotherhood of Angels and Men".

Archangel Bethelda

Bethelda speaks to us through her red below.

For education she says, "This is the way of the teacher – first to uplift the soul, secondly to expand the mind, thirdly to vivify the understanding, and fourthly to coordinate body, mind and soul.

In conclusion she tells us, "Be love, your angel self, that through your beauty God's splendor is revealed."

Utmost Aspirations

Clearly feeling our divine image within and appreciating our developing seventh sense of intuitive hearing, what then may one's hearty good aspirations be? There are plenty. You understand.

That stereo speaker was material. It is the earth thing that sounds out music, and represents the vocal self that outpours our creative aspirations, like *writing* music, poetry, doing creative good.

Since age seventeen I've aspired to creative service. Well, let's make a list of creative aspirations. OK?

Teaching

Healing

Bringing loving harmony

Clarifying one's loving heart

Divine love

Mental clarity, high and whole

Learning

That's seven. I love the last one, learning. One finds that he/she learns more after college. I have a masters, and a doctorate for experience. And I'm learning more each year, and my learning directly aids the creative outpour, helping others, oneself, and above.

Regarding Above, there are some nice realities – heaven is in-part here, in our joyous, loving, creative blessings of perfected harmony. The good that we do also aids Above. We even sanctify the Supreme Being when we see beauty and beam, "Ah such beauty. Sanctify Thee dear God." That's another reality in nature. God's presence is in every being and atom; and we, gifted greatly on earth, can even sanctify Him.

And nature's principle that what you give you too receive, happens. In sanctifying God, when seeing and feeling beauty, a little sanctity too returns.

A superb aspiration that more and more are doing now each generation is working with *Light*.

Every Being here and above is working with divine Light – we're, in an inner sense, *solar*.

Way above in the upper Tree of Life, the divinities there experience eternal unity.

Our aspirations add to our lasting harmony and unity with all. Let's pick one to realize further – clarifying one's loving heart.

Yes, it's vitally important to raise and clarify the heart, one's love. One of the things you learn about Nature within is that raising continually the quality and perfection of our love is singly the most empowering thing to do. In India it's known as kundalini. We are speaking of our inner male-female empowering union. It is physically a third flow in our spine, blue upward and around the brain. When we develop our inner male female polar empowerment we get this blue flowing up the spine. This is an empowering means for accelerated evolutionary growth, an utmost aspiration.

You will see it working with everyone in our last section, the 'Solar Living' story.

To clarify one's loving heart feels fabulous, and everyone is working at it a bit to a lot. That truth about divine love given us by Peter Deunov is a nice element. Feeling, realizing and enacting divine love feeds to the Sun, to the divinities above and even to Supreme Being dear God.

You know how things in life come together. It's called the law of corresponding events, directly aided by near divinities in the invisible realms. My writing this and your reading is a corresponding event.

So a biggest aspiration is, yes, to Learn.

In the future I feel that people will be learning more through their seventh sense of intuitive hearing than from reading. And entertainment won't be Hollywood, it'll be as it's been for tens of millennia, mainly Wesak. You'll experience Wesak in the beginning of 'Solar Living', in the opening chapter 'Sublime Mountain'. People experience and learn beautifully.

Let's create a nice vital learning. We understand that one of the key things for progress is one's 'priorities'.

Priority Order
Ordering One's Life Priorities

Put these five priorities in their order of importance for you, the most important first.

Happy life progress
Living one's full life-span
Service given to others   (e.g. family)

Perfected health
Divine love

You have priorities that are specific to you. List them in order of importance.

Yours

1. _____
2. _____
3. _____
4. _____
5. _____

Here are mine, in order.
1. Divine love
2. Service given to others
3. Working with light
4. Happy life progress
5. Perfected health
6. Living my full life-span

Richard

Superb Wonderful Wealth

Every century there's brilliant wealth bestowed. Fifteen millennia ago Egypt's emperor Ra Ta said, "Have trust and faith." 6,400 years ago Hermes Trismegistus gave us the whole story of life in two pages, his 'Emerald Tablet'. In the fifth century BC Heraclitus told us about life being like a violin and bow – how things are at once individual and together.

Are these bars together or apart, or both?
Right, they're both together and apart.

Heraclitus says, ""They do not apprehend how being at variance it agrees with itself literally, how being brought together with itself there is a connection working in both directions, as in the bow and the lyre."

Again, truth 'sings'. Hmm. Isn't that – "bringing together" – in *two words* saying what we mostly do?

Then five hundred years later Jesus gave us a lot of 'bringing together'. "Whoever drinks from my mouth shall become as I am, and I myself will become he, and the hidden things will be revealed to him." Our harmonious union thrives with intuitive joyful hearing.

A nice nugget came to us in the 16th century, from the visionary master Nostradamus.

"To a humble family will fair child be born

from a Balkan country will this Eagle fly
to dwell in the land of the Coq
his name the same as mine
the world will long recall
his voice the peoples of the earth will hear
and following upon upheaval and disaster
a New Age will be born."

This Eagle has flown magnificently, giving us over 6,500 lectures in forty nine years. The land of the Coq is France. Nostradamus's first name is Michael. The 'Eagle's' name is Omraam Mikhael Aivanhov.

Today's greatest wealth is in simply 110 books, the forty of Geoffrey Hodson and seventy of Omraam Mikhael Aivanhov. We don't have to reinvent the wheel. Life and nature's greatest is channeled from Above to us, as ever.

Here's an example in verse. This from *way* up, through Archangel Bethelda.

**"I would sing to you of joy,
the joy of the Gods
as they revel in the land of joy.
The land of joy is the land of dreams,
where every dream comes true.
Where every thought and answering thought
thrills with joy.
The land of joy is the land of the Gods,**

there lives the God in man;
For men are Gods, and the Godly part
dwells in the land of the Gods.
The land of joy is beyond the mind,
through the gates of eternal peace.
Angels share that land with men,
and these are the Gods who sing;
Thrills of gladness fill the air,
by joy we live and breath;
Everything there is full of joy,
like bursting buds of spring;
Throughout all the land is the freshness of
morn, of dew, of bud, of flower.
Lightly the angels pass on their way,
wafted on wings of joy;
Nature wears a perennial smile,
a smile that is ever new;
Laughter rings through the woods and dells,
for the joy of eternal spring."

"Angels share" – again, **togetherness.**

"Nature's perennial smile" and "Eternal Spring" – our progressing joyious Golden Age, God's kingdom of heaven on earth.

Eternal Spring and heaven on earth correspond with the upper Tree of Life's eternal unity, heaven eventually everywhere.

We know about the wonderful realms in the cabbalistic Tree of Life, and also another planet in the universe. UFO people are on a planet thirty light years out. Their spiritual understanding is as ours was, a few thousand years ago. They are shorter in height with bigger heads. They are scientifically advanced. For UFO fuel they use atomic element 106, that has a half-life of half an hour and puts a 50,000 volt square wave on their flyer surface, making it antigravity propelled, and much more.

Most advanced of all peoples are earth's Agarthans, who are over 6 ½ feet tall and live around 450 years each life. The Agarthan's leader is, as always, Melchizadek, mentioned in the Old Testament. Melchizadek is ever-living, like the divinities highest in the Tree of Life. Melchizadek is also guider for earth's seven orders of angels, and partner to the Tree of Life's highest regent, Metatron. Agarthan people occasionally come up to earth's surface to help a person. It happened for me a few years ago.

I prayed, "Dear God, I've done everything I can to increase my inner male-female polarity. Please help."

A few nights later I was lightly awake and saw the etheric body of a lady, upside down, right over me! I silently looked at her for 3 hours, then got up. Wow!

Three weeks later I went to my Buy-right grocery store. I was the only customer there. A clerk even walked away. After a few minutes I was walking by the store's diary products and in the distance saw a lady. Looking, as I filled my small basket, I saw her three more times down aisles. Then, she was twelve feet ahead of me looking at detergents. At Mt. Shasta, in the town's grocery store, an Agarthan man was seen who bought some detergent, paying with gold.

The lady at my front was seven feet tall, and dressed similarly to when she was with me at night. She turned and looked at me smiling.

I too smiled at her and thought, "I should smile with sunlight," and did so. Then she too smiled at me, widely, with sunlight.

That was precisely what I needed, the inner male-female empowering wealth beautifully flowing further every year.

Here's a place the polarity wisdom is available for you.

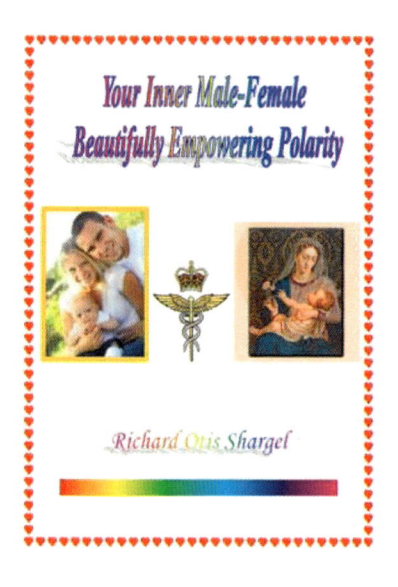

Contents

One's Inner Male-Female Union

Hearing – Symbolism, the Higher Language –
Dreams, Significant Happenings

Angel Speaking at Night Through Cat Sunny

Polarity and Family

Giving and Receiving – Life, Nature's Lovely
Laws of Progress

My Prayer for Inner Male-Female Union –
Most Gorgeous Result

Another Lovely Blessing for Us Today

Singing One's Divine Love –
Your Solar Heart Here and Above

Divine Brilliance Through Archangel Bethelda

Our Magnificent Polar Life-Wholeness

Attainment Now, Globally

Your Solar Future   Divine Loving Harmony

Being Your Mini-Sun

Heavenly Father and Divine Mother, *everything* polar in Nature, helps tremendously. For example, water dissolves salt, as you know. Masculine is out-going, feminine is receptive. Water receives, water is feminine.

If you're a male and in water you can receive polar power beautifully, "Oh, lovely water, divine loving light to you." If you are a female and in sunlight, "Oh, lovely sun, divine loving light to you."

Every presence of a person of complementary gender - she or he - helps one another polarity-wise.

Togetherness and complementary beauty splendidly abounds. Avian Verse dramatizes your presence among our fabulous angels of air. Much is learned.

Avian Verse

Brilliant Ballet from Above

In the 1960's, as a medical service worker, an inner voice led me to begin a study of philosophies, religions and spiritual truths. I eventually became aware of the teachings related to Jesus' own training among the Essenes, with France a likely source. Although I had read a few of Master Aivanhov's books on nutrition and symbolism, it was discovering a gold label *Fraternite B;anche Universelle* that I became nearly overwhelmed with joy at what this meant.

History's entire Universal White Brotherhood of initiates, adepts and sages, by both lineage and fraternity, were seen linked through the work of Masters Peter Deunov and this Omraam Mikhael Aivanhov – an action of profound vitality for humanity and the world's future.

Here then, is what happened for both me and you.

I live on a hill overlooking San Francisco Bay, with acres of meadow and wetlands in between. The view encompasses two mountains, distant cities, three bridges, and vast reaches of hills and salt water. One afternoon I stood on the rear deck in a fifty-mile gale in rapt fascination, watching a flock of swallows play in the vigorous cross-gusts. High winds swirled every which way. With superb skill the swallows deftly danced, I sharing their joy right through the final surprise. All of a sudden, from two hundred feet over the meadow, one swallow froze its wings in a blazing fast shallow dive. Imagine a bird six inches wide from one hundred and fifty yards away on an arrow-straight path hitting forty miles per hour through gale cross-gusts, zipping thirty feet past your head. Mother Earth's eloquent chorus of meaningful was just beginning.

I decided to begin predawn meditations at the rear of my garden where the view of sunrise upon the entire region is most direct. The third day began magically.

5:45 a.m. early June A quiet of incredible softness.

An awakening of infinite beauty bursting with promise rises through vistas of sea, wetland, meadow and distant cities right before you. There, resting on the hills of the sunrise-to-be, a soft pregnant cloud pillow veiled with color. Just now, all the Earth scintillates with portent. And there to the right, from the Bay shallows, an avian ballet begins, as a line of eight calling Canadian Geese sweeps below you over the meadow, climbing in a giant three-quarter mile circle toward you. A circle of flight anointing the sacred sun in a moment to rise, sanctifying earth and saying, "You have it well within you. Go for it. Now"

The next morning at dawn a third avian ballet, equally wondrous, begins. Geese fly a line of circles up towards you. Then, a few days later, at sunrise meditation another group of sea birds fly circles up towards you. This happens six time in this three weeks. Next, a Great Snowy Egret, away from its accustomed flyway, discovers a gentle updraft over the meadow. First it glides a perfect circle a quarter of a mile in front below. Then uphill closer another circle, and with perfect ease another and another, until it circles high above with you at the center, then behind with two more, all coasting in the constant breeze toward you.

    Now the imperative is firmly ingrained, and as well the shape of tasks ahead, directed to start with something that could be begun now, done well and thoroughly. Even so, the next morning before dawn, during my meditation, an old thought surreptitiously pokes its nose up, "With all my faults and shortcomings compared with the magnitude of the work ahead, can I really do this?" Immediately the innate harmony of Sun and Earth sings through air angels again. A Canadian Goose flew straight up the meadow. In five years I had not seen one goose over my meadow. Now there were nine in three days. This fellow, with all the concentration he could muster, flew swiftly straight over my head, house, and vehicle parked in front, as if to convey, "Really. What in heaven's name do you need? Claim the opportunity! It is yours. Cannot you see, in the exquisite harmony all around, that none of what you need to do is difficult? Just keep up the momentum. Don't ever stop. Press joyfully onward. Shed the excess: let

the creative energies flow .. let Nature happen. It can be so easy.

You humans struggle so much. Which of our bird movements takes undue effort? Be like Swallow, Canadian Goose and Great Snowy Egret. Cultivate the supreme joy of flying high, effortlessly."

That three weeks of high experience was the most wondrous great thing ever in my life. And, of course, this is for you, too. I realized then that angels of air were singing beautifully for us.

Then, years later, I realized *more* where this divine help to us came from.

In his last year of life, the master teacher O.Mikhael Aivanhov said "After my transition I will then be helping you all." Well, he is. And he was involved in creating this avian verse aid through air angels and birds for us.

The next chapter here corresponds. The chapter is on this subject of our together serviceful help.

Collectivity, Divine Loving Togetherness

In my book for children, 'Sunshine Playground', after emphasizing love, it was right to emphasize loving *harmony*.

Big illustrations for harmony are our beautiful symphonic chorales, church choruses, and other utmost music. When we have a beautiful harmony in civilization it'll fully be the Golden Age.

Littlest children understand. "I love the harmony with my mommy. This is where I came from before I was born – a realm of perfect harmony and light."

Well, good soul, let's experience some harmony again in song – verse.

Invitation

in a dream I spied a goddess
beckoning radiant from a balcony
one whisper 'cross a moonlit mist

transformed upon sky's pastel sheen
in heady portent, pain to joy away did burn
like liquid pearl there softly shone
true mirrored bliss, bold life eterne

She whispering with a smile
no mortal'd feign,
"What more would now you have me do?"

> when on an instant..
> thorn of karma gone!
>
> I bowed with contrite heart
> "Love incarnate, e'er remain!"
>
> and turning, drew I nearer
> more to rapture's throne
> while in my heart
> her warming image kissed

That was the first time I met a Divine Mother representative. It was a lovely inner female-male union polarity event. Another occurred during meditation, when again I saw a helpful Divine Mother representative. The third was the wonderful tall lady from Agartha.

Then too, of course, every time we are with a person of complementary gender our inner polarity is enhanced.

Your polarity is so vitally superb to *advance.* Any way you can advance your empowering inner polarity is superb, helping you and all.

Being a musician I had an inspiration to sing to above, with these lines.

Midnight Metamorphosis

Diamonds glaze a burnished sky
becoming ebony
The sun's last blush at last retired in
pastelled memory

A gentle kiss of stillness tucks each
being in its fold
And tenderly bestirs afresh each
form in Nature's mold

There dwells inscribed within
each star
a dream in secret rhyme
Where angels speak, where
Love herself weaves
mysteries sublime

Therein somehow, beloved dear,
we brothers all do play
While children of a younger year
will welcome earth's new day

Now night, her garments tucked about earth's
gently guarded sleep
Tends minds that on tomorrow's stage with livened
hearts will leap

Rest well in nightfall's slumber pure
Each life a sacred trust secure

The Celestial Queen with brood well-nursed
Directs by causal energy rehearsed

Our destiny affirmed again as dwellers of one Heart
Its beat a rhythm sanctifying Charity's full part

Where She Herself in radiant harmony and bliss
With understanding mirth! Bestows
life's raptured natal kiss.

Solar Harmony
Happy Wise Working with Light

Our Celestial Queen, Divine Mother, births greatly here and everywhere. She of course has magnificent solar empowerment from the Supreme Being. Another way of saying this reality is that Divine Mother and Heavenly Father are a major part of God's creative Being. Through our Sun, God's divine loving Light nourishes us all and every atom on earth. It's known that, way in the future our other planets will have people living on them. Solar harmony is beautifully enriching and learning to us.

The sun channels our greatest lovely learning. How? People in mainly Europe know. Eastern Europe is the world's fastest learning, nicely developing area now. Bulgaria is where it happened a century ago. Now Russia has eight hundred study groups in the universal wisdom initiate science teaching. We have 70 volumes of these highest lectures translated into English.

You had a teaspoon of this lovely, advanced wisdom channeled from way above, in our talk about the Nostradamus Eagle, Omraam Mikhael Aivanhov, and his lecture 'The Seed'. Master Aivanhov told us what his mother did to tremendously give him 'gold' before he was born.

This gift of mothers during their child's gestation is called 'Galvanoplasty', 'plating gold'.

Just after conception Mikhael's mother prayed, "Dear God, please may this person be a leading spiritual teacher of mankind." And he is the best, most fully helpful wisdom master teacher of all history, partly because it's recent, in today's advanced understanding. O. Mikhael Aivanhov has channeled virtually *all* we need, generations-ahead.

Our contemporary life-wisdom is definitely solar.

One of the elements is 'Link with your inner spring of sunlight'. Another is 'Be your mini-sun'.

It's known. Earth is gradually becoming a mini-sun. Like the moon, the planets mirror light back to the sun; yet too, moon, planets and people also mirror back *life*-light to the Sun.

This is a principle in Nature. Humans' inspired service radiates to heaven upward. The truth, 'A child's smile radiates to the most distant star' works beautifully with us lots of ways.

And so, collectively, when hundreds of millions of us learn and use these advanced life-truths, our golden age of God's kingdom of heaven on earth becomes achieved.

To be a mini-sun, with accelerated evolutionary growth, read the Aivanhov lectures. www.prosveta.com. What's mainly most key? – to have a high *priority* for faster evolutionary development. I did this years ago and feel three and a half lifetimes ahead. What you learn, like and do is yours the rest of this life and lifetimes-ahead.

Our Peter Deunov quote was about divine love. Here is my favorite Omraam Mikhael Aivanhov quote, from his book 'Spiritual Alchemy'.

"He who possesses purity in his heart, wisdom in his intellect, love in his soul and truth in his spirit can transform and improve everything."

Our developing seventh sense of intuitive hearing gives us truth to our spirit. However, much *quicker*, truth to our life and spirit comes with reading our world's top master initiate teachers. Another truth that stays with me is the Aivanhov recommendation to identify with God's image within oneself.

That adds a lot to our divinity and servicefully empowered inner beauty. And, you remember, "When you experience beauty you can sanctify God."

Sancifying the Supreme Being when feeling nature's beauty is a way of beaming Light. When we see beauty we may radiate "Sanctify to You beloved God." We dearly love working with Light.

We are Light, a God-sprout of His divine loving Light through the spiritual sun.

Learning to work with Light is so beautifully superb – we love it. You will too then have tens of thousands of brothers and sisters who study and do the Teaching.

6400 years ago Hermes Trismegistus channeled a lot to us about Solar wisdom. His "Emerald Tablet" gives us a two page treasure on solar truths.

The Emerald Tablet
Hermes Trismegistus

Truly, without deceit, certainly and absolutely:

That which is Below corresponds to
that which is Above,
And that which is Above corresponds to
that which is Below,
In the accomplishment of the Miracle of One Thing.
And just as all things have come from One,
through the Mediation of One,
So all things follow from this One Thing
in the same way.

Its Father is the Sun;
Its Mother is the Moon.
The Wind has carried it in his Belly.

Its Nourishment is the Earth.

It is the Father of every completed Thing in the whole world.

Its Strength is intact if it is turned toward the Earth.

Separate the Earth by Fire: the fine from the gross, Gently and with great skill.

It rises from Earth to Heaven,
and then descends again to the Earth,
and receives Power from Above and from Below.
Thus you will have the Glory of the whole World.
All Obscurity will be clear to you.
This is the strong Power of all Power
because it overcomes everything fine and penetrates everything solid.

In this way was the World created.
From this there will be amazing Applications,
because this is the Pattern.

Therefore am I called Thrice Greatest Hermes,
having the three parts of the Wisdom of
the whole World.

Herein have I completely explained the
operation of the Sun.

The miracle of One Thing is obviously Life's fabulous evolving and creative perfection.

Father, Mother and the Power of all Power is our inner male-female empowering divine unity. Our major power, in this sense, is our kundalini third spine flow, bringing us huge divine male-female empowerment, needed for aiding our growing golden age of loving harmony and unity.

So here for you, beloved dear, is our true science fiction story of the Golden Age just begun. Our Aquarian age began in February 1986., and is beautifully full and whole to come.

Our Luminous World Family

Solar Living — Story of Our Solar Future, Life Centuries Ahead

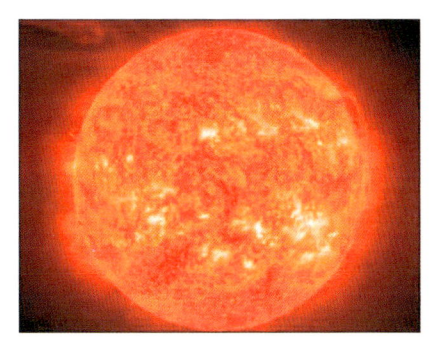

The Known Future - Clairvoyant Foresight

Today incidents of foreknowledge are relatively common. The sensing of events prior to their occurrence, answers in prayer, foresight through contemplation or meditation, hearing what another is thinking to say, certain dream episodes, are links ahead. Life irreversibly flows forward. This moment that we feel together *is* the future. The imminent forthcoming may be sensed, and sometimes even seen or heard.

It is the clairvoyant initiatic master of universal wisdom, a leading world magus such as Geoffrey Hodson or Omraam Mikhael Aivanhov who, hearing with tremendous clarity, gives us preciously magnificent discoveries.

We ask not why, nor how; rather it is our role merely to marvel in the unfolding of the life-transformative wisdom of the intelligent universe, endowed from living realms way above. The story "Solar Living" casts the intuitive sensitive master's vision of God's Heaven on Earth. The solar civilization's people ahead we may now nicely emulate. Harmonious perfection breathes closer to fullness, even our childrens' lives beautifully whole in luminous divine loving brotherhood.

Chapter One

Sublime Mountain

The moon enters Taurus, earth's hour of Spring's joyous bloom, as the Tree of Life's genii focus heavenly fire amongst the convening initiates. Every cell of life and atom of stone resonates with the hour of Spring's wakening, Mt. Everest's beautiful deva radiating music and life worldwide. A tall figure arrives by astral travel, his first moment in the courtyard of the mountain cathedral. Torrents of overwhelming Light rush through him as he enters, taking a seat with bewildered joy.

As a solar archangel breathes an opening anthem through the gathering, the man thrills to the celestial harmony of the Spheres, feeling his teacher's presence through the luminous warmth of one of the teacher's aides. While the man's feelings beam his need to enter the master university at large, he feels the solar regent Michael approaching and hears the instruction, "Talk to the child of your creative heart." With the word 'child' the man receives an image of a baby shriveling and wonders, "What is this child? And how am I not fully talking to the child? Maybe the image represents my work, or even somehow, me."

The spoken vision which the astral form of the man vividly recalls bears crucially on his mind, and he regards the message as vitally important. Entering into the great hall of the initiates, he hovers before the altar of the universe, around which is gathered in conference – as for millennia - several great masters of universal truth.

The intensity of light, fullness of colors and celestial music continue to reverberate through the man, just as he experiences at sunrise, yet now with a more familiar sense of divine presence. The subject being presented in conference is 'sacred voice of heart'. The man knows immediately now that his baby is his own contribution to the living cosmos. From his healing experience he feels, "The vitality of my work needs a healthier physiology. I must train and exercise my thoughts to guide, part by part, piece by piece, the life I have given birth to, but have left too much in the hands of the natural world. I must accelerate breathing life and structure with my creative gift to humanity and above."

Noticing people he has seen before at home conferences, and a few brotherly friends, he feels the Wisdom Master's creative cosmic light and divine love in a brilliant formula-prayer resounding through every cell of his being. The healer then anticipates what he may experience rising back at 2000 meters.

Now near a fringe of the conference grounds, with the Everest summit directly ahead, he feels, hears and sees the beautiful huge mountain deva, luminously vibrating with the Music of the Spheres.

Thrilling in inspiration before the majesty of the rainbow-colored archangel, the man pauses in contemplative focus before the assembly's emanating magnificence of new life, and feels, through his intuitive powers that not only the earth's brotherhood of Light but the entire universe of loving harmony is strengthened, their powers being more focused and effective in unique lovely tasks, in loving unity serving the throne of the Absolute, our source of all life, through and above even the highest Tree of Life realm, Kether. Fully energized and inspired, the worker glides back to greet friends.

Three also present astrally, enjoying their merging in presence and thought together, and seeing Merrien come their way hail him, "Oh beloved dear brother of light, how wonderful to have you with us. Tell us what is happening with you? You seem as bright in good feeling as even the grand deva. Isn't the conference splendid?" So delighted to see his sister and two brothers, he joins their ecstasy of good will. "Ah your auras blend with such beauty of music, how superbly perfect I feel this moment with you. Aren't the heavens especially magnificent in these heights, transmitting all the universe's gifts to our millions of brothers and sisters? From the moment I arrived I'm sure you've felt, as have I, the creatively building emanative thought-forms growing from the inspiration of all masters of our Brotherhood, so beautifully in harmony."

"Yes!" remark all three, in divine loving harmony. "Our master teachers are even alone replenishing, vivifying and rebuilding ever more splendorously the harmony of our ancestors. Thank goodness we are one world in wholehearted brotherhood and don't have to contend with the old boundaries of selfish-interest, nationalism and all the rest. The Tree of Life's sephira Chokmah at last governs through the work of the archangels, divinities and those of recent millennia who've put their hands to our wheel of life.

Isn't it wonderful, dearest Brother, what the master Teachers taught today about furthering our sanctifying power of powers in order to help, with ***Telesma***, birthing children on the planet Uranus?"

Merrien is exhilarated at the mention of the manifesting element, telesma. "From the moment divinities taught us how to use the power of telesma, I have been practicing. I am beaming through me telesmatic cosmic Light and Love to the planet, nourishing Uranus' living forms, those beautifully delicate beings. I am beaming them divine-loving light toward their luminous destiny. And in so doing, I feel the resonant glow of Chokmah and Binah's pure music-lightning joyously throughout me."

As Merrien describes his lovely experience, the Himalayan sunrise spreads a thousand hues of brilliance in front above. Grandly inspiring bursts of radiant cloud, over what feels like the whole universe, sings choruses in triple forte to the souls of the sister and three brothers, filling them even more with telesmatic illumined Life.

Though no one mentions it, a momentary reflection of something an Egyptian sage said seven millennia ago sends a precious hymn through us. The tall sister, in her aural raiment of dazzling-light rainbow colors, invokes a prayer to the ever-loved God of all Being.

"Holy most sacred Highest Source, Throne of God." Singing in upward tone, she pronounces the name of God in region Kether. "e h h h e e e y y a a a a a." A rush of living energy courses through every being assembled, to the very root and rock of the hillside.

"Father empowering Spirit, divine form-giving Mother, I rise in my upper self to You, returning our gathered cosmic Light and divine Love to Thee- divinities all. We gratefully receive your splendidly thrilling, enriching and luminous Presence through this magnificent Himilayan sunrise. Thank you from our deepest heart for the wisdom and inspiration garnering through this year's Wesak conference of masters here and Above.

We pray that the evolutionary increase of living forms throughout the solar system be at least as powerfully harmonious as we on earth - even as perfect as enjoyed throughout your splendorous life-giving Tree of Life.

Haloed God, most sacred and high be your name Yod Heh Vau Heh. Thy Will is most bountifully everywhere manifest."

As the solar disk appears above the horizon of Himalayan peaks, the devout family of four, among earth's fraternity of Light, fly to greet two friends eight kilometers near. A waking of higher empowerment continues through the people of the earth and solar system, felt with compassionate joy by Merrien, his sister Marria and their younger brothers.

Near the Temple's entrance the four disciples discover the new pair on their way out and are impressed with an element of earnest devotion. Now Merrien's family greets the two travelers from their home region. "Warm greetings dear brotherly friends. How splendidly wonderful to see and be with you. We are both impressed and enriched in admiration by your dedication to the high purpose of this lovely Wesak conference, traveling all the way here in body. We feel with delight your experience with the spiritual grandeur of the mountains and temple! As we draw close into combining auras with you, we anticipate the ecstasy-of-merge, and are specially happy feeling that you also anticipate and know."

A ring of seven mountains from Annapurna to Everest enclose the sacred site, at which for millennia initiates have annually gathered, at this same moment in early-Spring.

The six vitally expanding figures, radiant with Light and divine Love for one another and their common service, appears from afar as a micro-galaxy, a lustrous embryo millennia in gestation, now perfectly whole by their devotional convening in such beautiful luminous harmony.

The two sisters and four brothers arrive at the Temple's garden to hear the conference's benedictory instruction, through the wisdom masters' nearby source, regent Michael of our solar realm Tiphareth.

One of his archangels speaks. "Children of fiery divine Light, people of planet earth, the time of a whole flowering of your solar soul has arrived. Your evolutionary advancement to harmonious world brotherhood, with your Kundalini strength creatively risen, birthing life itself through the power of your words, is ready to expand to bring birthing on other planets.

Recall these three elements of the Teaching. 1. As your thought is founded on the ideal of your creative task, so too the creative forces of the cosmos are met, by the principle 'like vibrations harmonize by luminous loving affinity'. And so the illumined Intelligences far above hear and come in aid to help you. 2. As long as you have made friends with one divine idea, as long as you love it and nourish it making it your constant companion, it will put you in touch with all others and they, in turn, will give to you greatly. And 3. Sanctify the sublime height in every soul and being.

These three keys give you much of the creative force to enact life. Such expansive work makes you higher creators with earth's role throughout the universe.

Further your skills of male-female polar harmony. Practice applying your Buddhic body of divine Love to direct creative thought-forms together, as one spiritual people. As visionaries, beam your creative love to vibrate in harmony with what we have already established as budding life on the planets, adding your own special qualities from earth, Malkuth.

And therein too, secure your own future in our universe, enhancing our beloved solar civilization's participation in building life through the universe, so that substantially and most truly we realize further the kingdom of God, heaven throughout all regions of our beautifully living cosmos.

The details of your inner work, what to do to project your Kundalini empowerment outward in creative life-giving throughout the Kingdom, will come to you telepathically, as you direct your intuitive contemplation into the higher realms, for example resonating with divine Mother and heavenly Father, where motion originates in the sephiroth Chokmah and Binah, in our Tree of Life's high region, Atziluth.

So now work at your luminous helms with confidence. Steer upward through the Temples of Cosmic Light and the Divinely Loving Spheres of the most sacred holies. Advance your evolutionary growth continuing in the initiatic schools of Light - astrally at night, in meditative practice during the day.

Help build further our luminous worlds, and

teach those less advanced in their learning, sanctifying all, spirit to spirit, giving praise and thanks to the Highest."

Chapter Two

Breakfast in Sofia

As Merrien and his sister of light Marria prepare to return homeward, their brother Davienn gathers the scores for the conference's music. These songs sing in his higher bodies, memorable for the work of expanded life-giving ahead. Brother Aumier makes an etheric talisman from the truth, "True humility is to pray, to have deep respect for all things sacred and to safeguard what is sacred within oneself and around one."

As the family journeys northwestward home the prana of the conference and sunrise continue enriching and strengthening them as they remain in astral flight together. Their thoughts focus on their own role in participation with Binah's primal form-giving power.

Realizing that their bodies will strengthen from nutrition, the four look forward to a breakfast together with the home brotherhood, who are sensed now within the approaching aura of the city.

Sofia is peacefully still. No sounds interfere, from the magnetic commute rail, or from the personal vehicles and busses, propelled by their antigravity magnetism and solar power. Even talking in public is some by ESP, the city's people having access to our deific solar presence both day and night.

The whole experience of living has become luminously intimate, and each citizen of the universal brotherhood exercises her and his full faculties of sublime power. The earth too has become a mini-sun.

As the astral bodies of Merrien, Marria, Davienn and Aumier blend back into their meditating physical forms, the room and its sacred flowers and pictures resonate highly. An aura as that of the Tibetan temple can be felt all around one. The fasting which was useful in order to be at the conference, renders their spirit beautifully receptive, the presence of the Masters and Archangels feeling like a vitally breathing divine Love. Rejoined in their bodies, they concentrate their harmonious meditative repertoire silently together, deepening their furthered understanding and power recently gained.

After awhile they sing together a benedictory song of high celebration. Marria adds, "Esteemed beloved dear Brothers, I am thrilling to the living presence of the Tibetan sunrise, experiencing further how to enliven the sublime in people. It is a matter of beaming fiery telesma through the music of creative thought, synthesizing life - just as the heavenly fire through Kether and Tiphareth sculpture the living earth and planets. I sense you feeling these ways too. In a moment we will have the opportunity to practice our new gifts during breakfast."

The city of Sofia has retained all its sacred radiance, centuries now since the world catharsis. Where, during old times, one felt like remaining in silent meditation at an entire month's visit to Sofia, today the city's every grain of life, magnified more-so, sings rainbows of Light to the celestial realms a thousand times more, gracing every divine eminence throughout the universe.

As the brilliance of the period of the Bogomils in old times reflected the ancient universal wisdom, so too the earth's highest teaching center, Sofia's World University, - the worldwide Teaching for people of all endeavors and needs, - thrives forward across centuries ahead, in luminous strong nurture to the universe.

As their hearty breakfast beckons, - its harvest mainly from ocean farms, - the four maintain their meditation heights at their oval dining table of pale yellow crystal. They eat in silence, reveling in their nourishment, at once both physically and etherically.

Davienn beams a song to the solar regent Michael, while savoring his food and appreciating its solar origin. Aumier beams the words of one of the ancient mantra which have gathered enormous power over the millennia, "Holy, holy, holy Lord. Heaven and earth are full of Thy glory. Glory be to Thee, O Lord, most High." Then, adding:

> "I thrall responding, every cell aglow
> in heeding Deva's call
> a pulse within me breathing Light
> to fuel my effort's all
> as creatures of every shape and hue alike
> reform to earth's new day
> we brothers, sisters kin of Love and Light
> have a Kingdom's role to play."

Like a star perfectly emanating life, Marria, Merrien, Aumier and Davienn beam their Spirit in a focus of selfless, transparent power, strengthening and enriching their brothers and sisters throughout the solar system. Aumier and Davienn beam Telesma through poetry and music - Merrien and Marria through understanding creative thought in aid to the universal Brotherhood above. Even Uranus too is nurtured

Once again, their home temple resonates with subtle vibrations of solar spirit - to the distant corners of the universe - as the four in harmonious unison reverberate with the heart of the Teaching..

Love returns from their Uranian friends.

"Thank you, dear sisters and brothers. We play deliciously, absorbing your gifts instantly received. It is so beautiful to feel and experience us as one people, one in ideal and activity even with the entire great Universal Brotherhood throughout the Tree of Life.

We reflect your gifts of divinely loving telesma in solar Light back to you in our hearts and admiration, to you all, sanctifying life in the grand and glorious evolving expansion of our living universe.

We dearly love you. In livened furtherment, God's richest blessings be ever yours."

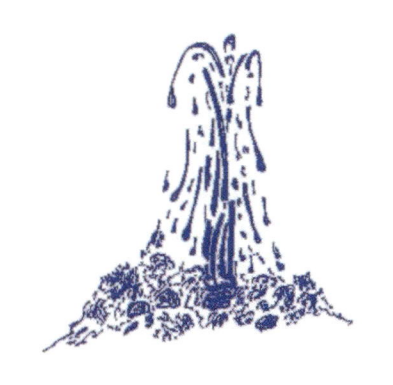

Chapter Three

The Market

    A heavenly music perfumes the air amongst shoppers busy in their gathering hour. Baskets of floral scented spirogeia, lemon lilac and astral heather lace the aisles of the outdoor market as the women tag needed items with their light-stili. Many recognize one another and thrill to warm embraces of heavenly light, even at a distance. In a unison of solar toned harmony the hearts of the shoppers, lights and sounds of the market resonate in harmony with the divine above, whose magic has steeped its dew into every element and corner of the marketplace. Where in ancient times a cacophony of disparate noises dispelled a few nature spirits, the age now and henceforth enjoys a perfected rhythm of inherent harmonies, attuned with care to the high divinities who gladly attend their fellow beings with utmost wisdom and love. The Golden Age is come, evident in every living presence, abounding with the common beneficence, each soul magnifying the efforts of his neighbor, in sum radiating end upon end glories to the heavens above, now descended into our very midst, each person inhaling the multinutritive essences of the solar logos, here steeped throughout the marketplace's fruits, vegetables and flowers in splendorous variety.

In the market's center, a light fountain cascades etheric power of intensely rich, pranic energy into each item of food. Thus retained, all of food's original vital solar energy remains for direct assimilation. Not only is the earth protected from environmental upheaval, but also the sun's pranic energy is maintained fully in all things, such as food, drinking water, and fabrics for clothing.

Into the radiance of the market glides Marria, fresh from silent transit through the public thoroughfare. She harbors an eager expectancy at what the sea farms may have produced in her absence - and equally more-so, whom she will meet of her many brothers and sisters in this, Bulgaria's Sophia, her happy home and global spiritual center.

Through Marria there breathes an exhilaration of luminous beauty, in the light and warmth of her presence. Her brothers and sisters, likewise replenishing their food supplies, grandly nourish all near and far,

What it means to be finally free of negative thought, feeling and action is everywhere additive in blessing, in synergy to all life. Earth responds to the unblemished good of her human inhabitants, its new regent, Uriel, with solar Michael, having freed negative's harm, in which people so often heeded low temptations. Uriel, Michael and Melchizadek help wonderfully.

Having elevated the reproductive instinct to high empowerment, mankind has purified and magnified this sacred force, men and women further claiming their birthright as emerging mini-Gods.

The path to stir the collective Kundalini forces into securely purified activity had been arduous and long, our learning being accelerated through hearing and adhering to the initiatic wisdom. Now all the world in resplendent eloquence testifies to the work of those millions who lent their creative quintessence to birth our magnificent solar civilization, radiant here every hour.

Immediately recognized, Marria is greeted with a joyful embrace by three of her sisters, "Ah, our beloved sister returns from her explorations at world conference, adding nourishment at home to her big Tibetan journey. You look so lovely luminous - Tell us!"

"Dearest ones, it is you too who appear with the aura of heaven about you. I am blessed to again be with you, and am so delighted at our presence here in the splendid market. Our lovely fountain of light reminds me of the Himalayan sunrise. You all must come with me next year and then you will know. Everyone experienced a most glorious furthering of their powers.

Life in the solar system is growing straight and strong, ever more magnificently. Our whole family of illumined beings in the Tree's hierarchy heralds your attainments, and smiles with pleasure at the bounty of the centuries ahead for us all. The Music of the Spheres is here for you to feel, experience and know.

Our choirs of archangels sing beautifully, adding and attuning our souls in joyous musical achieving.

I am interested to discover what new forms our innovative harvesters of the sea have provided. We are so gifted in these years - as our very perception expands, nature too diversifies her bounty of color, music and fragrances. Look. There is a new variety of lumifern. And lovely sea greens from the Sargasso Sea."

"Marria, you are a wonder. It is the dearest blessing to have you back with us. Yes, we will supremely enjoy together the celestial concert. We trust that our brothers Merrien, Aumier and Davienn are likewise bursting with good from the conference."

"You will hear! Aumier has brought us poetry, Davienn music, and Merrien, his initiatic healing work. The whole conference was as uplifting and perfect as ever.

The immediacy of the splendorous beings in our spiritual quest to God's universe is ever present, and most powerfully appointed. Great good attainment sings from every realm and plane of the Tree, our task of course continuing to increase the frequency and variety of our creative harmony with heaven."

The pleasant radiance of the marketplace accords well to the shoppers, a divine light of most agreeable comfort being clearly felt throughout aisles laden with produce from a gratefully purified planet. A long-cultivated focus of earth, human and celestial energies has cascaded into Sofia's heart; the education centers, homes, conference gathering halls and market-places. The market's varieties of nutritious food remind one of the global spiritual, universally life-enriching learning for all, now being provided by our world's schools and universities.

A perfectly coordinated, universal system of spiritually elevated education has evolved. World religions having merged, embracing the universal teaching with a single voice in unison, poetically portray truth in affinity with the wisdom of God's living Tree of Life. The 'one world' referred to by the sage's last words -- "Death is a happy bridge between this world and the next, which is one world" -- is more closely understood, to the gratitude of many beings above!, the magnificent work of sun's regent Michael allies the hearts of all men and women. And so confidently forward stride the world's children of divine Loving Light into yet further splendors to be.

Chapter Four

Choir of Angels

Returned now to her hearth of residence, Marria finds her brother Davienn in meditative rapture. Their family sanctuary resounds with the tone of sacred bells, glowing with the multihued aura of the flowered meadow. She loves joining her brother in his communion with the angelic divinities. In the sacred teaching, all souls are encouraged to engage and develop their lovely spiritual gifts. As the great music of the ages has ever shown humans how, - the music of the spheres having become itself heard through the sensitive genius of inspired composers, - Marria and Davienn tune their souls to solar music, emanating from the prime Source. And so there's happy rapture for the pair, their bodies resonating, every cell singing in unison with the divine chorus of the angelic Tree of Life, which archetypally births earth's beings.

Here then is method in action, cultivated through centuries, in which heaven's Light is breathed through one's soul, the high energies of divine light conveying magical telesma to our lives' well-being.

Opening to their luminous source above, perfectly reflected in God's seed within, Davienn and Marria by the perfected freedom of selfless concentration upon the celestial hierarchies, radiate life's choral symphony, experiencing the ecstasy of the blessed realms of perfected light through the heavenly music, beautifully bestowed to us through archangels.

Archangel Bethelda

The red below is her music to us.

Cosmic harmonies, ever beautiful, – in conveying one's heart near, and as well, to the fringe of the Infinite, – sing treasures enormously wonderful in essence and fullness.

All the old masters still remain, and are **heard** through an intimately communing awareness to the divine source, one's spirit and seventh sense now whole-hearing.

Even the old music instruments, with names such as Stradivarius, Amati, Guarnerius and Bergonzi, as well still channel masterworks through composer and violinist.

Free of awkward inharmonies, even in literature, citizens now as one world thrill to the eminence of grand art, born through centuries in golden tones of celestial light and song.

And so it is upon an impetus of fraternal love and devotion that Davienn and Marria, having relished together a taste of the angelic choir, call their brotherly and sisterly friends together.

Extrasensory communication through the luminous logos has become enjoyed with widespread expertise by most residents of Sofia and neighboring regions. The world's inhabitants are at last fully awake, their senses hugely expanded through conscientious achieving, according to each person's uniqueness, aided immensely by luminous beings throughout the beautiful Tree of Life.

Marria, sitting comfortably in her meditation sanctuary, tunes mentally into people's astral links, sensing live vibrations in her dear spiritual sisters and brothers. Their presence is felt. Marria knows she is with them all, and they with her. A smile illuminates the perfect features of her lovely face as the experience of their presence feels thoroughly superb.

Immediately she welcomes them all, embracing each with special recognition, honoring their communal presence.

Then all at once, in grateful response they beam their gratitude for this beneficent happy hour. A pause follows, wherein their unanimity of feelings radiate multicolors of light in loving harmony with the high illumined beings present.

Marria speaks, "Dearest beloved family, most treasured brothers and sisters. Your warmth is as the Sun itself. We in household here, Merrien, Aumier, Davienn and I, most cordially invite you to a gathering in the courtyard of the Temple of Divine Light, listening together to the celestial harmonies of the Angelic choirs and the Tree's Music of the Spheres. We plan to meet one hour before sunrise, the morning of our next full moon. We shall thrive above in magnified rapture of our luminous togetherness.

Afterwards we will share a meal, and then discuss preparations for the next arrival of a solar archangel. He is to be with us on the occasion of a solar flare, heralding the birth of sentient forms on the new planet, our tenth, Hermes.

The universe delightfully grows, and so precious it is playing our part. Therefore, what you sing my dears - a concert hour in the angels of solar Tiphareth's presence - shall be our next family's celebration."

With unbounded joy, glorious waves of lovely energy sing from the group, reverberating through the household, saturating the auras of the family four with the warmth of their loving hearts. With gladdest outpouring, the assembly affirms the angelic gathering to soon unfold.

Merrien, with joyous expectancy anticipating the celestial music, has returned to his work, coordinating for the region what remaining healing is necessary. Mainly for accident victims, the exercise of advanced subtle energy techniques, using Sunlight, restores the patient's inner perfection to a healthful luminous harmony. Medical science has long discovered means to treat the entire person instead of just symptoms. We've learned the science and methods of Solar respiration.

Most disease is gone, health becoming the maintenance of a perfected harmony, all body systems vibrating in unity with the splendorous Tree of Life.

Healing instruments extract and concentrate packets of telesma for rapid healing. With Merrien's health training giving him skills to focus solar telesma to ill people, he focuses his creative brilliance into powerful straight healing.

Today is Friday, June third. A patient, nutritionally depleted, with worn body systems due to hard overwork, is seen to also have a marked underfeeding of the brain from the nourishing solar plexus. As the man waits in the meditation anteroom, adorned with olive oil lamps, skylights open to the sun and sky focusing pranic telesma into the room, its walls display symbols creating bridges upward. The man feels calm, contemplating the splendor of the divine Sun. His consultation is brief, the man's systems being restored by application of a radiant field of solar Telesma feeding his needed resonant frequencies.

This Tree of Life in the universe also is *within each person*. Malkuth's earth regent is no longer Sandalphon. Earth's regent is Uriel. Up the central pillar is earth *Malkuth*, moon *Yesod*, sun *Tiphareth,* and *Kether* at the top. The rainbow embraces God's absolute realm, the *Ain Soph*.

Our human aura is enlivened with the seven rainbow colors. And moreso, our inner sprout of God has the Tree of Life's attributes.

Today, world systems of support to the eight billion living worldwide are in a phase of perfected-tuning. The earth is protected from environmental harm by humanity's transformation of negative feelings to mass ***divine love given earth***.

Three healing centers benefit from Merrien's creative help.

As the day of the celestial choir approaches, Aumier and Davienn remain happily immersed in study and meditation. Marria works in their home's garden - roses receive their archetypal form from Venus - cultivating garden plants which breathe the qualities of Netzach and Yesod's etheric beauty.

Marria's brilliance is a magnificent blessing to the brotherhood. As well, the perfection that her body, heart and mind have attained is an inspiration to people. Splendorous is God's handiwork, everywhere thriving, paramount in grace and sanctity. The garden too radiates its lovely vibrations to the celestial harmonies enjoyed here and above.

Life flames high and joyous. The city's sunlight is fiery liquid, the air impregnated with pranic telesama, waters of Kether purifyingly strengthening all inhabitants. The descent of sanctifying Telesma and ascent of divine love through the heart, mind and will of earth's brotherhood are in creative balance. The solar system is nourished from its loving human nucleus.

As the flare's birthing presence is felt emerging, a

word trumpets across the flash of the Tree's sephira Binah. Tzaphkiel, Binah's regent, is speaking an event being accomplished.

All the splendorous intelligent beings in earth's solar logos, Tiphareth, thrill to the birthing note. The enteric form of the new planet Hermes fills in with atoms of light, coalescing the planet's mass in a synergy of telesma birthing.

All members of the fraternal gathering are attentive to the symphony of Song radiating. Sunrise at Sofia unfolds in a heavenly rainbow of pristine brilliance with a melody from 'Hermes Trismegistus, Egyptian Bearer of Beautiful Wisdom', his "Emerald Tablet" that Jesus and most top masters know, singing in harmony through our solar ether.

Every cell of life sings its welcoming tone in response, the holy Tree and all its illumined presences do their archangelic tasks with renewed joy and incredible strengths, helping all. The planes of heaven and earth's solar living resonate in a loving accord of perfected unity.

Merrien, Marria, Davienn and Aumier are dazzled by the celestial music of the solar logos, and are inspired by the presence of the angelic brethren, as is each member of the brotherhood participating in the birthing of a sister planet.

Now, at the moment of the sun's emergence over

the horizon, all sing their unique lyric to the grand event - Marria of cosmic beauty; Aumier of divine love; Merrien of luminous light, and Davienn of God's nourishing Word.

The angelic chorus of moon's Yesod is then joined by those of the Tree's higher sephiroth. Every nerve is aglow. Light, strength and substance are firmly instilled. Everyone feels the glorious height, creatively eloquent in a solar symphony of divine Loving Light.

Live rays of Tiphareth's expansive majesty radiate to the most distant star. An ever thriving of new life, birthed each moment through this sacred living act of God, breathes life onward in sanctifying praise and thanksgiving to our heavenly Father and divine Mother, life abounding ever, infinitely.

The brotherhood rejoices, heartily fulfilled. Our planets rest with glad spirit, their creative bounties received, with new creatures gaining life.

Chapter Five

Science of the Sun – Solar Respiration

Secrets of the universe – centrally, Nature's principles - are revealed. Humanity's Golden Age is well along in their application.

Enormously instrumental to perfect health has proven the precept that it matters vitally **how** one lives. Threaded through each age has come more of our perfected whole way and means.

Human nature having grown through adolescent stages needed to learn sometimes by hard experience – study, hearing, learning, making bridges to the divine realms, thus attuning us to be in loving harmony, within and about. Thus steeped in nature's true ways, we breathe cosmic light and divine love every moment.

The body knows which biochemical substances it needs, making them from sunlight with the bridge to above nicely active. We remain steadfast in our learning and development.

Received energies from both earth and sun come day and night. With learning it becomes much easier to master and perfect further evolutionary growth.

By concentration in silence, luminous learning's progress proceeds nicely. And to think we learned this from trees! Trees are constantly growing, making earth's first food in their leaves, and outpouring oxygen. "Do like us. In silence make creative life-food and spiritual oxygen, for breathing from Above and lovely life-progress."

A multitude of diversions are shed in order to focus powerfully on our own heavenly well-being.

Winnowing self-interest and nationalism are transformed and creatively applied to harmonious global growth. Light, the increasing levels and frequencies of cosmic light (e.g. intelligence), with of course its attendant warmth (divine Love), are universally creative. Divine loving light, as always, is centrally key.

The ancients of Atlantis operated machines by concentrating and focusing light through giant crystals.

Our lasers make focused light for production. Our solar plexus use of Light apprehends Nature's realities and truths. Even astral travel helps.

Brilliant learning occurs too through angels, archangels and divinities above.

Daily nutrition may be supplemented meditatively with solar divine Light.

Universal light is creatively breathed. Communication with each other - as do our high powered divinities - is a matter of focusing and speaking the light of lovely brilliant harmony.

As well, closely associated, is our use of celestial *fire*. The archangel of fire radiating the birthing, celestial music of Chokmah is a dear, dear Friend. The fiery pathway through Geburah and Netzach is well known.

These natural ways are fertile to everyone's understanding and use. And thank God for initiate masters. They bring to great progress the universal wisdom teaching. Marria and her brother Merrien are well acquainted with the master initiate teachers and are helping apply the esoteric wisdom to society's solar science.

There is an old formula. $E = MC^2$ "Energy

equals mass times light, squared."

Together with a principle discerned by Erwin Schrodinger stating that 'within every energy system there is an inherent element of uncertainty'. The principle of relativity is thus magnified. Physics leaves unexplained many realities with regard to subjects and experiments. It is here that solar science is beautifully instructive.

Einstein's theory of relativity considers the immensity of massive energy. Fine. Let us substitute 'thought' for light. The $E=MC^2$ relationship becomes, "An idea developed by the power of creative thought can, in full output, achieve an effectiveness (E) in magnitude equal to the power of Light (thought) – squared."

We are given the example of the velocity of light squared in demonstration of the intelligence's creative immensity. Here then is an essence of the creative emanation of the universe. Here is a foundation of civilization, an emanating intellectual power, proportional to the square of light. You are the proof.

By the way you live you demonstrate these powers, this sacred fire, traditionally identified as a quintessence of the living God within each person. What is this quintessence? The loving warmth of Cosmic Light, spiritual Intelligence imbued with divine

Love.

The originating polarity of love and light, giving prime movement throughout the universe from the creative union of the Tree of Life's realms, flames vitally within all. Society depends on practical applications of universal Light in the subtle, mental and intuitive work common in our evolving growth as a race.

Applications of the universal science flourish. Uncertainty vanished. Witness the birth in Egypt of Hermes Trismegistus. Light hugely magnified occurred in his learning experience from divinity Isis. Such events still beautifully happen here in Sofia.

How does the exponential brilliance of light's power manifest through humans? Such force was described by Hermes: "It receives power from above and from below. This is the strong Power of all Power, overcoming everything fine and penetrating everything solid. From this there will be amazing Applications."

Such power of all powers is centered through the merged male-female fountain coursing in our third spinal blue flow upward. From one's root chakra Hara center, our sushumna nadi flows up.

At last free of erotic dissipation, one's kundalini power multiplies in a purified concentration of tremendous force. The power of powers, divine spiritual love, empowers us creativity, beautifully.

Amazing applications abound – even astral travel to realms in the Tree of Life, such as solar logos Tiphareth and beyond.

Moreover, the Essene perfection of ancient days thrives beautifully further. Through one's beloved partner is experienced a living deity. No longer dispersed into a refuse of sensory pleasure, life thrusts upward with fabulous empowering.

Numerous methods of self-purification insure the preservation of divine power consistent with the idyllic hymn's line, "A spirit as powerful as God and one with God."

Divine force transfigures our being with torrential power, mankind participating in the universe's amazing applications. "God's Kingdom, the power and glory, forever," nicely abounding through one's creative thought and service.

One of the diversions in old times had been an effort to reach extraterrestrial understanding by radio telescope. A purely physical method, it saw relatively little, whereas master initiates had been directly intuitively receiving and beautifully learning from above.

Now we have the means, - our sensitive intuitively hearing *seventh sense*. Most of us use it to learn in life's universal School. It's a tremendous advance for individuals and mankind.

Destructive x-rays had been used in medical diagnosis. Today we examine phenomena with skilled vision and understanding.

Again the 'keeper of the mysteries' smiles with compassionate understanding: "Perfect the way you live. Learn to use light at all levels."

Thus our society has achieved its harmonic social *synarchy*, we carrying our creative thyrsus further ahead.

Chapter Six

Word from the Archangel

Builders of the golden age had long exhorted the powers above to bring back initiates. 'Bring back to earth the initiate wisdom teachers. Jesus, Socrates, Verdi, whom had briefly appeared in body. We need the entire cadre of master teachers of every skill and genius.' Mankind has been subtly led through art, music, theosophy, initiate traditions. Today again, the Tree of Life regents and divinities, including our solar Michael of Tiphareth, share the teaching to a world fully awakened to reality's truths, our world working for all, in luminous fraternity ever. Ascended masters *are* here, directly helping from above with their soul and spirit.

The six world religions are now melded, in furthered rebirth of their universal understandings. Truth and reality explicit, practical, comprehensive and eternal, live and breathe within everyone. And happily, our broad bridges to the splendorous regions give immediate access. With a calm and attentive focus, Merrien's household senses divinities.

A primary creative achieving is the invocation of deity Eheieh, in affirmation of pure being, lasting and unchanging.

In high Kether is the pure source of utmost being. Kether's regent Metatron is brother to earth's Agartha divinity Melchizadek. Melchizadek guides earth's angels.

Work focusing and concentrating energetic power beautifully advances us through, for example, our love to Kether, Metatron, Tiphareth, Michael. These are four of sixty two paths we've ever had in the Tree of Life.

Here we grasp the upwelling force arising from the reservoir of limitless Loving Light and the Supreme Being. It is centrally through Kether that divine power is drawn. When you derive through region Atziluth's path of Kether, you creatively, wonderfully gain, contributing excellence.

You find yourself realizing with complete conviction the supreme brilliance of God's universal Life in nature, creating form like clay in the hands of a potter. With these keys to magnifying your male-female power of powers, worded in accord with civilization's traditional vision of the living Tree, the presence of regent Michael also grows, His each syllable indelibly inscribed in the devoted hearts of our attentive, admiring brotherhood.

Thus too, Marria's invocation of Kether at the Himalayan conference lives in fond memory among her brothers. God's emanation through Kether resonates in spiritual work through us all, the power of powers bursting forth with inspired creatively harmonious activity. Bridges to heaven are further active, our solar civilization thriving. Unity with the solar logos is universally enjoyed, and everyone's spiritual mobility beautifully expanded. Capital materialism vanished.

Though rocket activity remains mainly for material transport, many people travel astrally to favored planetary regions including the spiritual sun.

And occasionally an explorative journey is made into the mists of history. It is just this urge now that Aumier feels, in his curiosity as to origins of the power of powers through the polar union of our *male-*

female complement. He wonders how people in old times regarded our formative male-female being.

In their home's meditation sanctuary, Aumier focuses his concentration upon the brilliant light of Kether and intones the region's name of God, 'Eheieh'. Then he enacts a formula bridging the archive of history and finds himself astrally in a land between two great oceans, on a path in a forest.

Making his way between redwood trees, Aumier picks up an inscribed rock at the site of an old church. The rock's markings are barely legible, with but six words readable. He memorizes "burnished sky, secret rhyme, natal kiss", and satisfied with his discovery, returns to his home sanctuary finding the room's flame of devotion still lit.

Then Aumier tunes in to the frequency of Sophia's archeology laboratory, requesting an akashic examination of his rock. An hour later the laboratory calls back and a full reading of Aumier's rock is provided. With a smile of understanding, he ponders his find:

Midnight Metamorphosis

**Diamonds glaze a burnished sky
becoming ebony
The sun's last blush at last retired in**

pastelled memory

A gentle kiss of stillness tucks each
being in its fold
And tenderly bestirs afresh each form in
Nature's mold

There dwells inscribed within each star a
dream in secret rhyme
Where angels speak, where Love herself weaves
mysteries sublime

Therein somehow, beloved dear,
we brothers all do play
While children of a younger year will
welcome earth's new day

Now night, her garments tucked about earth's
gently guarded sleep
Tends minds that on tomorrow's stage with livened
hearts will leap
Rest well in nightfall's slumber pure
each life a sacred trust secure

The Celestial Queen with brood well-nursed
directs by causal energy rehearsed

Our destiny affirmed again as
dwellers of one Heart
Its beat a rhythm sanctifying Charity's full part

Where She Herself in radiant harmony and bliss with understanding mirth! bestows life's raptured natal kiss.

Delighted by his find, Aumier notes the poem's reference to love seven times, to light five times, to humans as brothers/sisters, and to the creative role of angels' speech, aiding here.

"Metamorphosis is precisely what our race has undergone, motivated as 'dwellers of one Heart,'" he muses. Then he observes that in the poem's last line is a reference to joy in the union of Chokmah and Binah's origination of male-female polarity, as well as the spiritual happiness with mature union according to initiate understanding. In the poem's every line breathes an emphasis on developmental activity.

Transformation is a subtle nurture, in thought and feeling, and in strong willed creativity. Loving harmony 'overcomes everything fine, penetrating everything solid.'

And so, upon a tapestry of beauty, song, poetry and light, the future is woven by countless hands near and far. The marvelous Tree of Life bears fruit upon fruit, given the flavor and aroma blooming throughout the gracious work of the living Tree's industrious, splendorous Divinities - everywhere bestowing Kether's sanctifying fire of divine luminous love, eternally.

Chapter Seven

Solar Schooling - Initiate Education

Marria, returning radiant from introducing a college friend to his new teaching job at her university, smiles sanctifying light to brother Aumier, beaming her heart's heavenly music to him, "God's kindest happiness, dearest one. You have found a lovely artifact." He responds, "Yes, precious Marria, splendorous-heart. It's the drama of peoples' reunion of the feminine and masculine power of powers, as humanity dissolved lowness, returning to our original purity by perfecting one's inner masculine-feminine."

What had been an ages-long problem is past, healed through sanctifying divine-love, women experiencing heavenly Father through man, men the divine Mother through woman, each person exhilarating.

In western America a poet called humanity's reunion in wedded power a *metamorphosis*. The butterfly of male-female union in us all becomes our phoenix of superhuman empowerment. Our clairvoyant manifesting hearts help manifest life in pure accord with the power of God's supreme Light and Love.

As Merrien returns after a week at his healing center he finds Marria meditating in their sanctuary of Light. He joins her, she communicating with Kether's regent Metatron and Tiphareth's Michael.

After awhile Merrien senses Marria's communion completed.

He says, "Thank you so deeply, Marria, as I thrill to the beauty, music and perfume of the divine Mother through you. People used to spend lifetimes receiving God's Heavenly Father and Divine Mother polarity. I revel in this infinite presence through You." She responds, "And I, dear brother Merrien.

It is through the window of your dear soul."

A luminous presence radiates everywhere now as the couple beam the glow of spirit through one another. Universes of exquisite beauty, perfume and music are both theirs and ours.

Then Marria speaks, "What strides did you make this week in healing?" He says, "Well, precious dear, the Agarthans have an improved channel to the spiritual Sun. The people of North America, long separated by oceans east and west and a narrow isthmus southward, are more integrated worldwide, and the world's aged are more inspired to remain creatively spiritually expansive. And with you, dear Marria?"

She says, "The divine Mother is empowering more and more women to endow their **newborn as initiates**, and she is helping to further master training in universities. Of course, many supernal Beings together help us.

Divine Mother's role is more and more to detail the activities of one's spiritual Heart within schools' lessons, the sacred Teaching available in our students' creative learning.

We are discovering ways to become closer in our effects upon others, to the manner of archangels, spreading peace, harmony and loving-light wherever they go, to all that they see.

What do you think; which higher illumined Being might we hold as a model, to resemble and rise to, receiving particles from, in order to teach and heal with our solar science?"

"Well, dear Marria, I think – and Davienn would agree – Chokmah's Cherubim, as they are pure music. Remember? Sculpture is structurally more lasting than painting. And music, in mere minutes conveys wonderfully beautiful life-empowering.

I would nominate the singing Cherubim as our models, in that they are messengers of God's primal birthing lyric to all nature and life. And in doing so they fructify the Tree's next sephira Binah with universal polarity, birthing humans' male-female complement."

"Admirable, Merrien. Yes. I am wholly in accord. The Cherubim shall be reached, studied, communicated with and emulated. Their function is to sing to God, 'Holy, Holy, Holy.' When we sing in harmony we create a little bond with the Cherubim, receiving their particles of telesma so that the forms emanating through us too reflect purity, beauty and harmony."

Marria's day at school comes to mind, and she shares its highlight with her brother.

"During our seminar today our graduate students reported their research into areas of solar music, the zodiac's vernal power accelerating perfected-purity, and our emanating life through creative inspiration.

My colleagues doing research were delighted by the students' excellent and enthusiastic progress. Your alma mater grows in excellence, Merrien."

He replies, "To think that only a century ago our form-birthing work was in a pilot phase, and now eleven couples have born children through telesmatic thought projection, or as it had been known in the past, 'the power of the Word becoming flesh.' All thanks to the arrival of master initiate teachers and our impetus together expanding humanity's great education."

"Yes, dear brother. An astounding age we live in, and such golden heaven ahead! Our master teachers look forward soon to another sabbatical in the Himalayas with earth's Agarthan divinity, Melchizadek.

The family of humans, angels and archangels expands in empowered harmony. And Sofia's children too enjoy their share." Marria reflects on the beauty of her neighborhood's Garden of Light elementary school, seeing a class in progress. The teacher is showing a video portraying children frolicking with fairies and elves of our sylvan forests.

Then Marria's attention focuses toward a junior high class in Sofia, its students rapt in a biology lesson.

The class's teacher speaks, "I would like to say a word about your indelibly preserved memory. Within the solar plexus and heart are recorded your seventh sense intuitive understanding. 'I have a gut feeling.' Together with the brain then, a person commands an enormous power of recall. This is why, through regressive hypnosis, many past events are recorded, like Jesus' letter to mother Mary.

Likewise you, being a replica of the living cosmos, may link with any realm or being in the universe, and in doing so magnetically attract vibrations of their lovely virtues.

For example, in studying the nature of the Cherubim you discover that they embody perfect pure music. And through their extraordinary intelligence the Cherubim channel a divinely loving music through which emanates our universe's loving life.

Now, rising toward the Cherubim's sublime heights you may choose to play and hear the lovely 'L'Enfance du Christ' or an 'Ave Maria', while selflessly beaming your loving light upward. Connecting so, with the music of your soul singing upward, you receive lovely nourishment.

Numerous angelic intermediaries help send your love above.

All else along the magic bridgeway happens

because you have raised yourself to vibrate close in harmony to beloved ones above. You *become* music, your vibrations attuning to a higher pitch, a more powerfully creative Light singing through you."

The young people hearing these words need no notepads. The initiatic wisdom shared is indelibly affirmed in their souls, maturing to bloom ripe in their perfected lives.

Continuing, the teacher adds, "So keep this precious memory active. Relive prior heights of inspiration and happiness as often as possible, renewing and reliving your harmonious, divine experience.

I would like to return now to the subject of Light. You will benefit from this knowledge for years ahead.

When you are gathered together in silence, concentrate, for example, on your solar being. Much nicely depends on it. You may surround yourself in solar Light, and you will be receiving God's divine loving Light.

Join your voice to master initiates and say, for example, "I admire you." If you like, for your aura you can visually surround yourself with purple, hazel, blue, green, yellow, orange and red light.

It's also nice to work with white light, for white has all colors within.

"White light gives you the omnipotence of

purple, the peace and truth of blue, the wealth and eternal youth of green, the wisdom and knowledge of yellow, the vigor and vitality of orange, and the activity and dynamic energy of red."

Once you succeed in contemplating nicely on light you sense it as a vibrant, pulsating ocean of happiness, peace and joy. Then too you sense it as perfume and music, the cosmic music that we call the music of the spheres, the song of the universe."

Merrien responds, "Beautifully done, beloved sister. I thrill in joining you, visiting our schools. The young people are doing so exceptionally well.

I am happy especially to know that our students learn about Light, empowering their lives with divine Light." "Yes, Brother, this is a vitally essential life-focus for us all, well-learned in youth. Our teachers carry on the initiatic tradition earnestly and skillfully. The students are growing strong through the wisdom of life-science as loving, creative brothers and sisters in the Universal Fraternity of divine loving Light."

Chapter Eight

World University

Sun-splashed groves of redwood, flowering peach, maple and magnolia grace the lawns between ivory-hued towers as teachers, staff and students weave their way to desk and class. Hundreds of bright and pastel shades fill campus flowerbeds, surrounding statuary of the millennias' eminent prophets, masters and artistic geniuses. Every moment, everywhere the celestial rainbow of multicolored spiritual iridescence beams a heavenly light of vibrant happiness. A sanctifying music of bright harmony and peace softly fills the ether, silently, powerfully caressing each stride of the campus walkers.

You can feel it - an immensely intelligent and resonant, luminous harmony everywhere pervades, from even the friendly motion of the trees' branches to the genius of the classroom seminars and the spiritual research of both student and teacher.

A pair of flame-haired girls dressed in the pale flowered cottons of Spring, popular with today's youth, chat as they enter Domine Hall. "Berramy was so outrageous on stage yesterday as he sang the Fraternite's hymn with our Earth Angels choir." "Yes, wasn't he! I hope he'll record especially his 'Spirits of Kether' interpretation. I reached the Heavenly Father so deliciously through him, and heaven through the music."

At the entrance to their classroom a subject board greets the two girls, with the title of today's lecture: 'The Chemistry of Spiritual Living.' Within, their classmates eagerly await arrival of disciple Marria's friend, Professor Claire Blanche, co-originator of the celestial harp, an instrument detecting and amplifying the sun's incredibly beautiful music, like Chokmah's Music of the Spheres.

A hush fills the room. Professor Blanche, in a white and orange robe with necklace of lotus pearls enters, smiling, "Today, I want to talk to you about the masters Deunov and Aivanhov, and the understanding of our luminous seventh-sense intuitive hearing.

The chemistry of life's anointed presence on earth, the vital energy of Truth's thyrsus of quintessent grace, lending vitality to every cell and atom abounding, is conveyed through the music of God's divine word. You have already learned that your four activities of spirit, - prayer, meditation, contemplation and identification, - powerfully correspond with the emanating brilliant harmonies in the cabbalistic Tree of Life.

In Peter Deunov's lovely 'Prayer to the Supreme Being', he gives us a deeply explicit idea with which to connect and correspond, *identifying* with the divine essence we so admire and adore, just as we might identify, for example, with heaven's splendor reflected in the beauty of a flower, a choral hymn, a ballerina, a child's smile; and specially too, identifying with the divine in one's beloved sister, brother, parent or partner.

And then, in the process of visually and mentally identifying, you propel your being into the realm of heaven, soaring upward thus - to the Universal Soul with your spirit, to the Cosmic spirit with your soul, thereby completing the polar union of your male and female subtle self with the masculine and feminine Cosmic Spirit and Universal Soul. In Master Deunov's 'Prayer to the Supreme Being', he illustrates for us beautifully.

"Dear God. May I feel Thee very close to myself as a close friend from whom I may never part. Be Thou a light in my mind so that I may feel Thee in it. Be Thou a life in my heart so that I see Thee within it, as I see Thee outside myself."

A hand is raised from the second row and acknowledged. "Professor Blanche, I feel it would be wonderfully useful to discuss how the masters enact these principles of correspondence and connecting with the sephirotic realms of the Tree of Life." The teacher responds, "Precisely!, this is where we go now. In a moment we will hear one of the exact statements on the subject which the teacher Aivanhov made in 1938, on spiritual grafting, and then another in 1967 on the subject of spiritually merging with the solar realm Tiphareth.

As you are already aware, it matters a great deal which words you think to use in greeting the sun at morning meditation. From one point of view, it reduces to the question, 'Just how earnest are you, how high your sights, how broadly helpful to others is your ideal?'

Today our spiritual leaders regularly employ astral travel and other gifts to explore the universe's Tree of Life. The development of such gifts begins with a perfected communion with our spiritual sun. Master Aivanhov gave us the best way. Listen and receive a portion of his lectures, 'Spiritual Galvanoplasty' and 'A Master Must Be Like the Sun and Remain at the Center.' Afterwards we will discuss your ideas and how we practice the Teaching. Listen to the lovely

Teacher."   An audio is playing, Master Aivanhov speaking.

"The phenomenon of galvanoplasty – plating gold - teaches us how to nurture the purest and most noble thoughts and feelings in our minds and hearts in order to bring to full-flowering all the qualities our Eternal Father has placed in us since the creation of the world. When we have developed all these qualities to the full we shall resemble our Father; we shall have the visage of perfect love, perfect wisdom and perfect truth. We must work according to the laws of galvanoplasty every day of our lives. Firstly, by implanting in our mind thoughts of durable, incorruptible materials - thoughts of pure gold. Secondly, by carrying constantly in our heart and soul, the image of some truly exceptionally being, Jesus or another great Master. Thirdly, by 'plugging in' to the central powerhouse from which flow all the life-giving forces in the universe. If we do this, as we are immersed in the solution of cosmic ether, all these forces will begin to work in us and accomplish something marvelous. Day by day, subtle particles of matter will flow from our spirit into every part of our body, into every cell, into our face. Under their influence our faces and even our bodies will change until, one day, we shall be a true portrait of love."

Professor Blanche continues. "Subtle particles of telesma from the sun transform us on an ongoing timeline. Now, let us ask the question as to what we can do to accelerate, enhance and maximize this flow of transformative solar power, for substantial increase in our evolutionary growth, even at once!

Here is the initiatic master Aivanhov giving us a huge blessing of exactly what you may daily do to fully increase the beneficence of your future."

"A true master is like the sun: he remains at the center. He showers an abundance of blessings on his disciples, and gives them his light, strength and warmth, as well as his ideas, but he never abandons his position at the center. Not realizing that such a thing would lead to disaster, many masters have married one of their disciples, with the result that the others abandoned them. A master who does this is not a true sun. In fact, he is more like the moon, for the moon is a symbol of someone who is unstable, sentimental and easily influenced - it is attracted by the earth. There have been several moons in our solar system, and some of them fell down to earth! You may not believe me, but this is all on record in the archives of initiatic science.

Initiates who are strongly influenced by the lunar side of their nature, that is, whose emotions and affections are strongly developed, are drawn towards human beings and end by succumbing and abandoning their position at the center. But those who are true suns are guided by their reason and remain inflexible. This does not mean that they are hard-hearted and cold or egotistical. Not at all. Quite the reverse, in fact. They give all their love, light and strength to their disciples, but they remain where they belong: in the center. Even the most ravishing beauties, even a princess cannot sway them. They stay where they are. They say, 'I will give you my light and my affection, but let me stay where I am.'

You can see how the sun sheds light on a question which is not at all clear to a great many men and women. When you begin to think in this way, you will be freed from many things that torment and worry you. So this is what the sun teaches us - all for the sun, and the sun for all.

And now, let me give you some formulas that you can use during sunrise meditation. very lovingly, say these words in your heart:

As the sun rises over the world, so may the Sun of truth, freedom, immortality and eternity, rise in my spirit.

As the sun rises above the world, so may the Sun

of love and immensity rise in my soul.

As the sun rises above the world, so may the Sun of intelligence, light and wisdom rise in my intellect.

As the sun rises above the world, so may the Sun of gentleness, kindness, joy, happiness and purity rise in my heart.

As this luminous, radiant sun rises over the world, so may the Sun of strength, power, force, dynamic energy and activity rise in my will.

As this luminous, radiant, living sun rises over the world, so may the Sun of health, vitality and vigor rise in my body.

Amen. So be it, for the kingdom of God and his righteousness.

Amen. So be it, for the glory of God.

This is a very powerful magical formula.

I have given you so many exercises. You have enough for a lifetime. Use them and you will all be as radiant, shining and beautiful as the Cherubim and Seraphim, as true children of God. The brothers and sisters will walk through life praising the Lord and spreading his glory throughout the world, so that the kingdom of God and his righteousness may be established on this earth as soon as possible. Then life will be filled with gladness and joy, poetry and music. All men will vibrate in harmony and live together as brothers. Rivers will flow, flowers will perfume the air, birds will sing divine melodies. The whole of life will sing the song of the glory of God. There will be no more wars, no more destruction or distress, no more illness or crime. For the first time, the earth will be really and truly a land of the living.

Work to make this come true. Orientate your lives, in a spirit of harmony and unity with all the members of the Universal Brotherhood, toward the highest and most beautiful regions of creation. This is what the teaching is all about."

Claire Blanche adds, "Historically, as more people entered into communion with the sun, civilization emerged from a separatism of self-interested, warring nations toward the unified, harmonious, loving world community we have today.

All throughout the millennia numerous artists, philosophers, prophets and poets contributed. Hermes, Jesus, Socrates, Leonardo, Bach, Mendelssohn, Deunov, Aivanhov and many others emblazoned our foundation of living wisdom with their fountains of Light. As a result, today we advance our research into the nature of the living universe, from experience with the subtly magnificent Intelligences in the realms and planes of the cabbalistic Tree of Life, such as you, a minute ago, inquired about.

In Tiphareth, by contemplating the lines of Master Aivanhov's solar formula prayer, we connect with the archetypal birth-source of our lives. You I'm sure appreciate the virtues perfected! Let's just look at the list - truth, freedom, immortality and eternity; love and immensity; intelligence, light and wisdom, gentleness, kindness, joy, happiness and purity; strength, power, force, dynamic energy and activity, health, vitality and vigor.

We now sense a lovely quintessence of one's essential living. These virtues are how gained? With, for example, this delightfully detailed sunrise communion we heard.

The words of your heart extend to the solar logos, and the solar logos returns to you its gifts; all the qualities of power, health and harmony - immensities indeed!

Let us choose topics from the audio lessons for our discussion. Dear ones, where do your lovely inquisitive hearts lead you today?

Five students immediately raise hands. "Yes, Emelia?" "Professor, Blanche, I am intrigued by the idea of our acquisition of strength and light by meditative identification. How does music participate in such experience?"

"Well, class, here is a fine topic for our seminar -

the relation between the light of evolutionary growth and music.

First, may we appreciate the reception of the solar logos' music through the inspired ear of the classical composer.

Emanative creativity originates through one's spirit. Nothing is spontaneously born alone

God's formative archetypes in nature, in the spiritual sun, emanate from the Tree of Life's 'music of the spheres'. What about it, Emelia, have you experienced these moments of inspiration?"

Rising at her desk, Emelia answers. "Indeed, I think one of the best was my poetry written on my flight to Spain. As I contemplated life's plateaus of love in relationship with my brothers and sisters, family and friend Harlain, one metaphor after another filled my page. And I do acknowledge that the angels nearby me helped in conveying the light of my heart with verse."

As Emelia finishes, the class remains silent. In a moment, a young man raises his hand. "Ah, Therimy, you are a violinist. Perhaps you would like to tell us your thoughts about the relativity of music and light."

"Yes, I would. First though, may I say how that, by living in perfected harmony with all illumined beings, we find wondrous expression through our divine heart. I have had this happen so often. In particular, writing my string sonatas, I find the hand of heaven attending me closely and constantly.

As to music and light, I take the idea of their blend to be life-emanative at the highest meaning of the word. As the Bulgarians say, - 'videlina', life-light - enlivens all beings. To me, music's life-light is the song felt in everything from one another's smile to the birth of a new child."

The teacher acknowledges Therimy's insights with her own understanding smile, "Thank you, dear young man, for those good words. You are indeed blessed in your art." Again, a pause, and a hand is raised. "Yes, Vivia! Do add your insight."

Vivia, with a visage of great depth in her eyes and a countenance of intuitive warmth, speaks, "I as you know have done considerable research in Nature's wisdom through the master teacher, Omraam Mikhael Aivanhov. There is a single line from one of his meditations which I find utterly fascinating. He refers to man's power of manifesting life in the very heavens above! I find such activity utterly astounding for people in the late twentieth century. I brought to class the quotation.

The Master comments about choral singing. "Just as the union of a man and woman on the physical plane gives birth to a human child, so the joining of voices is a creative act which gives birth to forces and energies that are active throughout space.

The union of the two principles through song is a reality which very few people think about or work with. But if you learn to sing consciously, you can free yourself from the pull of earth to a point where you feel that currents flow upwards through your spinal cord and your whole being ignites, radiating colors. The vibrations of your vocal cords trigger an outpouring of energies which unite on a higher plane to beget heavenly beings."

Vivia continues. "To beget heavenly beings! by uniting through song with heavens in the Tree of Life. This seems so incredible, yet it accords well with what we do on earth in our idealism's acts of creative emanation. For instance, this year's community-wide aid in helping manifest life on one of our sister planets, Uranus.

Here is my nomination for a wonderfully eminent activity in the creative union of music and light."

Sonja speaks up with a question. "Professor Blanche, how did you develop the sound transducer for your celestial harp? This certainly must have entailed a scientific use of the mutual energies of light and sound."

"Yes, Sonja. We adapted as close as possible the archetypal solar form of the harp, refining with molecular electronics the sensitivity of a carbon plasma at 2400 degrees centigrade, to receive solar sound from the infinite other frequencies of telesma.

Well, dear students, you journey through the realms of the powerful universe-birthing Tree of Life. In closing our seminar today let us extend what we have considered. Logically, where does our contemplation of the 'Music of the Spheres' union of light and sound lead?

I think our minds are together, I hear you thinking as I, "We enjoy the experience of being lovingly luminous like the sun. In our inspiration we receive beautifully. And some travel astrally to solar Tiphareth. We join in frequencies of love thousands of hertz in pitch, in the heavenly ecstasies earned by lifetimes of diligent spiritual growth.

Astral travel happens for a person, in part, when pure purple is expanded at one's crown chakra.

Purple is the spirit of divine omnipotence and spiritual love. Purple is a very powerful color which protects one. It is an extremely subtle, mystical color which enables the astral body to leave the physical body and visit other worlds more easily. And it also helps us to understand the love of God.

The other six rainbow colors heighten us magnificently too. For example, blue corresponds to the spirit of truth. It pacifies the nervous system, heals the lungs and has a beneficial effect on the eyes. Blue light also is associated with music, helping develop one's musical sensibilities.

We powerfully gain when fully expanding our aura with rainbow colors meditation. One surrounds oneself with each color, one at a time, purple to red.

Doing so, the energies of that color radiate out to all, adding to one's aura."

Blanche closes with "Wonderful, precious dearies. Again our class seminar has gained for us. Hearty sincere joyous blessings.

Perfected glory to all, everyone thriving in divine harmony."

Within the brilliant divine-loving harmony of earth, humanity and above thrives the perfected clarity of our hearts - humanity gaining in divine loving luminous, harmonious unity

An action of good help is to think of oneself *as* **perfection.**

Our loving harmony in humanity grows. Here is a true science fiction story of society's perfected unity.

Our Luminous World Family

Story of Our Solar Future

Life Centuries Ahead

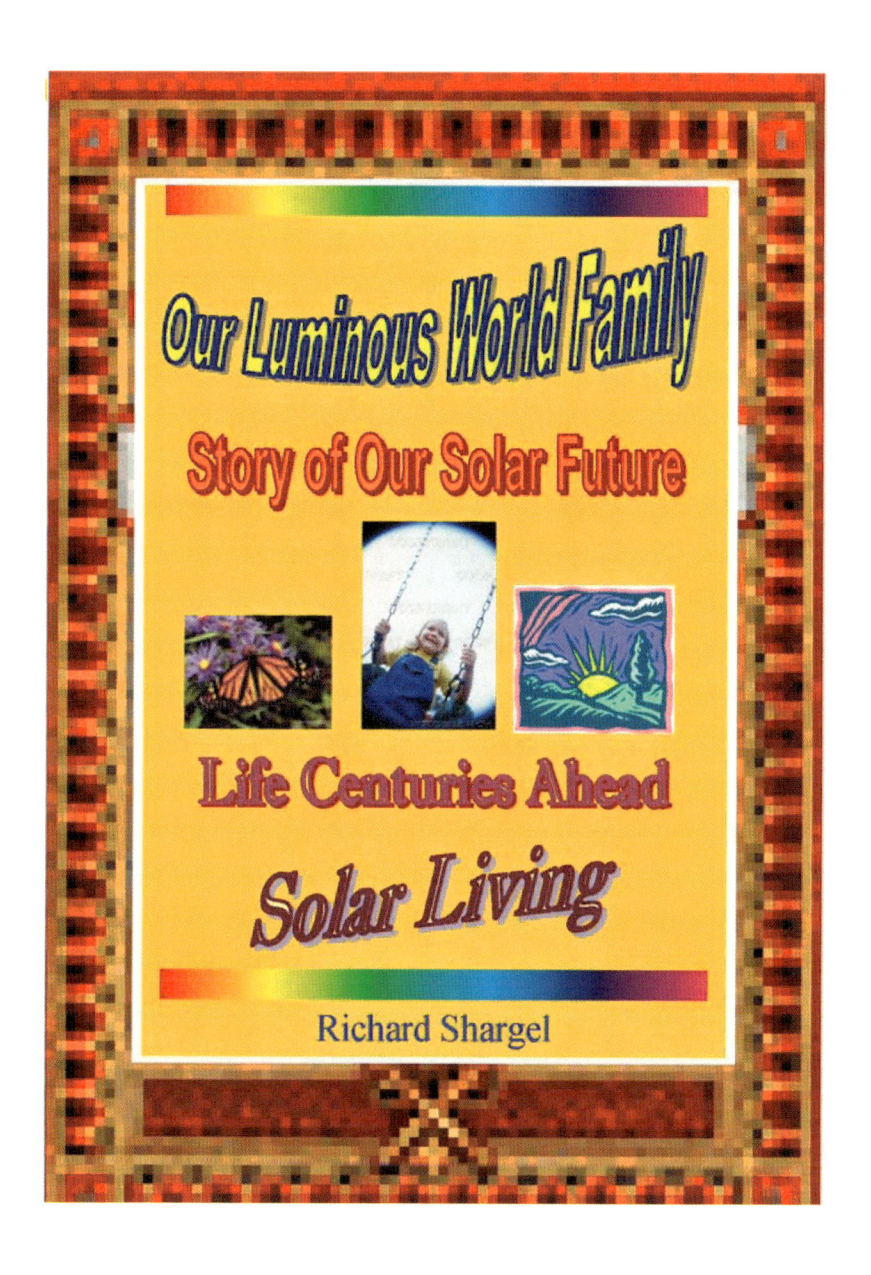

Solar Living

Richard Shargel

Here is a story of our happily empowered lives ahead. Divine love, good-will and joyous service are centuries-ahead and beautifully progressing.

"May the angels and archangels open the floodgates and pour out their generosity on the children of God, on all mankind.

Omraam Mikhael Aivanhov

May there be an abundance of light and understanding, an abundance of joy and happiness so that mankind may, at last, accomplish the exalted mission for which it is on earth: to *reflect and express the Creator and the glorious beauty of heaven*."

Made in the USA
Charleston, SC
05 June 2012